Aspects of Bilingualism in Wales

Multilingual Matters

Please contact us for the latest information on recent and forthcoming books in the series.

Derrick Sharp, General Editor, Multilingual Matters,
Bank House, 8a Hill Road, Clevedon, Avon BS21 7HH, England.

MULTILINGUAL MATTERS 19

Aspects of Bilingualism in Wales

Colin Baker

MULTILINGUAL
MATTERS LTD

British Library Cataloguing in Publication Data

Baker, Colin,
    Aspects of bilingualism in Wales. —
    (Multilingual matters; 19)
    1.Education, Bilingual — Wales
    I.Title
    371.97′009429   LC3736.G7W3

    ISBN 0–905028–51–1
    ISBN 0–905028–50–3 Pbk

Multilingual Matters Ltd,
Bank House, 8a Hill Road,
Clevedon, Avon BS21 7HH,
England.

Typeset by Photo·Graphics, Honiton, Devon
Cover designed by Julia Morland
Printed and bound in Great Britain by
Colourways Press Ltd, Clevedon BS21 6RR.

Contents

Acknowledgements

This book contains a number of paradoxes. It is written in the English language about the Welsh language. It is written by a monoglot Englishman surrounded and sustained by a nuclear, extended and academic family of Welsh speakers. In its original intention it was to be an analysis of aspects of bilingualism in Wales. In outcome the book goes beyond analysis. From the beginning there existed the conviction and assumption that minority languages need to be fostered and maintained. As a result of exploring data and literature on the minority language in Wales, it became difficult not to make interpretations and develop arguments. It is acknowledged that a move from customary academic prevarication to provocation is pathed with problems. The philosopher will be able to detect some hidden ideology. The psychologist will be able to detect some underlying personal characteristics. The sociologist will be able to detect some hidden assumptions about society and social relationships. Despite the script being read by a number of critical, perceptive and helpful colleagues, errors of judgement remain. The responsibility for these rests solely with the author.

An academic interest in bilingualism stems from W. R. Jones, a tutor and a friend. A debt is owed to Professor Roger Webster who provided the initial opportunity to research and later teach in a Welsh University. Professor Phillip Williams encouraged me to research and write. He continually provided perceptive criticism in the most sensitive manner and gave unselfishly of his time and wisdom. His comments on the first draft were of great help. Three other experienced experts read the full draft: Derrick Sharp, Professor Iolo Williams and Dr B. L. Davies. Derrick Sharp encouraged the development of the book and provided invaluable comment on the draft. Professor Iolo Williams generously provided encouragement and advice on the book, and his depth of understanding of Welsh cultural activity has been of great help. Dr B. L. Davies, a meticulous and devoted tutor from undergraduate days, used these coveted skills to sift the draft and remove vagaries of language. Maldwyn Thomas read substantial parts of the draft, and provided invaluable advice, constructive criticism and great encouragement. Two colleagues provided perceptive criticism and expert and essential advice on the compilation of

Chapter 1: Gwilym Jones and John Jones. To both I owe a debt of gratitude. The Rev. E. T. Roberts, who appears more anonymously elsewhere in the acknowledgements, assisted greatly in the compilation of the appendices. While on sabbatical leave in the U.K., Professor Stephen Kemmis made some valuable comments on the nature of the material.

Chapters 6 and 7 have their origins in research activity with two practical educationalists. J. Philip Davies gathered the data that provided the foundation for Chapter 6. Emrys Price-Jones gathered the data and provided part of the analysis for Chapter 7. Both have followed in the excellent Welsh tradition of teachers carrying out important educational research. As E. Glyn Lewis (1981) states: "Schoolmasters in Wales were among the first educators anywhere to undertake what were admittedly modest investigations of the consequences of bilingualism and to identify the needs of bilingual children" (p. 333). Philip Davies and Emrys Price-Jones in becoming my students also became my teachers.

Bernard Jones, Secretary of the School Curriculum Development Committee in Wales, Stephen Steadman, Euryn Ogwen Williams of S4C, John Gwyn Jones of Yr Urdd, J. Bryan Jones of Mudiad Ysgolion Meithrin, the Directors of Education and Chief County Planners in each of the eight Welsh Counties, Ifor Jones and Muerig Williams have each provided help and advice. Chapter 6 is partly based on an article published in The Counsellor. I am grateful to Rev. Dr Bill Rees, the editor, for permission to use and modify that article. Copyright of the Census data upon which Chapter 1 is based is vested in H. M. Stationery Office, and acknowledgement is paid to OPCS and UMRCC for help with this database. The results of the Microcomputer survey in Welsh speaking Schools in Wales, presented in Chapter 8, are based on research funded by the Economic and Social Research Council, Award reference no. C 0025 0004. Particular thanks go to Martin Kender of ESRC who greatly encouraged the research.

Dilys Parry, an expert human word processor, gave sympathetically of her time and computer skills, transferring handwritten scripts to disks and printer. Her patience and care were exemplary.

Finally, my personal interest in the topic of bilingualism stems from being accepted by marriage into a Welsh extended family. From the propositional knowledge gained from research and reading, they have helped to add tacit knowledge of bilingualism and biculturalism. My wife and my two bilingual children, in particular, provided the context in which to write this book. It is to them the book is dedicated.

Colin Baker

Introduction

Bilingualism is often about minorities in the majority. It is probably true that the majority of people in the world are to some extent bilingual. Yet where bilingualism is found, the issues that arise often concern minority interests. For example, Spanish in the USA, Frisian in the Netherlands and Gaelic in Scotland give rise to minority political, social and educational issues. Wales is no exception. Where a regional or minority language exists it is usually the small in the face of the large.

Given that bilingualism is a world-wide phenomenon, it is odd that until recently the topic has received little attention. In comparison with the mainstream research in anthropology, psychology, sociology, education, politics and government, bilingualism and biculturalism have been a minority interest. There are examples of sustained and valuable contributions stemming from individual academics, Round Tables and academic centres. However, considering the geographical distribution, the political and social importance and the cultural and educational significance of the topic, the amount of research and literature available is not extensive.

The tide seems to be turning. Recently there has been a renaissance amongst minority language groups. A new interest in maintaining or restoring minority languages and cultures has arisen. Wales is a good example. The rise of the Welsh Nationalist Party (Plaid Cymru), the Welsh Language Society, the movement for Welsh medium schools and the advent of S4C, (a television channel partly devoted to Welsh language broadcasts), are a few of the symbols of a Welsh language renaissance.

Yet the danger is that the renaissance is in interest and not usage. In the following chapters a number of different analogies are used. Most come from recent sources. A castle crumbing under attack from anglophone culture. A dried-up lake with small and ever decreasing pools of water. Malnutrition and attendant death. Each analogy has the same perilous feeling. Each analogy has the smell of decay rather than the sweet scent of a renaissance.

In the context of increased world-wide interest in minority languages, the book seeks to take the temperature of the Welsh language. Since the book is not a post-mortem it is not historical. But just as a doctor is concerned about the future as well as the present health of a patient, so the book goes further than contemporary history. In examining the survival prospects of the Welsh language, the book involves geography and pedagogy, statistics and semantics, communication studies and curriculum theory, technology and psychology. The issues raised in the book are not only of significance in Wales. The effect of television, other mass media and the micro-electronics revolution are part of the nervous tension in many minority culture and language situations. The nature of minority language education is a central theme in the book. Heritage language education research, curriculum development, educational policy and provision are examined. Each topic is contextualized in Wales but is significant in most minority language situations. All the evidence examined ultimately raises political questions. The appropriate treatment, preventive or restorative, that ultimately needs to be applied is, in the last analysis, a matter of political debate. The book seeks to inform, even stimulate that debate.

1 Where are the Welsh Speakers?

The Distribution of the Welsh Language

Introduction

The history of the Welsh speaking population in the 20th century is a history of decline. At the turn of the century, the 1901 Census suggested that approximately 50% of people in Wales could speak Welsh. In the next 30 years, a 13% drop occurred: only 37% of Welsh people spoke Welsh according to the 1931 Census. The 1981 Census showed an all-time low on Census figures of 19.0%. The decline in the Welsh speaking population is not only in terms of the proportion of the general population in Wales. The decline is also in absolute numbers. In 1901 there were approximately 930 thousand Welsh speakers. By 1931, this figure had dropped to 909 thousand and by 1981 to a little above 500 thousand. Figure 1 illustrates this decline in proportional terms.

This chapter does not focus on the reasons for such a decline. Instead it attempts to investigate present and future trends in the use of the Welsh language using the Welsh language database extracted from the 1981 Census. What, for example, are the geographical distributions in the use of the Welsh language? Is there a heartland of language usage, or several heartlands, or a uniform spread? What are the age distributions? Is it older people who predominantly speak Welsh in comparison with younger people? Such a trend would indicate some pessimism about the future of the language during the remainder of the century. Are there signs of a revival in the language with more younger people speaking Welsh than their parents? Are age distributions similar across Wales or are there local differences? Such localized trends might suggest that the future use of the Welsh language will be in selective areas.

The chapter seeks to examine evidence from the 1981 Census to provide clues as to the state of the language and a glimpse of its future.

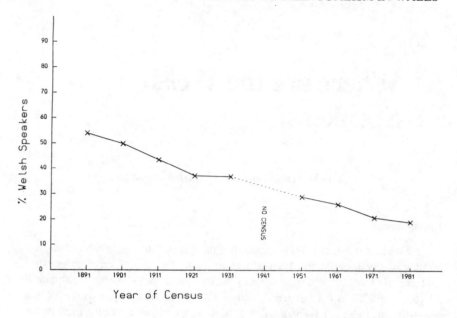

FIGURE 1. *Welsh Speaking Population Census Figures, 1891–1981*

While accurate prophecy is impossible owing to the great complexity and variety of present and future factors affecting the health of the language, certain trends do seem discernible and important. Recognition of such trends may affect the health of the language by being taken into account in future strategic planning and policy.

The 1981 Census

On the 5th April 1981, the population of Great Britain completed, or had completed for them, a census form. The result for the researcher is superficially a near perfect database. Banished are the limitations of trying to generalize results from a small sample of people. For example, were we to look at the use of language in a small village or a small number of villages in Wales, a problem exists as to the generalization of the results. While statistically generalization has certain rules, in reality researchers often hope their findings and interpretations reach further than strict statistical generalization allows. On the surface, Census data avoid this pitfall.

Included in the 1981 Census were a short series of questions on the Welsh language, which could be read and answered in Welsh or English:

For all persons age 3 or over:
(a) Does the person speak Welsh?: Yes/No
(b) If the person speaks Welsh, does he or she also:
Speak English?
Read Welsh?
Write Welsh?

Results showed that 19.0% of people, 503,549 out of a population of 2,645,114 in Wales, were said to speak Welsh. Before examining in detail the results, two initial considerations need to be discussed: the nature of the question asked, and the nature of the Census database.

The Language Questions used in the Census

The results concerning use of the Welsh language need to be critically considered in the light of the phrasing of the question. Superficially the question is straightforward and simple. The only answers were Yes and No (Ydyw and Nac Ydyw in Welsh). Since it is a question of fact rather than of opinion, it may appear that answers will be valid and reliable. Appearance, however, is not reality.

Ambiguity. What problems may be generated by these questions? First, there is the potential ambiguity of the phrases "speaks Welsh", "reads Welsh" and "writes Welsh". Chapter 3 will examine these problems in detail. Specifically here, positive responses to the "speaks Welsh" item could range from those who are fluent Welsh speakers to those who have spent a week or less on a Welsh learners course. The range might also extend from those who speak "pure Welsh" with no interference from English to those who speak a pidginized form of Welsh (to babies, for example). The question covers those who speak Welsh all the time in a variety of contexts and those who speak Welsh for a minute or less a year. The outcome of this ambiguity may be that the figures are an over-estimation of spoken Welsh. To set a cut-off point as to who is and who is not Welsh speaking is artificial, highly subjective and ultimately impossible. The existence of continua of use of Welsh from learner to expert and from those who speak Welsh all the time in a variety of contexts to those who rarely speak the language, suggests that a complex issue is not capable of being investigated by a simple question. The danger is that the figures, unintentionally, may convey a more healthy or unhealthy picture of the use of Welsh than is warranted.

Social desirability   A second potential problem is the social desirability response effect well known to questionnaire designers. Take two examples. "Are you a friendly type of person?" and, "Are you ever late for appointments?" It tends to be socially desirable to answer "yes" to the first question and "no" to the second. When faced with socially desirable questions, respondents quite unconsciously may give a "halo" version of themselves. With respect to the Census question, a small number of respondents might have said they could speak Welsh, but in fact could not. Socially desirable responses may also occur in the other direction. A small number of respondents may occasionally speak Welsh but respond negatively to the question, perceiving themselves as English speaking. For example, somebody with a very Anglicized self-image may intentionally or unintentionally deny using Welsh. Also the enumerator may have affected responses. Known as the experimenter effect, a Welsh language or English language enumerator may occasionally have unintentionally influenced the language used to answer the Census questionnaire, and the answers to the Welsh language questions.

While the social desirability response pattern must not be exaggerated, nevertheless due to this effect, the Census figures may present a more or less healthy picture of the number of people speaking Welsh than is valid. As Baetens Beardsmore (1982: 71, 72) states:

> "In situations where ethnic, political or prestige factors hinge on language questions considerable distortions in census responses can arise as a result of attitudinal dispositions. In Wales respondents have been known to deny any knowledge of Welsh, even though they were highly competent in the language, because of the emotional bond between Welsh nationalist politics and knowledge of Welsh. In Belgium respondents have claimed knowledge of French when in fact they could hardly manipulate the language because the census was interpreted as a referendum which would indicate the linguistic community the respondent would like to be identified with rather than his true knowledge of one or more languages"

Research on the Irish language also shows how fallible Census figures can be. In the 1971 Irish Census, 28.3% of the population returned themselves as able to speak Irish. This represented a figure of approximately 816 thousand people. Yet the Committee on Language Attitudes Research found that, in reality, only 9.3% of the population spoke Irish, numbering about 277 thousand people in total (Greene, 1981).

Acquiescent response. Apart from the social desirability response effect and the experimenter effect, a further psychological response mechanism may slightly bias the results. The acquiescent response set concerns the slight tendency of respondents to answer "yes" rather than "no" to a question. To prefer to be positive rather than negative to an answer is a known tendency in questionnaire response (Kline, 1983). In terms of the Welsh language Census question, an acquiescent response set will tend to produce an over-estimation of the size of the Welsh speaking population. It is possible that an example of the acquiescent response set is found in the figure of 2340 children age 3 and 4 years of age reported as being able to read and write Welsh. Of children aged three and four, 28% of that group who are Welsh speakers are said to read and write Welsh. While "read" and "write" contain as much ambiguity as "speaks" and while social desirability and genius will affect this unlikely result, acquiescence is also a likely contaminating factor.

Residence. Only residents in Wales were asked the language questions. There exists a population of Welsh speakers scattered elsewhere in the U.K. The size of this population is unknown. In large cities, Chester, Liverpool, London and Birmingham, for example, there are sizeable clusters of Welsh speakers. The proportion of these who speak Welsh is difficult to assess. Although not included in the Census, there also exists a population of Welsh speakers abroad, for example in the U.S.A., Patagonia and Canada.

Different versions of the Census. In the English language version of the Census, the question is ambiguous, failing to distinguish between ability to speak Welsh and actual usage of Welsh. Such a question may be answered negatively by those who are able to speak Welsh but do not do so in practice. It may also be answered positively by beginners in Welsh language classes. In the Welsh language version of the Census, the question is phrased as follows:

Ar gyfer personau 3 oed neu'n hyn:
(a)   A yw'r person yn gallu siarad Cymraeg? Ydyw/Nac Ydyw

(b)   Os yw'r person yn gallu siarad Cymraeg, a ydyw
         hefyd:
         Yn gallu siarad Saesneg
         Yn gallu darllen Cymraeg
         Yn gallu ysgrifennu Cymraeg

The oddity is that the English and Welsh questions are not exactly the same. In the English version, the phrase is "Does the person speak Welsh?"; the Welsh version translates as follows "Is the person *able* to speak Welsh?" It appears that the Welsh question concerns DEGREE (i.e. ability) and the English version confuses DEGREE and FUNCTION (see Chapter 3). With the Welsh version of the question a negative response may be given by those who feel their ability is too restricted to be labelled "Welsh". The English version allows a positive response in the same circumstance. Both the English and the Welsh version of the question, though different, may inexactly estimate the total usage and ability to use Welsh.

To summarize: the Census question about the Welsh language differed in one important respect according to whether a person answered the Welsh or English version of the Census. The phrase "speaks Welsh" is both ambiguous and exclusive. On the English version it may include those barely able to speak the language and exclude those who can, but do not, speak Welsh. On the Welsh version the question may include those who can speak Welsh, but do not in practice, and exclude those whose ability is self-perceived as inadequate to be called "Welsh-speaking". The question is open to socially desirable and acquiescent responses but is closed to Welsh speakers across the border of Wales.

These inbuilt limitations make for overestimation and underestimation to act concurrently. Whether the final effect is one of exaggeration of the health of the Welsh language or of understatement is unclear.

Nature of the Welsh Language Census Database

General publication of Welsh language figures from the 1981 Census is undertaken by the Office of Population Censuses and Surveys (OPCS, 1983). The data from the Census are also available for analysis on computer. The results to be presented later in the chapter are almost all based on manipulating this computerized database. A brief description of the nature of the database may be useful in understanding the results.

The data are stored on the computer in terms of counts at Enumeration District level (ED). For example, the county of Gwynedd can be broken down into 694 ED's containing between one and 826 persons per ED. ED's containing less than six people are excluded from the computerized database due to possibility of confidential personal data being revealed. Enumeration Districts can be joined together to form Wards. Thus in Gwynedd, the 694 ED's can be categorized into 142 wards. Next in the hierarchy is Local Government Districts of which there are 5 in Gwynedd (Aberconwy, Arfon, Dwyfor, Meirionnydd and Anglesey). Table 1 illustrates the hierarchical nature of the database and Table 2 and Map 1 provide details of this database for Wales as used in the results to be presented.

TABLE 1. *Hierarchical Structure of Census Database in Terms of Area (Gwynedd)*

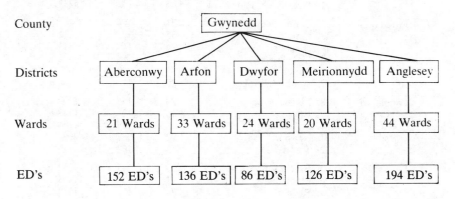

Figures to be presented may very slightly differ from official OPCS statistics owing to data adjustment by OPCS to prevent any possibility of infringement of confidentiality (Denham & Rhind, 1983). Also the results have deliberately excluded census responses from shipping around the coast. Such adjustments may cause very slight differences from official OPCS figures, but certainly not enough to affect the interpretation of the results. Since 56% of ED's in the U.K. changed between the 1971 and 1981 Census, no computer comparisons of decennial changes are considered.

Analyses of Previous Welsh Language Census Data

Since 1985 it has been customary to examine in detail the geographical distribution of the Welsh language (Southall, 1895; Williams, 1937;

TABLE 2. *Census Areas in Wales*

County	District (1)	No. of Wards	No. of ED's	Total No. of Welsh Speakers (2)
Gwynedd	1. Aberconwy	21	152	17742
	2. Arfon	33	136	37053
	3. Dwyfor	24	86	20033
	4. Meirionnydd	20	126	20944
	5. Anglesey	44	194	39295
Clwyd	6. Alyn & Deeside	24	140	5130
	7. Colwyn	17	131	13099
	8. Delyn	24	140	11497
	9. Glyndwr	21	120	16349
	10. Rhuddlan	12	117	8271
	11. Wrexham Maelor	36	233	15232
Dyfed	12. Carmarthen	21	154	30461
	13. Ceredigion	35	205	34831
	14. Dinefwr	24	113	25343
	15. Llanelli	11	158	36901
	16. Preseli	31	210	16097
	17. South Pembroke	20	115	2580
Gwent	18. Blaenau Gwent	20	165	1799
	19. Islwyn	13	125	1848
	20. Monmouth	27	159	1766
	21. Newport	20	287	2994
	22. Torfaen	13	189	2143
Powys	23. Brecknock	33	147	9232
	24. Montgomery	41	171	11103
	25. Radnor	24	117	1023
Mid Glamorgan	26. Cynon Valley	14	151	7130
	27. Merthyr Tydfil	10	142	4802
	28. Ogwr	25	265	10232
	29. Rhondda	11	202	7369
	30. Rhymney Valley	21	217	6616
	31. Taff-Ely	16	193	6542
South Glamorgan	32. Cardiff	21	594	14712
	33. Vale of Glamorgan	18	234	5972
West Glamorgan	34. Afan	11	104	5131
	35. Lliw Valley	8	133	24788
	36. Neath	16	143	9024
	37. Swansea	20	401	18465
TOTALS:	37 Districts	800 Wards	6669 ED's	503549 Welsh Speakers

1. District numbers are located on Map 1
2. OPCS (1983)

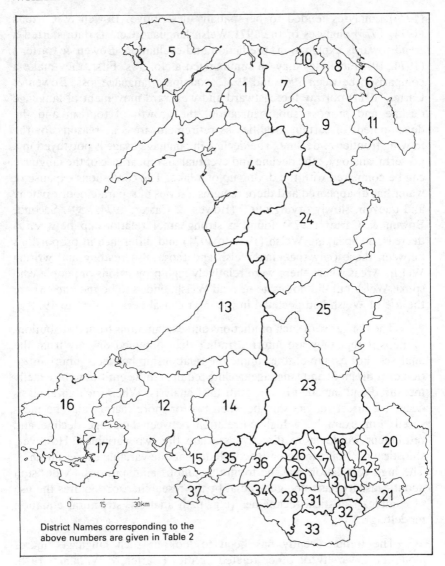

Map 1. *The Districts of Wales*

Williams, 1953; Thomas, 1956; Jones & Griffiths, 1963; Bowen & Carter, 1974, 1975; Thomas & Williams, 1978). Such examination locates areas of higher and lower usage of Welsh, noting heartland areas or islands of language usage. Analyses of the geographical distribution of the Welsh language have changed since the 1971 census. Previous to Bowen & Carter

(1974), analyses tended to be spatially descriptive. Bowen & Carter's (1974, 1975) analyses of the 1971 Welsh language Census data started a trend towards explanation, prediction and evaluation. Bowen & Carter's (1974, 1975) analyses may be summarized as follows. First, they make a comparison between 1961 and 1971, examining language loss. Bowen & Carter (1974) portray the eastward and westward movement of language decline and propose suburbanization, the growth of tourism and the development of certain localities as retirement areas as reasons for the moving frontier of decline. The decline in language usage is portrayed in a powerful analogy; "the decline and eventual disappearance of the language can be compared with the drying up of a lake. The continuous expanse of water has disappeared and there remains a series of separate pools; patchy and uneven, slowly drying out." (Bowen & Carter, 1974: 439). Second, Bowen & Carter (1975) found a strong areal relationship between a decrease in speaking Welsh (1961 to 1971) and difference in proportions between those only speaking Welsh and those also reading and writing Welsh. Areas where there were relatively high proportions of people who spoke Welsh but did not write or read Welsh tended to be the ones where the use of Welsh had declined in the inter-censal period, 1961 to 1971.

The danger with such predictions and explanations from distributional maps is that they are inferred rather than obtained directly from the analyses. For example, to examine the relationship between suburbanization or retirement and language decline requires these entities to be exactly measured and included in one statistical analysis. When such an analysis occurs, a direct relationship between two or more factors may be measured. For example, a high correlation between language decline and retirement would more directly associate the two variables. However, statistical analysis cannot easily conclude that one variable causes another. The high correlation may be totally fortuitous and spurious. A decision about causality has to be guessed at by the researcher, or requires the use of complex statistical techniques (e.g. path analysis, structural equation modelling).

The trend recently has been to look at such language figures alongside a variety of other related entities (Carter & Williams, 1978; Williams, 1982). Included in such multivariate analyses are variables such as social class, immigration, emigration, political affiliation and religion. Carter & Williams (1978), for example, find in their factor analysis a core heartland (Y Fro Gymraeg) of Welsh language and culture, a relationship between language loss and urbanization and industrialization, and a relationship between the Welsh language and rural traditions. Williams

(1982) found that the 48 variables included in the analysis reduced by factor analysis to eight groups of variables. The first factor was termed Welsh culture and grouped together speaking Welsh, religious non-conformity and voting for Plaid Cymru. A spatial analysis of the distribution of the factor showed that it formed a distinctive westward region from Anglesey to Carmarthenshire. The areas around Bala, Dolgellau, the Llŷn Peninsula and certain market centres scored particularly highly on this dimension. The Welsh cultural periphery where Welsh culture and language were found at their weakest included the North Wales coast from Llandudno to Chester, the former border counties of Brecon and Radnor, South Pembrokeshire and the Severn coastal plain comprising the major urban-industrial corridor of Newport, Cardiff, Penarth and Barry.

The analyses to be presented in the remainder of this chapter will focus on two concerns.

1. A map of the geographical distribution of the Welsh language from the 1981 Census data is presented. Such a map forms a factual foundation from which further analysis and discussion can commence. The issue that will particularly be considered is the concept of Y Fro Gymraeg. That is, the existence of a Welsh language heartland.

2. Using two different analyses, the changing pattern of language distribution will be examined. Two questions are posed. What differences are there between literacy and oracy? What does the balance of age differences in the use of Welsh predict about the future of the language?

Analysis One: The Distribution of Welsh Speakers

General

Map 2 shows the distribution of Welsh speakers throughout Wales using ward level as the unit of area. This distribution is also detailed in Table 3.

Following the tradition of Welsh language maps from previous Census, the distribution is given in terms of proportions and density of Welsh speakers rather than in absolute numbers. The rationale for using proportions is given by Bowen & Carter (1975: 115): "the 'Welshness' of an area is dictated not by absolute numbers but by relative dominance".

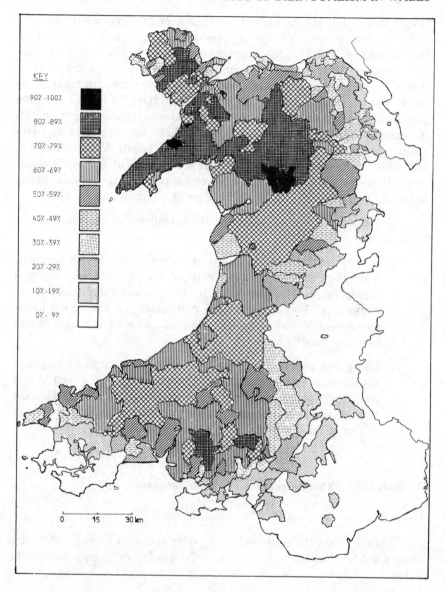

Map 2.   *The Distribution of Welsh Speakers, 1981 Census*

TABLE 3. *Distribution of Welsh Speakers across Counties by Wards*

% Welsh speakers	Clwyd	Dyfed	Gwent	M/ Glam	S/ Glam	W/ Glam	Powys	Gwynedd	TOTAL Wards
90–100	–	–	–	–	–	–	–	5	5
80–89	2	7	–	–	–	–	–	46	55
70–79	4	32	–	–	–	1	7	25	69
60–69	4	32	–	–	–	2	3	19	60
50–59	7	17	–	–	–	1	4	24	53
40–49	7	12	–	–	–	1	5	11	36
30–39	6	5	–	–	–	5	5	5	26
20–29	23	2	–	1	–	5	7	2	40
10–19	39	8	–	19	–	18	18	5	107
0–9	42	27	93	77	39	22	49	–	349

It must be observed that there is a pitfall in this choice, as density or proportion is not the same as distribution of Welsh speakers throughout Wales (Lewis, 1983). High percentages of Welsh speakers may relate to a relatively small number of people. Low percentages of Welsh speakers may hide a relatively large number of people. In both Powys and South Glamorgan there are approximately 21 thousand Welsh speakers. In Powys, the percentage of Welsh speakers in the general population is 20.2%. In South Glamorgan it is only 5.8%. Table 3 therefore provides raw figures for each district. Further details may be found in OPCS (1983). Despite this pitfall, the mapping of Census data is normally by proportion due to the misleading nature of mapping absolute numbers (Rhind, 1983).

Both Map 2 and Table 3 show that Welsh speaking areas are predominantly to be found in Dyfed and Gwynedd, with Clwyd and Powys containing small pockets of Welsh speaking territory. Gwent and South Glamorgan contain no ward where more than 1 in 10 people speak Welsh. Only five wards contain over 90% Welsh speakers: Caernarfon (Ward No. 12 – South), Penygroes, Porthmadog (Ward No. 6 – East), Llanaelhaearn and Llanuwchllyn. All five wards are in Gwynedd.

The areas where the Welsh language is relatively strong (over 80% density) are noticeable for their spatial isolation. In Gwynedd the Llŷn Peninsula and parts of the upper Conwy Valley extending to Blaenau Ffestiniog and Bala emerge as the strong heartland areas. In South Wales a heartland exists around Llanddarog and Llannon extending to Cwmaman and Quarter Bach. Appendix 1 lists all wards where over 70% of people speak Welsh.

A very noticeable break appears between the South and the North. In the 1971 Census analysis, Bowen & Carter (1975) noticed this break along the Severn-Dyfi Mid Wales area. Since 1971, this break has become much more distinct (see Maps 3 and 4). Between Machynlleth and Aberystwyth extending eastwards to the English border is a distinct area of increased Anglicization since 1971. It seems increasingly possible to talk about geographically separate North and South Welsh language communities. As the lake continues to dry up, smaller and more fragmented pools form.

Much of Bowen & Carter's (1974, 1975) description of non-Welsh areas holds as true in 1981 as it did in 1971. The North-East coast from Llandudno to Queensferry, South Pembroke, the Gower coast and vast areas on the English border all show very low densities of Welsh speakers. With the exception of the Llŷn Peninsula, the coastal regions tend to contain relatively lower densities of Welsh speakers, with relatively higher densities being located in the interior. Such interior areas tend to be rural in nature. Not only may Welsh speaking areas throughout Wales be increasingly geographically isolated from each other, but also such predominantly rural areas may themselves contain communities which are separated, at least spatially, from each other.

While there are many interesting features on Map 2, the intention is not to describe the spatial distribution of the language in detail. Rather the intention is to focus on one issue: the concept of a Welsh heartland (Y Fro Gymraeg). This has been an issue of debate among both Welsh language activists and academics.

Y Fro Gymraeg

The idea of Y Fro Gymraeg appears to have two origins: one academic, one popularist. The academic origin stems from Bowen (1959) who made a distinction between traditional and modern Wales, between "inner" and "outer" Wales (also termed *Cymru Gymraeg* and *Cymru ddi-Gymraeg*, translated as *Welsh Wales* and *Wales without Welsh*). Bowen (1959) argued that although there is little geographical unity in Wales, there are areas of cultural and linguistic unity – the Pays de Galles. Using the 1951 Census data, Bowen (1959) spotlighted the relative paucity of areas with between 40% and 80% Welsh language density of population. Heartland areas were therefore defined as places where over 80% of inhabitants spoke Welsh.

The popularist origin of Y Fro Gymraeg stems from Saunders Lewis's famous radio lecture on February 13th 1962, entitled *Tynged yr Iaith* (*The Fate of the Language*). He stressed the need to establish the primacy of Welsh in various administrative areas in Wales. Although Saunders Lewis did not articulate precisely the idea of Y Fro Gymraeg, he is customarily regarded as inspiring consciousness of the idea.

These two origins have developed into two pursuits of the idea of a Bro Gymraeg. Saunders Lewis's lecture became one inspiration for the institution of Cymdeithas yr Iaith Gymraeg (The Welsh language Society) in July 1962, and this in turn spawned Adfer.

In the political sense, it is Mudiad Adfer (Recovery) that has most publicized the idea of a Bro Gymraeg. Mudiad Adfer believe that the Welsh language and culture have no future outside Y Fro Gymraeg. Therefore, efforts to save the language and culture must be concentrated within clearly designated areas.

There is a contrast between Adfer's ideology and general opinion. To many Welsh speaking people, the idea of separated Welsh communities may be anathema. Many Welsh people have a distaste for the potential selectivity, exclusion, privileges and obligations which can result from creating preservation areas or language zones (Jones, D.G., 1979). Adfer is a minority movement within a minority language. Yet paradoxically support for the concept of a Bro Gymraeg comes from academic research studies.

Bowen's (1959) analysis of the 1951 Census data led him to identify an 80% language usage boundary that seemed to suggest the existence of a Bro Gymraeg. The Census results of 1971 led Bowen & Carter (1974, 1975) to a similar conclusion. This time, using 70% density of Welsh speakers as the boundary line of a Bro Gymraeg, Bowen & Carter (1974) also found that the areas adjacent to this demarcation line related to the areas of greatest decline in the use of Welsh since the 1961 Census. Bowen & Carter (1974: 437) concluded that –

> "Although many optimistic disclaims are made denying the sharp cultural differences in Wales, there is a most clear spatial break between Cymru Gymraeg (Welsh-speaking Wales) and Cymru ddi-Gymraeg (non-Welsh-speaking Wales). This polarization has been recognised in a spatial sense by most workers on the topic".

Betts (1976) extended Bowen & Carter's (1974, 1975) analysis by specifying which communities and towns fitted into a three-fold category:

heartland zones where over 70% of the population speak Welsh; transitional zones where between 50% and 70% of people speak Welsh; and "Anglicised Heartland Towns" containing below 50% density of Welsh speakers. Williams (1977, 1978) has criticized such area delimitations for their crudity and simplicity in using one question on a Census return as the basis for designating administrative and cultural regions. For reasons given earlier in the chapter, the language figures are unreliable and inexact. Also the language question on the Census form does not give any indication of the cultural nature of the area. However, rather than dismissing the notion of Welsh language and culture areas, Williams' (1982) own research tends to support the possibility of identifying heartland areas. Further support for the cultural basis of heartland regions comes from Carter & Thomas (1969), Carter & Williams (1978) and Williams (1979).

Maps 2 and 3 reveal that there appear to exist heartland areas in terms of the 1981 Census data. Taking Bowen & Carter's (1974) 70% isopleth as an approximate measure of a heartland area, Map 3 identifies such areas. Wards within the 70% isopleth are listed in Appendix 1. The isopleth is a boundary, a line on a map distinguishing areas of different language usage.

Before proceeding, one limitation of using isopleths, and indeed categorizing varying percentages into groups as in Map 2, must be mentioned. Using 70% as a boundary line is essentially arbitrary. It is always possible that using a slightly higher or slightly lower percentage than 70% may provide a very different picture. The same critique can be made of Map 2, where categorizing percentages into 10 groups could produce an occasionally false image. For example, a ward with 69% Welsh speakers next door to a ward of 70% Welsh speakers becomes separated on the map. The latter is included in a heartland area (Map 3), the former is excluded. The more appropriate representation requires not 10 categories as in Map 2, but a hundred. Such a map should provide a continuous rather than a discrete mapping of density with all possible shadings between black and white (Rhind, 1983). The specification of an isopleth to define a heartland area may then become less arbitrary. Inspection of a distribution of wards in terms of percentage Welsh speakers showed no obvious break or trough (see Table 3). Therefore 70% was used as an isopleth to define heartland areas due to its previous use by Carter & Bowen (1974, 1975).

Clearly identifiable in Map 3 are a number of heartland areas: a central and south western area of Anglesey, much of mainland Gwynedd, and four partly separate areas in south west Wales. A comparison with the

70% isopleth from the 1971 Census data (Maps 3 and 4) reveals considerable change. The heartland area has not only shrunk, but in that ten years has fragmented into separate pieces. In the 1971 analysis there were two major areas of heartland: Gwynedd and Dyfed. By 1981, the Gwynedd area has changed little in size or shape. It is the Dyfed area which has fragmented.

The reasons for such fragmentation require further research. Educational policy, immigration, emigration, industrial, economic and cultural change may each play a part. What does appear to be clear is the spatial definition of not one language heartland, but several. If the 70% isopleth is acceptable as an approximate boundary of a heartland area, then in terms of Bowen & Carter's (1974) analogy, the separate pools in the lake are becoming more shrunken and more separated. The further the pools are separated the less chance may exist of brooklets of communication between them.

There is, however, a crucial difference between the identification by research of heartland areas and the advocacy of the official designation of such areas. Validity in identification of Broydd Cymraeg does not in itself make the case for recognition and official designation of such areas. The case for Broydd Cymraeg is essentially political, cultural and psychological in nature and not merely geographical.

There is also a need to be very cautious in assuming that heartland areas necessarily contain the most active communities in terms of Welsh language and cultural maintenance. Ambrose & Williams (1981) have shown that within an area of apparent language decline, there existed distinct sub-zones. Such small zones may contain active Welsh language communities where the language is thriving. The opposite pattern may also exist. Ambrose & Williams (1981) found that in a zone where over 80% of households contained a Welsh speaker, the potential for the frequent use of Welsh failed to be turned to account. Such research points to the danger of assuming that, for example, rural heartlands are the better breeding grounds for the survival of the language compared with anglicized towns. Towns may contain active and prospering cells of Welsh language and culture. Rural heartlands, while showing a high density of Welsh speakers, may through less community interaction and declining institutions (e.g. chapel) be a less powerful minority language and culture generator than is customarily supposed. When are absolute members of Welsh speakers (e.g. in towns and cities) more important than high proportions? Ambrose & Williams (1981) conclude that the Welsh language is not necessarily safe in places where over 80% of people speak the language, and that the

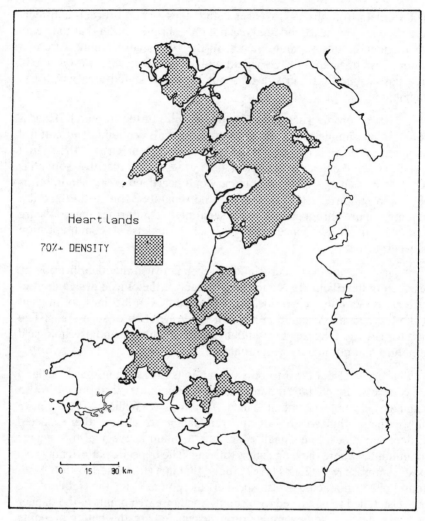

Heart Lands

70% DENSITY

0   15   30 km

MAP 3. *Welsh Heartland Areas, 1981 Census*

language is not necessarily dying where only 10% of people speak Welsh.

For some, the rescue of a dying language comes through language planning, and particularly by different policies for different geographical areas. Colin Williams (1981) provides a thorough and balanced consideration of territorial language planning, focusing on Wales but in a compara-

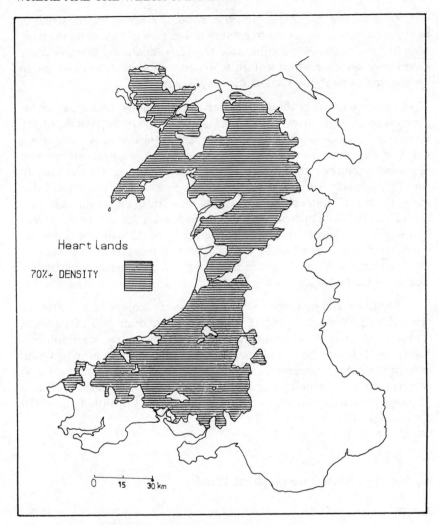

MAP 4. *Welsh Heartland Areas, 1971 Census*

tive context of Finland and Canada. Williams (1981) sees two opposing and conflicting forces at work: the rights of an individual regardless of language and culture, and the rights of groups of distinctive linguistic and cultural character. For example, the individual right of freedom of choice in education or equal access to vocational opportunity may be at the cost of the preservation of a minority language. On the other side of the issue, "If we choose the group-rights approach in Wales, we admit that the needs of both speech communities are so great that they cannot be met on the basis of individual rights. We also institute the legal separation of one culture group from another which in turn will lead to a strengthening of group distinctiveness and group boundaries" (Williams, 1981: 63).

The resolution of the conflict between individual and group rights depends mostly on Government. MacDonald *et al.* (1982) have portrayed American bilingual policy as assimilatory and transitional. A melting-pot policy attempts to assimilate the various minority language groups into American culture with English as the channel of communication. In contrast, Canada has a legislated policy which seeks to provide for a linguistic and culturally pluralistic society. The British Government has yet to consider the issue in depth, and has yet to make a decision on the extent of the rights of Welsh speakers as a distinct group. As Williams (1981: 61) notes, there has been a "failure to specify in a clear and consistent manner just what constitutes the language rights of the Welsh -speaking minority". Chapter 2 further examines this issue.

Language zoning is not solely a product of ideology (e.g. Adfer) or research (e.g. Williams, 1982). Canada and Finland are two examples of countries where political consideration of such zoning has occurred (Williams, 1981). It may be that political consideration of some form of Welsh language zoning is opportune. Just as an earnest ecologist may wish to preserve an area of natural beauty and restrict development, so may a language preservationist see in the 1981 Census maps disturbing trends in the ecology of language.

Analysis Two: Future Geographical Trends

Introduction

To predict the future is to court danger. Suggesting the future course of the distribution of the Welsh language is bound to be inexact and partially inaccurate. Changes in government policy, mobility, educational provision, and in the cultural and economic climate may each make prophecy false. Yet paradoxically, careful and well grounded predictions may be useful in that they can in themselves create change. Take a simple example. If prediction showed that one specified area of Wales was in danger of a great decline in the density of Welsh speakers, then restorative action might be taken to avert the decline.

Predictions about the future of the language need to take into account likely immigration and emigration patterns, social and vocational mobility trends, assessments of likely cultural change in rural and urban communities, changes in educational provision at every level from nursery schools to adult classes and many other economic, social and political changes. Such a task would be a mammoth undertaking, but potentially very productive.

The analyses to be presented are of a modest nature. Two different analyses examine the same issue from very different perspectives. The issue is simply this. Where is the speaking of Welsh decreasing? Where does it seem stable? Where is it increasing? The two analyses are as follows:

1. Bowen & Carter's (1975) finding that the difference between speaking Welsh and reading/writing Welsh was a strong indicator of a *previous* decrease in the use of Welsh is examined in terms of the 1981 Census data. The gap between literacy and oracy is regarded as a predictor of areas where *future* decline may be likely. Where people speak Welsh but do not read or write Welsh, such an area may decline in future language usage. The decline may be slow. Oral Welsh may still be used and useful. The expectation is that Welsh oracy without literacy is like a body devoid of limbs. It may have life, but, because of limited useful-ness, survival may be difficult. A further rationale is given by Bowen & Carter (1975) in terms of a parallel to colonialization. Where the vernacular is used as a means of oral communication and the colonial language is used for all formal, official and written transactions, then the pressure is great to value the official language at the expense of the vernacular. Demoting the import-ance of vernacular literacy may be tantamount to consciously or unconsciously promoting the virtual extinction of the vernacular language.

2. What age trends exist in the use of Welsh? Do older people form a high proportion of Welsh speakers? If Welsh is predominantly the language of the elderly, then language decline is to be expected. Or is there a resurgence of usage of Welsh among the young? This might provide an optimistic note for the future of the language. What are the regional patterns in a comparison of the age distribution of the language? Is there a uniform age increase or decrease throughout Wales? Are there definable areas of age increase and decrease?

The Difference between Oracy and Literacy

Nineteen per cent of the population in Wales claimed to be Welsh speaking. In comparison 15.2% claimed they could read Welsh and 13.7% claimed they were able to read and write Welsh. An important statistic is that only 72:1% (363,116 out of 503,549 people) of the Welsh speaking population is literate. In simple terms, for every four people who speak Welsh, one cannot read and write in Welsh. This is very close to, but marginally poorer than, the 1971 Census result, when 73.2% of Welsh speakers were literate (Bowen & Carter, 1975).

There is bound to be some difference between oracy and literacy, irrespective of the Welsh minority-language context. In the U.K. approximately 5% of the adult population are illiterate in English. Allowing for a nominal 5% difference between oracy and literacy, there is still a 23% difference in the Welsh Census data which appears to be due to the minority language context.

It is possible that the global figure of 72.1% literacy masks two variations: variation with age and spatial variations.

Age variations in Welsh literacy. A histogram (Figure 2) of variations in the percentage of Welsh speaking age groups who are literate, shows that as age progresses, literacy decreases. This is a note of optimism for the future. For example, 78.2% of the 15 to 24 year old Welsh speaking age group declare themselves literate as opposed to 63.0% of the 65 years+ age group. As Bowen & Carter (1975) suggest, this trend may be explained by the older section of the Welsh speaking population being educated through English. Welsh was spoken at home, but often forbidden at school. Literacy was achieved in English rather than Welsh owing to educational practice.

Promising though the age trends in literacy may be, the overall picture is still gloomy. Even in the younger age groups, the gap between oracy and literacy is still very significant. Allowing for 5% being illiterate owing to low ability or similar reasons, the education system and other institutions which promote literacy appear not to be succeeding in fostering Welsh literacy skills. At least 1 person in 10 who speaks Welsh leaves school without Welsh literacy skills apparently owing to the minority language context. One in every 10 Welsh speakers appears to find being literate in the minority language unimportant or does not find sufficient help in achieving literacy.

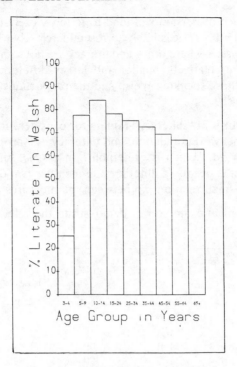

FIGURE 2.   *Literacy Age Differences*

Spatial variations in literacy.   Following the tradition of Bowen & Carter (1975) the difference between oracy and literacy can be mapped spatially. Where are the areas of greater and lesser literacy in Welsh? The method of Bowen & Carter (1975) was to examine such differences in terms of the population of an area. For example, if there are 100 people in an area, ten speak Welsh and eight read and write Welsh, the difference between oracy and literacy is 2%. Yet it is clear from this example that there are two alternative methods of calculating "illiteracy". First, in that ward, two out of the ten Welsh speakers are illiterate (i.e. 20%). This may be called Welsh speakers illiteracy. Second, there are 92 people (92%) from the total of English only and bilinguals who are illiterate in Welsh. This may be called Population illiteracy.

Which measure of "illiteracy" is preferable? Population illiteracy, while not irrelevant, is the measure of least interest in this analysis. It is a ratio which locates the dispersion of proportions able to read and write

Welsh. Since such dispersion will tend to follow closely the dispersion of Welsh oracy ($r = 0.99$), it is likely to resemble closely Map 2. The more interesting analysis is where oracy and literacy are not so highly correlated. Where are there relatively smaller and larger differences between the proportions of those speaking Welsh and the proportions of those reading and writing Welsh?

Two measures of "illiteracy" remain for consideration: illiteracy as a proportion of the ward population, and illiteracy as a proportion of Welsh speakers in a ward. Which is preferable? In essence the two measures contain different concepts of illiteracy and measure two different entities. There is only a small relationship between the measures ($r = 0.32$).

A hypothetical example will demonstrate the relevance and limitations of each measure.

	Total no. in Ward	Total Welsh speaking	Total Read/ Write Welsh
Ward 1	100	10	2
Ward 2	100	10	8
Ward 3	100	90	80
Ward 4	100	90	20

If the concern is "illiteracy" within the total population of a ward:
Ward 1 has 8% illiteracy (difference between oracy and literacy)
Ward 2 has 2% illiteracy (difference between oracy and literacy)
Ward 3 has 10% illiteracy (difference between oracy and literacy)
Ward 4 has 70% illiteracy (difference between oracy and literacy)

If the concern is illiteracy within the Welsh speakers in a ward:
Ward 1 has 80% illiteracy
Ward 2 has 20% illiteracy
Ward 3 has 11% illiteracy
Ward 4 has 78% illiteracy

In the latter concept of illiteracy (proportion of Welsh speakers), the example shows Ward 1 to be as perilous as Ward 4. Amongst the Welsh speaking population, illiteracy is high in both wards. In the former concept (proportion of total ward population) the example shows Ward 4 to stand out for illiteracy, while Ward 1 is similar to Ward 2. The limitation of one concept is the strength of the other. This is demonstrated in a comparison of each illiteracy measure with areas of differing Welsh speaking density.

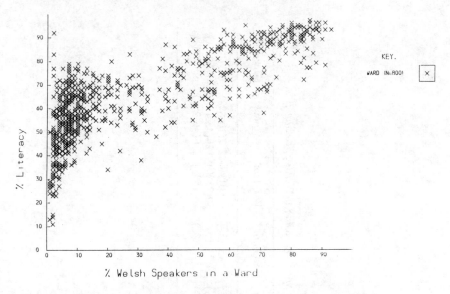

FIGURE 3. *Scatterplot of Welsh Oracy and Literacy, 1981 Census*

Welsh speaking base. When literacy amongst Welsh speakers within a ward is compared with the proportion of people speaking Welsh within a ward, a high correlation is found ($r = 0.79$, $p < 0.0001$). This means that where a high density of Welsh speakers exists in a ward, literacy amongst those Welsh speakers tends to be higher. Where there are relatively few Welsh speakers in a ward, illiteracy amongst these speakers tends to be greater. Figure 3 provides a visual representation of this relationship in terms of a scatterplot. Wards containing over 70% of Welsh speakers tend to show the higher amount of literacy among those speakers. Wards with less than 20% of Welsh speakers contain the greater illiteracy amongst that 20%. Illiteracy in Welsh is mostly to be found amid Welsh speakers in wards where Welsh is spoken by the few rather than the many. The personal cost-benefit balance for Welsh speakers who are in a minority may tilt against being literate in Welsh. Literacy in such areas may have low currency value. However, the scatterplot (Figure 3) also reveals something the simple correlation hides. In areas of less than 20% density of Welsh speakers, there is great variation in literacy. Areas of similar Welsh language density contain different patterns of literacy and illiteracy. Such areas variously contain 20% to 80% literacy amid those Welsh speakers. Table 4 details the distribution of these areas across the eight counties of Wales.

TABLE 4. *Distribution of Literacy in Wards with less than 20% Welsh Speakers, using a Welsh Speaking Base*

	Clwyd	Dyfed	Gwent	M/Glam	S/Glam	W/Glam	Powys	Gwynedd
20-39% Literacy	2 (2.5%)	3 (8.6%)	36(40.4%)	10(10.4%)	2 (5.1%)	4(10%)	7(10.8%)	0 (0%)
40-59% Literacy	32(39.5%)	21(60.0%)	46(51.7%)	56(58.3%)	9(23.1%)	30(75%)	28(43.1%)	0 (0%)
60-79% Literacy	47(58.0%)	11(31.4%)	7 (7.9%)	30(31.5%)	28(71.8%)	6(15%)	30(46.2%)	5(100%)

Chi-square = 139.25 d.f. = 14 p < 0.001

Among the 800 wards, the difference among Welsh speakers ranged from 96.9% literacy in one ward to 10.6% literacy in another. Table 4 concentrates on three bands of literacy. Wards where less than 20% speak Welsh are not randomly distributed in terms of these three literacy bands among the counties. Gwent stands out for relatively high illiteracy in areas of low Welsh density. South Glamorgan and Gwynedd reveal the most promising picture, with relatively low illiteracy among Welsh speakers in low density Welsh speaking areas.

Population base. The hypothetical example of the four wards illustrates the danger inherent in using illiteracy expressed as a proportion of Welsh speakers in a ward. In Ward 1, two people literate out of ten Welsh speakers gives a comparable percentage figure to Ward 4 with 20 literate out of 90. Important and interesting as the Welsh speaking base illiteracy figures are, they do not take into account the relative size of the Welsh speaking population in a ward. In Ward 4, 70 people are illiterate; in Ward 1, only eight people. Thus literacy based on ward population is, with limitations, the favoured index (Bowen & Carter, 1975). The remaining literacy results use this ward population base.

The difference between oracy and literacy ranges from 0.13% to 29.9% per ward. Throughout Wales, there are regional variations in this difference. The shaded areas on Map 5 locate areas where there is a substantial difference between oracy and literacy (i.e. greater than plus one standard deviation from the mean). These areas are where there exists an oracy-literacy difference of greater than 11.77%. Table 5 provides a county by county breakdown of the oracy-literacy difference, and Appendix 2 lists all wards in the shaded area of Map 5.

On Map 5 certain areas of relatively high oracy-literacy difference fall inside heartland areas. Inside the 70% isopleth, areas of relatively high difference are, in North Wales, Dolgellau, Pwllheli and the area surrounding Lake Vyrnwy (Ward 23, Montgomery). In the South, the areas inside the 70% boundary are Llangyndeyrn, Llanarthne, Llanddarog, Lampeter, Ammanford, Cwm Aman, Landybie, Ystalyfera and the area called Quarter Bach. This provides a salutary warning. Strongholds of spoken Welsh language may not be the same as strongholds of Welsh literacy. Healthy areas in terms of Welsh oracy may be less healthy in terms of literacy.

What also may be a concern is the very large area of oracy-literacy difference in the South. All the Llanelli district, which includes Kidwelly, Burry Port, Llannon and the town of Llanelli itself, showed a substantial difference between the numbers speaking Welsh and writing and reading Welsh. This area extends to the south of Carmarthen, including the town of Carmarthen itself, through most of the Lliw Valley (Pontarddulais, Gorseinion, Pontardawe, Ystalyfera) to Seven Sisters and Ystradgynlais, Ammanford and Cwmamman and northwards to Llandovery. Appendix 2 provides further details.

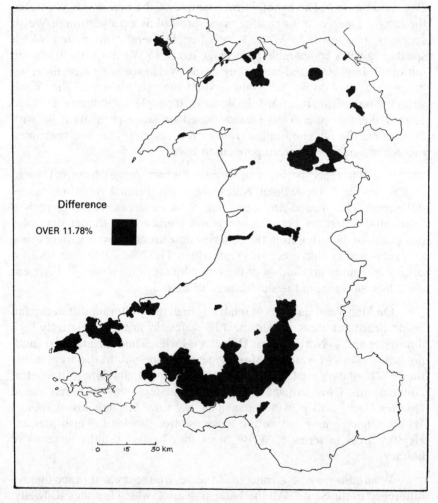

MAP 5.   *The Distribution of Oracy-Literacy Difference, 1981 Census*

TABLE 5. *The Difference Between Oracy and Literacy in the Counties of Wales by Ward*

% Difference	Clwyd	Dyfed	Gwent	M/ Glam	S/ Glam	W/ Glam	Powys	Gwynedd
11.8% to 30%	9	52	–	–	–	12	16	27
6.5% to 11.8%	41	48	–	6	–	8	15	75
1.2% to 6.5%	84	42	63	89	38	35	62	40
0.1% to 1.2%	–	–	30	2	1	–	5	–

1. Mean difference = 6.48%; Standard deviation =5.29%
2. The higher the percentage, the greater the difference between oracy and literacy.
3. The four groups were formed in terms of standard deviations from the mean (+2 to −2).

What is also noticeable about this area is that it joins together three counties: the south of both Dyfed and Powys and much of West Glamorgan. In 1971 much of this South West Wales area was within the 70% isopleth. The area contains many towns previously considered strongholds of the Welsh language in the South. The 1981 70% isopleth reveals that in much of this area the incidence of usage has apparently diminished. If the difference between literacy and oracy is a harbinger of future trends, then it is possible that within this southerly area the Welsh language may continue to decline in use.

Bowen & Carter (1975) suggested that areas of marked difference between oracy and literacy in 1971 had tended to decline in oracy between 1961 and 1971. That is, the oracy-literacy difference is a predictor of past inter-censal decline in Welsh oracy. Furthermore, they show that the 70% isopleth from the 1971 Census tends to co-incide with areas of greatest oracy-literacy difference.

In terms of the 1981 Census data, the relationship between oracy and the oracy-literacy difference can be examined more accurately. The question may be phrased as follows: What are the Welsh language characteristics of areas where there is the greatest Welsh oracy-literacy difference? Is this difference mostly found where there are few Welsh speakers or many?

Figure 4 is a scatterplot of the two variables, the difference in Welsh oracy and literacy, and oracy. The correlation between the two variables (0.65, p < 0.0001) suggests that the greater density of Welsh speakers in a ward, the greater the oracy-literature difference in Welsh. There is a problem with this correlation. Inspection of the scatterplot (Figure 4) reveals that the trend is not linear, as implied by the correlation. The trend is an inverted "U" shape or curvilinear. That is, where there are both few and many Welsh speakers in a ward, there is less oracy-literacy difference. The trend towards most difference is within wards with a moderate number of Welsh speakers. The oracy-literacy difference is often most present in regions containing between approximately 30% and 70% density of Welsh speakers.

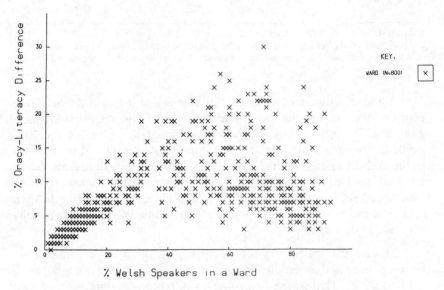

FIGURE 4. *Welsh Oracy and Oracy-Literacy Difference, 1981 Census*

Differences between Age Groups

Introduction.   Figure 5, Map 6 and Table 6 show age trends in the speaking of Welsh. A comparison is made on Map 6 between areas where there are substantially more younger people (5 to 24 years) speaking Welsh than older people (25+ years). The age group 5 to 24 years of age was chosen particularly to examine the possible effect of education (amongst other factors) in the last 10 years. Those between 5 and 24 years are either in the educational system or will have left the system since the previous Census.

It is impossible to prove that in areas where there are more younger than older people speaking Welsh, it is the bilingual educational policy that is to be given the credit. Age trends within a community, immigration and emigration may also play a part in such a difference. Nevertheless Map 6 does reveal that age trends are not randomly spread. There are linked areas which may hint at likely causes but require further research.

An "age" map, irrespective of causes of difference, also points to the future health of the language in terms of age structures in different areas. This future prediction will be far from perfect owing to the numerous variables previously listed. Also while children are at school they may speak Welsh of necessity. After leaving school, they may of their own choosing become monoglot English. Thus the percentage of people aged 5 – 24 years speaking Welsh according to the 1981 Census may provide an over-optimistic prediction of future trends. To take this into account, Map 6 only examines areas where the age difference is greater than plus or minus one standard deviation from the mean. Before further examining Map 6 in detail, a county by county examination of age trends will show the degree of optimism or pessimism.

FIGURE 5. *Histograms of Age Differences in Welsh Oracy*

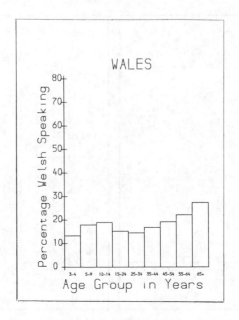

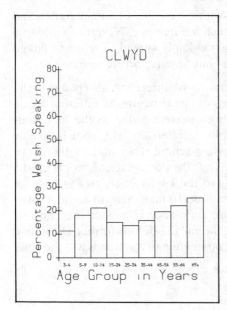

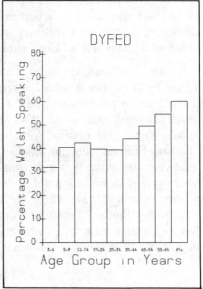

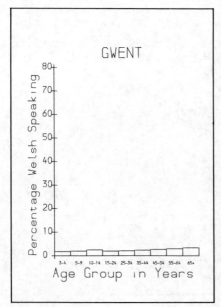

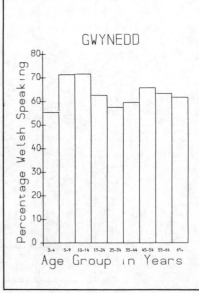

FIG. 5 *cont'd*

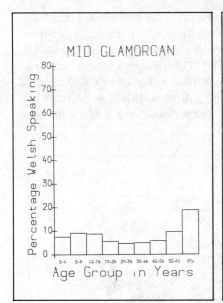

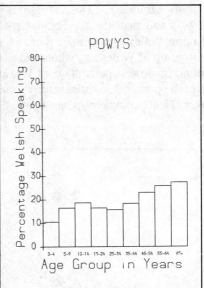

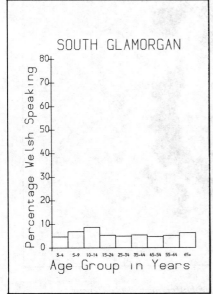

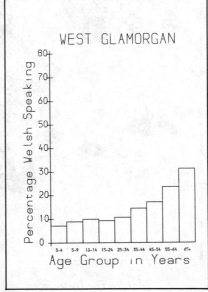

FIG. 5 *cont'd*

County variations. The histograms in Figure 5 are compiled from OPCS (1983) and provide a breakdown of age trends in nine age categories. Taking Wales as a whole, there is an "N" shape in the histogram. The histogram of Wales as a whole shows that between ages 15 and 44 are to be found the lowest percentage of Welsh speakers (15.5%). After 45 years of age, the percentage rises steadily, reaching its peak with those 65 years and over, 27.4% of whom speak Welsh. On the surface, the 2% to 3% increase

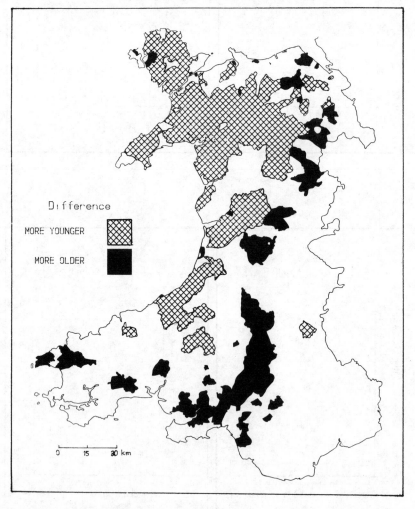

MAP 6. *The Distribution of Age Differences, 1981 Census*

of school pupils speaking Welsh over the 15 to 44 age group may strike a note of optimism. Given that children speak Welsh in Welsh lessons at school, and hence may be rated on the Census question positively, and given that an unknown percentage of such children will stop speaking Welsh after leaving school, the figures may not be so optimistic. A more realistic prediction for the future in terms of these national figures is that the 19.0% overall total will decline. The 19.0% figure is boosted by a higher percentage of more elderly people speaking Welsh. In ten or more years' time, when many of these will not be present, the total percentage of people speaking Welsh, on present data, is likely to decline again, unless offset by a rise in younger age groups speaking Welsh.

TABLE 6. *Language Age Distribution Differences by Wards across the Counties of Wales*

% Difference	Clwyd	Dyfed	Gwent	M/ Glam	S/ Glam	W/ Glam	Powys	Gwynedd
Over 8.4%	12	18	–	–	–	–	5	75
−1.1% to 8.4%	63	43	60	41	37	–	43	35
−10.6% to −1.1%	40	52	33	52	2	34	28	16
Below −10.6%	19	29	–	4	–	21	22	16

1. Mean = −1.1%; Standard deviation = 9.5%.
2. The higher the %, the greater amount of younger (5 to 24) than older (25+) people speaking Welsh.
3. The four groups were determined in terms of standard deviation units from the mean (−2 to +2).

If, over Wales as a whole, the age distribution is not encouraging, then examination of individual counties provides a more refined perspective. Table 6 and Figure 5 reveal considerable differences between counties in age distributions. As will be examined in Chapter 2, Gwynedd's bilingual education policy together with a relatively high density of population speaking Welsh in the county would lead to the expectation of a relatively high percentage of Gwynedd school children speaking Welsh (71%). In contrast with the national distribution, within Gwynedd a second peak is reached not with the 65+ age group but with the 45–54 age group (65.7%). In the Gwynedd figures, there may exist the expectation of the language holding its own in the next decade or more. At present 63% of people in Gwynedd say they speak Welsh. It seems unlikely that this will change substantially in the future, negatively or positively.

Dyfed and Gwynedd are traditionally the strongholds of the language. A comparison of age distribution reveals differences between the two counties. The Dyfed histogram reveals age decline in Welsh speakers. Overall 50% of people in the county speak Welsh. In the 65+ age group the figure is 60%. This drops to 54.6% in the 55 to 65 age group. As the age groups become younger, each step reveals a drop of about 5% until the 25–34 age group is reached. The age groupings between 5 and 34 vary little in the percentage speaking Welsh (close to 40%). If, as previously argued, the 5 to 15 age group figures are inflated for prediction purposes, then the Welsh language age distribution within Dyfed is decidedly pessimistic. The total percentage of 50% masks a difference of 60% older and 40% younger people speaking Welsh.

A similar picture to Dyfed is found in age distributions within Powys and West Glamorgan. The total percentage in Powys of 20.5% speaking Welsh masks considerable variation between the 65+ group and the 5 to 34 age group. As in Dyfed, there exists in Powys a steady decline from the 65+ group through to the 25 to 34 age group. The percentage of schoolchildren speaking Welsh does little to suggest that this decline will be reversed in Powys. West Glamorgan follows a parallel pattern. In this county, 16.4% of people speak Welsh, ranging from 31.3% in the 65+ age group to 9.3% in the 15–24 age group. From the 65+ group to the 35 to 44 age group, the use of Welsh declines almost linearly. Between 5 and 34 years of age the language reaches a low plateau of close to 10%. As in Dyfed and Powys, the age trends in West Glamorgan suggest a possible future decline in the density of Welsh speakers.

In South Glamorgan and Gwent there are no particularly striking age distributions. It seems unlikely for there to be great change within each county if age distributions are good predictors. In Mid Glamorgan and Clwyd, age distributions appear to contain implications for the future. Both counties have a much higher percentage of 65+ people speaking Welsh than their overall average. Both counties obtain lowest percentages in their 25 to 34 age group. But in comparison with Dyfed, Powys and West Glamorgan, each county shows a definite upturn in their schoolchildren age groups. In Clwyd, 13.7% of 25–34 age group say they speak Welsh in comparison with 21.2% of the 10–14 age group. In Mid Glamorgan the respective figures are 4.7% and 8.7%. Allowing for school age groups to contain inflated figures for prediction purposes, a small silver lining within the national dark cloud may be glimpsed in Clwyd and Mid Glamorgan.

Spatial variations. Map 6 both confirms and further refines the age distributions found across the counties. Two areas are distinguishable. The lightly shaded parts locate a region where younger people (5 to 24 years) form a relatively higher percentage than older people (25+ years) by more than one standard deviation. This first lightly shaded region, in simple terms, is where there is more than a 9.5% difference between younger and older people speaking Welsh, in favour of the younger element. The second region shaded black is where the age trends are the opposite; where more older people speak Welsh than younger people. Again the cut off point is one standard deviation in the opposite direction. Table 6 provides further details.

The lightly shaded region comprises much of Gwynedd extending to the rural south west of Clwyd, a smaller area close to the Dyfi including Talybont, Machynlleth and Cemmaes Road, a separate area north of the Teifi including Aberaeron, Llannon and southeastwards to Lampeter. Precise locations of these areas in terms of ward names are given in Appendix 3.

The black shaded region contains a number of small separate areas. A list of the wards is given in Appendix 4. The black shaded areas of age decline are not randomly scattered across the Principality. They form a loose chain which extends southwards from coastal Clwyd through Powys to West Glamorgan. This loose chain then extends westward through Neath and the Lliw Valley to Carmarthen, Narberth and finally to St. Davids on the Pembroke coast. If such age distributions predict, albeit imperfectly, future patterns in the density of Welsh speakers, then a decline may be expected westwards and northwards. The westward movement of anglicization is neither new nor unexpected (Bowen & Carter, 1974, 1975). The age distribution reveals the potential decrease in the use of Welsh along a westwards moving corridor which, in places, is relatively close and often parallel with the English border. The northwards corridor of change is not as strong as the westwards moving corridor. Nevertheless there is a visible broken corridor extending from St. Davids to the very south of Powys, the east of West Glamorgan and small areas of Mid Glamorgan, which suggests the potential decline of Welsh moving northwards from south-west Wales.

The question remaining in a consideration of age differences in the speaking of Welsh is, "In what kind of Welsh speaking communities are such differences found?" Where the age distributions are optimistic, is it high density or low density Welsh speaking communities that are fostering such positive possibilities for the future? Figure 6 provides the answer. The scatterplot compares wards with different densities of Welsh speakers in terms of their age distribution (younger-older). The correlation between

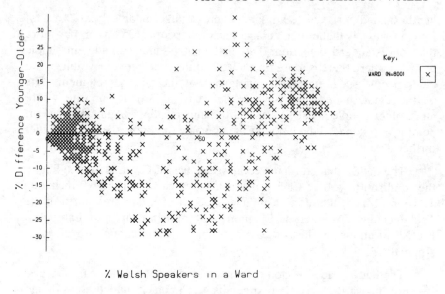

FIGURE 6. *Scatterplot of Welsh Oracy and Age Difference*

these two variables is 0·23 (p < 0.0001) which suggests a small but statistically significant relationship. This small correlation may be interpreted as high density Welsh speaking wards having relatively and marginally more optimistic age distributions. However, Figure 6 reveals that this is only part of the story. There is a suggestion of a "U" shape in the scatterplot. This means that wards where older Welsh speakers predominate tend to be wards of approximately 25% to 65% density of Welsh speakers. Wards with relatively low densities of Welsh speakers (under 25%) show little difference in the proportions of younger and older people speaking Welsh. In wards where there is a relatively high density of Welsh speaker (65%+), the tendency is for younger speakers to be present in slightly larger proportions than older people.

In heartland areas, the language is being maintained with the young. In areas between high and low density, the maintenance of the language seems most in danger.

Summary and Conclusions

The history of the Welsh language this century is a history of decline. In the 1971 Census an all-time low of 20.8% was reached. The 1981

Census, though revealing a drop from 1971, registered a smaller decennial decrease than previously. Are there signs that the language decline is tailing off? Can we expect the future preservation, even restoration, of the language?

The analyses presented in this chapter suggest a few silver linings set against the presence of a large foreboding cloud. The comparison of age groups speaking Welsh shows that it is amongst the relatively elderly that the language is most strong. This suggests that the future holds further decline in the total percentage speaking Welsh. Not all counties follow the same pattern. In Gwynedd, Clwyd and Mid-Glamorgan there are rays of light. More school children within these counties appear to be speaking Welsh than those in middle age groups. Figures for school children may be inflated. Children may fail to speak Welsh after leaving school for a variety of reasons. But allowing for this, it is possible that the educational system and other factors within these counties are working towards the maintenance of the language. This possibility will be further examined in the next chapter.

In Dyfed, West Glamorgan and Powys, the age distributions provide a cloud of pessimism. In these three counties, the percentage of school children speaking Welsh is well below the percentage of elderly people speaking Welsh. The age trends predict no increasing use of the language. Young people appear not be be reproducing the existing density of language usage.

A map of age trends further reveals a pattern in the potential decline and maintenance of the language. The future strongholds of the language seem to be in rural heartland areas: Gwynedd in particular, and also in small patches in Dyfed and Clwyd. The future decline of the language may take the form of anglicization continuing its westward march across the length of the Principality, and this may combine with a new frontier of decline moving from the south west of Wales in a northwards direction.

The gap between percentages of people literate in Welsh and those who only speak Welsh also suggests a northwards moving decline in the use of Welsh. The areas of literacy-oracy difference were located predominantly in the south west of Wales. While these are not always the same areas as those with declining age trends, the overlap is moderate ($r = 0.44$; $p < 0.001$).

Traditionally there have been two counties standing as strongholds of the Welsh language. According to these analyses, one castle is standing firm despite the constant threats of invasion. The other is under attack and in danger of crumbling to the majority language. Gwynedd apears to be defending successfully, Dyfed less successfully. A comparison of the areas where over 70% spoke Welsh in the 1981 Census confirms this pattern. In 1971 there were two distinct areas of Welsh heartland. One predominantly in Dyfed, the other in Gwynedd. By the narrowest of channels these areas in 1971 were not grossly separated. By 1981, the Gwynedd heartland had remained virtually intact. Its size and shape had altered little. By 1981, the Dyfed heartland had suffered serious erosion and had fragmented. Its size and shape had altered significantly.

Such fragmentation, such age trends, such differences between oracy and literacy, cannot but raise the question of the official designation of heartland areas. Two very different bodies of people have provided support for the idea of heartland areas. The first, Mudiad Adfer, is a political group of language activists. The other, a disparate group of academics, consists mostly of geographers. The former holds the fervent ideology that the salvation of the language can occur only by its concentration and designation in specified areas. The latter, through various spatial and statistical analyses, have located specific areas of Welsh language and culture. Williams (1982), in particular, has provided a methodology for locating heartland areas. The analyses presented in this chapter on the most recent Census figures appear to lend support to the location of heartland areas. They equally suggest that these areas may be fragmenting in shape and decreasing in size.

A Chronicler in the Bible recounts how King David conducted a Census throughout Israel and Judah. As a direct consequence, a pestilence fell upon Israel as a punishment, killing some 70,000 men. The 1981 Census of Britain revealed a loss of some 39,000 Welsh speakers since the previous Census, and signs of a dying language.

2   Policy and Provision in Bilingual Education in Wales

Introduction

In the late 1970's and early 1980's, language activists spotlighted television as a major source of anglicization. With the struggle for a Welsh fourth channel won, activists turned their attention to education. The slogan became "Addysg Gymraeg" (Welsh Education). The struggle launched was for educational institutions in the remainder of the 20th century to support and restore the Welsh language and its attendant culture.

By mere coincidence, the activists' emphasis on schools as important determinants of the future health of the language and culture gains support from recent progress in educational research. The work of Rutter *et al*. (1979) and Reynolds *et al*. (1976) for example, has shown that school organization and ethos is an important determinant in the outcomes of education. In Chapter 4, the Bilingual Education Model will suggest that school *context* is important in the cycle of education. It is only recently that educationists have become aware of the extent to which individual schools make a difference. But do they make enough of a difference to affect the future of the Welsh language? How important is the school system in Wales in the fight for the maintenance and restoration of the Welsh language? First, the problem will be briefly placed in an historical context.

An Historical Perspective

When William Williams, M.P. for Coventry, argued in the House of Commons in 1846 that Welsh people needed education to combat their lawlessness, he did not have in mind bilingual education. William Williams asked for an Inquiry and triggered off, unintentionally, an inflammatory situation. The Inquiry resulted in what became known in Wales as Brad y Llyfrau Gleision (The Treachery of the Blue Books). In the Blue Books, many of the ills and failures of the schools in the early part of the nineteenth century were blamed directly on the Welsh language (Davies, 1981). The Welsh language was described by the 1847 Blue Books Commissioners as "a vast drawback to Wales, and a manifold barrier to the moral progress and commercial prosperity of the people. It is not easy to over-estimate its evil effects". (Part II, p. 66.) Throughout much of the nineteenth and twentieth centuries similar, if less strong, negative overtones have been connected with speaking Welsh. The greater economic potential of English and the anglicizing influences of elementary schools, the railways, wireless, TV, telephone and motor car created a distance in status between the two languages. As Webster (1982: 204) summarizes "The desire of the nineteenth century nonconformist élite to 'get on in the world' also affected their attitude to the Welsh language. Although retaining Welsh as the language of the home and of religion, parents and teachers insisted that pupils spoke English exclusively in school". The Board of Education Report (1927) entitled "Welsh in Education and Life" describes rural villages, the historical heartland of the language, as "breeding grounds from which the professional classes of England – teachers, doctors, lawyers, ministers – are recruited" (p. 176).

The speed of the decline in the numbers of Welsh speakers, as witnessed by Census reports, brought an inevitable backlash. "Whereas the aim of the nineteenth century nationalists was to create an educational system that would give the Welsh the same chances as the English, today the demand is for an education that will preserve the Welsh language and Welsh culture" (Webster, 1982: 204). One marker for the historical turn of the tide was the establishment of a Welsh medium primary school in Aberystwyth in 1939 (Isaac, 1972). By 1950, there were seven designated bilingual Primary schools and today there are over 60 such schools or units in existence. Alongside these primary schools, there are also 13 designated bilingual secondary schools sited mostly in predominantly English speaking areas. Such designated bilingual schools are usually referred to as Ysgolion Cymraeg.

Current Perspective – Institutions

The most recently published school statistics from the Welsh Office (1984) provide a breakdown in terms of the following categories:

Primary Schools

Category A. Primary Schools "having classes where Welsh is the sole or main medium of instruction":   18.8%

Category B. Primary schools having classes where some of the teaching is through the medium of Welsh: 9.7%

Category C. Schools where some of the teaching is through the medium of Welsh to second language pupils: 4.5%

Category D. Primary schools teaching Welsh as a second language but not as a teaching medium: 43.4%

Category E. Primary schools where Welsh is not taught: 23.6%

Secondary Schools

(a) Secondary schools where Welsh is taught as a first language only: 3.8%

(b) Secondary schools where Welsh is taught both as a first and a second language: 33.2%

(c) Secondary schools where Welsh is taught as a second language only: 49.6%

(d) Secondary schools where no Welsh is taught: 13.4%

County Variations

Given that one in five people in Wales speak Welsh, then these statistics suggest that in at least three out of every four schools, Welsh is taught as a first or second language. For some this might appear satisfactory, for others anything less than 100% is intolerable. What may be more striking is the difference between counties. Table 7 examines each county on the following variables: the 1981 Census figures for the total percentage in the county and the percentage of 5 to 15 year olds speaking Welsh; Welsh Office DES statistics (1984) on the percentage of primary school classes and secondary schools using Welsh, and the percentage of children within each county assessed as fluent in Welsh by their Headteachers. The issue is this. Does the fluency in Welsh figure match the language background of the County and proportion of infant and junior classes and secondary schools where Welsh is used as a first or second language? Does the provision of Welsh teaching and assessed fluency match the language balance of the county? Or are provision and fluency ahead of language background, thus providing a possible indicator of some restorative action with regard to the Welsh language? Or is the trend more pessimistic, with provision and fluency below the level expected from the language background within a county? One caution in interpreting the table is that percentages of infant and junior classes do not necessarily relate to percentage of pupils. However, the two are likely to be highly correlated. A second caution is that percentages do not reveal quantity in raw figures.

Table 7. *Welsh Language Provision in the Counties of Wales*

	Clwyd	Dyfed	Gwent	Gwynedd	Mid Gla-morgan	Powys	South Gla-morgan	West Gla-morgan	Total Wales
% County Speaking Welsh[1]	18.7	46.3	2.5	61.2	8.4	20.2	5.8	16.4	19.0
% County Age 5 – 14 Speaking Welsh[1]	19.8	41.5	2.3	71.5	8.9	17.7	7.9	9.5	18.4
% Primary Pupils Assessed as Fluent in Welsh[2]	12.0	35.6	0.9	65.8	7.5	12.2	3.4	6.6	14.6
% of Infant classes[2] — Welsh is sole, part or main medium of instruction	14.0	44.7	1.6	68.7	9.2	13.0	4.3	8.2	18.5
% of Infant classes[2] — Welsh is taught/used as second language	80.5	34.9	0.0	31.0	68.8	38.9	20.0	40.8	41.8
% of Infant classes[2] — No Welsh is taught	5.5	20.5	98.4	0.2	22.1	48.1	75.6	50.9	39.8
% of Junior classes[2] — Welsh is sole, part or main medium of instruction	14.8	45.2	0.5	71.1	6.9	10.3	3.7	7.0	18.3
% of Junior classes[2] — Welsh is taught/used as second language	84.8	40.9	0.0	28.9	81.6	77.0	69.8	58.3	54.7
% of Junior classes[2] — No Welsh is taught	0.4	13.9	99.5	0.0	11.5	12.8	26.4	34.7	27.1
Secondary Schools[2] — % Pupils taught Welsh as a first language	6.3	24.6	0.0	53.3	4.8	6.6	2.4	4.0	10.2
Secondary Schools[2] — % Pupils taught Welsh as a second language	56.9	44.3	7.5	45.1	49.3	54.8	39.5	51.5	41.8
Secondary Schools[2] — % Pupils taught no Welsh at all	36.8	31.1	92.5	1.6	45.9	38.6	58.1	44.5	48.0

1. These figures derived from 1981 Census returns (OPCS, 1983).
2. These figures derived from Welsh Office Statistics (1984).

A low percentage may still relate to a large number of people or classrooms.

Table 7 reveals a good deal of variation between the counties. First it may be seen that in Wales as a whole 19.0% of the total population speak Welsh. Almost the same percentage of infant and junior classes use Welsh as a sole, part or main medium of instruction. Simply stated, first language Welsh primary school provision tends to reflect the language background of the total population. Taking this as a baseline, variations between counties may be portrayed. Gwynedd stands out on its own with provision being better than that predicted from the population language background. On the other end of the dimension, Powys stands out for provision being much lower than that predicted from language background. Clwyd, Gwent, South Glamorgan and West Glamorgan also tend to have less provision than the language background appears to predict.

Second, there are noticeable gaps between the percentage of the population in a county speaking Welsh and the comparable percentage of Welsh speaking 5 to 14 year olds. Gwynedd stands out again for a higher percentage of school children speaking Welsh than the total population. A similar trend appears to exist in South Glamorgan and marginally in Clwyd. Dyfed, Powys and particularly West Glamorgan show opposite trends. Education will not be the only factor causing these declining age trends. Immigration, emigration and age distribution in a county are examples of other factors which may help explain the differences. Nevertheless, educational provision *is* likely to be a major factor. In Gwynedd, the bold language policy, outlined later in the chapter, may partly explain the age trends. In South Glamorgan and Clwyd, the policy of second language provision appears to help explain their age trends. In both these counties, Welsh as a second language has received some consideration in the evolution of educational policy and provision.

Third, as must be expected, fluency in Welsh lags well behind Census figures for use of Welsh. Such differences will largely be explained by the balance between first language Welsh speakers and second language Welsh learners in a county. As Chapter 1 suggested, Census figures include varying levels of fluency. Provision of classes where Welsh is the sole, part or main medium of instruction tends to be greater than fluency. While this may mean such classes are not creating fluent Welsh speakers, the fluency figure includes younger children still to receive the full benefit of bilingual education. Therefore the opposite perspective may be slightly preferable. That is, provision is at least present for the fluency figure to be increased.

Fourth, all counties show a smaller percentage of secondary pupils taught Welsh as a first language than the percentage of pupils rated fluent in the primary school. This may be partly due to fluency still requiring a second language mode of provision. It may also be due to the data being cross-sectional rather than longitudinal. That is, the better comparison would be to follow the same pupils through from Primary to Secondary school. This would provide direct evidence of any decrease. The suggestion of these statistics is that about one in every four children rated as fluent in the Primary school is not given first language Welsh provision in the Secondary school. The Welsh Office (1984) statistics show that 14.5% of 10 year olds and over are rated as fluent in the Primary school. In comparison, 11.1% of first form pupils are taught Welsh as a first language in Secondary schools. Is the fluency figure inflated? Does Secondary provision fail to meet the demand and need? It is to such Secondary school provision we next turn.

Age Trends

In secondary schools, exposure to the Welsh language not only varies from school to school, but also with year and subject. While the percentage of pupils taught Welsh as a first language varies little between form I (11/12 years) and form V (15/16 year olds) averaging at about 10% of the pupil population, the pattern for teaching Welsh as a second language regresses as age progresses (although these conclusions are based on cross-sectional figures rather than longitudinal data). A graph demonstrates this decline.

Figure 7 shows that close to two-thirds of children commence secondary school by learning Welsh as a second language. By the third form approximately one child out of three has dropped Welsh as a second language and is not learning Welsh at school. During the last two years of compulsory schooling when pupils opt for various examination courses, close to three-quarters of children in Wales are not learning Welsh at school (Welsh Office, 1984).

The status of teaching Welsh as a second language in such Secondary schools has been highlighted by HMI (Welsh Office, 1983a). In a survey of Welsh in the Secondary schools of Wales they state: "Welsh as a second language in secondary schools is generally given no more place than the first modern language, whether French, German or another Western European language" (p.6). This survey spotlights one reason amongst others which may cause Welsh as a second language to decline in the Secondary school.

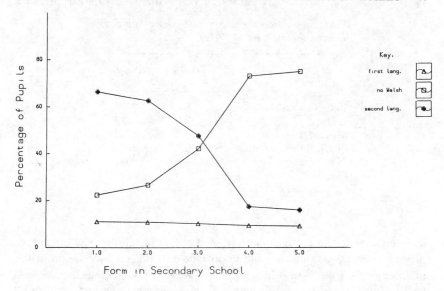

FIGURE 7.   *The Teaching of Welsh in Secondary Schools, 1983*

Apart from learning Welsh as a language in Secondary school, pupils may also be taught subjects through the medium of Welsh. Welsh Office Statistics (1984) suggest the relative infrequency of such teaching. Table 8 illustrates this trend. No statistics are given for fourth, fifth and sixth form pupils since a lower number of pupils take certain subjects due to the options system (see Chapter 6). That is after the third year, provision and choice of subject become fused.

Given that 14.5% of pupils are assessed as fluent in Welsh on leaving Primary school and that 11.1% of pupils take Welsh as a first language in forms I and III, then it is apparent that use of that first language in pursuing other school subjects is relatively low. Very little research evidence exists to suggest the cause of this. Lack of pupil demand may be one cause. There may also be problems of provision. If teachers are unable or unavailable to teach in Welsh, then provision may lag behind demand. The lack of availability of curriculum materials may also deter such provision. Alternatively, pupils for economic, vocational, social or language reasons may be given courses through the medium of English.

The first three subjects in Table 8 were chosen deliberately from almost 40 subjects that are available in Welsh. Each is connected in a

TABLE 8. *Percentage of Pupils taking Subjects through the medium of Welsh*

	Form I	Form III
Religious Knowledge	8.4	7.3
History	7.9	7.0
Music	7.7	5.2
Physical Education/Games	2.1	2.0
Mathematics	4.5	3.0
Chemistry	1.5	2.4

different way to the umbrella notion of Welsh cultural life. The distinctive history of the Welsh nation, the important part played by religion in the maintenance of the Welsh language, the Welsh musical tradition symbolized in the Eisteddfod and Cymanfa Ganu (hymn singing festival) are all areas where some expectancy of Welsh language teaching might exist. The most recent statistics suggest that as far as formal school lessons are concerned, cultural forms in Wales are not greatly transmitted via the indigenous language. Such transmission may alternatively occur by extra-curricular activities and by the English language. However, there are grounds in these statistics to suspect that the secondary school timetable is not a particularly potent agency in encouraging a multi-context use of the Welsh language. Use of Welsh to teach Mathematics and Science is particularly infrequent, hinting at the gap in education between a traditional language and moden scientific communication and culture.

Recent Trends

The limitation of presenting statistics for one year is that it suggests a static picture. It assumes that there have been few changes in Welsh language provision and outcome in recent years. On the contrary there have been changes, mostly positive in terms of increasing Welsh language provision.

First, Primary school fluency assessment figures have shown a steady increase. The Welsh Office figures show a small but significant increase over the period 1977–1982:

12.8% pupils assessed as fluent in Welsh at September 1977
13.7% pupils assessed as fluent in Welsh at September 1979
14.6% pupils assessed as fluent in Welsh at September 1982.

This increase masks a drop in the raw number of Primary pupils rated as fluent in Welsh. Owing mainly to a decrease in birthrate, the actual totals have declined. In 1977 there were 32,923 pupils rated as fluent in Welsh. By 1982 this had decreased to 30,847. Nevertheless, it is percentage of a year group rated as fluent which is possibly the more important figure. Such a figure represents density and saturation of Welsh speakers in an age population. Such density may be linked, for example, with the status, currency value and usage of Welsh in a community.

.The Welsh fluency figures do not show a uniform pattern over the last six surveys when a county by county analysis is made.

TABLE 9. *Fluency in Welsh in the Primary Schools of the Eight Welsh Counties, 1977 to 1982*

| | Date of Measurement | | | | | |
	Sept. 1977	Sept. 1978	Sept. 1979	Sept. 1980	Sept. 1981	Sept. 1982
Clwyd	11.2	12.5	11.1	10.6	11.2	12.0
Dyfed	32.7	33.7	34.4	35.1	34.6	35.6
Gwent	0.3	0.4	0.5	0.7	1.1	0.9
Gwynedd	63.1	63.6	64.5	64.5	66.2	65.8
Mid Glam.	4.5	5.1	6.0	6.4	7.0	7.5
Powys	13.3	13.7	11.1	12.0	13.8	12.2
South Glam.	2.6	3.0	3.2	3.8	4.5	3.4
West Glam.	6.2	6.4	6.5	7.7	8.4	6.6
Wales	12.8	13.5	13.7	14.2	14.8	14.6

Source: Statistics of Education in Wales, No. 3 (1978) to No. 8 (1984)

Generally, Dyfed, Gwent, Gwynedd and Mid Glamorgan have shown increases over the six surveys. Clwyd has similarly shown an increase over the last three surveys. South and West Glamorgan evidence a steady rise in fluency between the 1977 and 1981 assessments, but a fall in the 1982 assessment. Powys' figures fluctuate in a non-linear pattern, making a simple trend impossible to detect.

Second, the percentage of Infant classes where Welsh is taught has increased. In 1977/78, 56.6% of infant classes in Wales taught Welsh. By 1982/83, this had increased to 60.2%. With one exception, this increase occurred across all the eight counties in Wales, as Table 10 details:

TABLE 10. *Changes in the Percentage of Infant Classes teaching Welsh 1977/78 to 1982/83*

County	Percentage Change[a]
Clwyd	+ 3.3%
Dyfed	+ 1.8%
Gwent	+ 0.9%
Gwynedd	+ 1.3%
Mid Glamorgan	+ 5.4%
Powys	+15.0%
South Glamorgan	− 3.0%
West Glamorgan	+ 4.7%
Total Wales	+ 3.6%

a. A positive Value indicates an increase in classes teaching Welsh over the 5 years.

In Powys, Mid-Glamorgan and West Glamorgan there has been a noticeable swing towards more infant classes teaching Welsh. Only in South Glamorgan has there been a decrease in the percentage of infant classes teaching Welsh.

Third, the junior class figures are not quite so encouraging as the infant results. Between 1977/78 and 1982/83 there was a small percentage drop (1.8%) in the number of classes where Welsh was taught. That is, in 1977/78, 74.7% of junior classes taught Welsh. By 1982/83 this had fallen to 72.9%. Breaking down this overall result into a county by county analysis, the pattern is uneven.

Table 11 reveals that the national result hides differences between counties. In South and West Glamorgan the five year trend has been towards less junior classes teaching Welsh. A three year trend (1979/80 to 1982/83) provides the same pattern with a decrease of 6% in these two counties. In Mid Glamorgan, Clwyd and Powys there are more encouraging signs with an increase in junior classes teaching Welsh. In these three latter counties, the infant pattern was also relatively positive to the teaching of Welsh.

Fourth, there are recent trends in Secondary education which are more optimistic than the cross-sectional analysis of one year's figures. Between 1977/78 and 1982/83 there was an increase of 6.6% in the percentage of pupils age 11 to 16 being taught Welsh as a first or second language. Counties vary from this overall increase.

TABLE 11. *Changes in the Percentage of Junior Classes teaching Welsh, 1977/78 to 1982/83*

County	Percentage Change
Clwyd	+ 2.9%
Dyfed	− 0.4%
Gwent	− 0.2%
Gwynedd	+ 0.2%
Mid Glamorgan	+ 2.0%
Powys	+ 4.9%
South Glamorgan	−12.9%
West Glamorgan	−11.9%
Total Wales	− 1.8%

The most striking feature of Table 12 is that in all eight counties of Wales the percentage of pupils being taught Welsh has increased. Gwynedd, Dyfed, Clwyd and West Glamorgan stand out in this respect. Each of these counties has evidenced increases above the national norm.

TABLE 12. *Changes in the Percentage of Secondary School Pupils (Forms I to V) taught Welsh 1977/78 to 1982/83*

County	Percentage Change
Clwyd	+ 9.3%
Dyfed	+ 9.5%
Gwent	+ 2.1%
Gwynedd	+13.1%
Mid Glamorgan	+ 2.8%
Powys	+ 2.0%
South Glamorgan	+ 4.1%
West Glamorgan	+ 9.1%
Total Wales	+ 6.6%

The final trend to be examined concerns changes in the percentage of pupils taught subjects through the medium of Welsh. While no figures are available for the Sciences in 1979/80, the trend over three years (no figures are available for 1977/78), provides some interesting patterns.

In Music and Mathematics there has been a small but significant increase over three years in the percentage of pupils being taught through the medium of Welsh. The publication of "Mathemateg Cambria", a Welsh language Mathematics course for the 11–16 age range, has helped further Maths teaching, suggesting that positive changes rely partly on suitable curriculum material being made available. This is an issue examined in Chapter 5.

TABLE 13. *Changes in the Percentage of Secondary School Pupils taught through the Medium of Welsh, 1979/80 to 1982/1983*

Subject	First Form	Third Form
Religious Knowledge	0.0%	−0.1%
History	+0.4%	+0.5%
Music	+1.8%	+1.0%
Physical Education	−1.4%	−1.0%
Mathematics	+1.6%	+1.0%

While there has been a marginal increase in teaching History through the medium of Welsh, Physical Education (including Games) shows a decrease over the three year span. In a subject which is not classroom based, which may have links with present and future leisure activity, and which tends to be different from the dominating culture of the curriculum, there is evidence of decreasing use of Welsh. In contrast, the HMI report on Welsh in the Secondary schools of Wales (Welsh Office, 1983a) commends one school where no more than 10% of pupils were "native" speakers of Welsh, but where development and consolidation of Welsh as a medium of communication was encouraged throughout the curriculum, including in PE. The HMI's state that "the school has shown commendable progressiveness and vision, and this is a pattern which others could follow and adapt" (p.33).

Conclusions

Whereas parental choice, pupil aptitudes and preferences, curriculum resources and the freedom of schools to make decisions sensitive to their context all need to be given their full weight, the statistics suggest that the health of the Welsh language is not being given restorative help by the use of that language throughout the curriculum.

The position is not static. A growth in the availability of subjects through the medium of Welsh has been observable over recent years. It is also evident that availability is not always matched by pupil preference. Welsh speaking children who have a choice of pursuing the same subject through English or Welsh, may elect for the former. Language preference, peer or parental influence, teacher preference, vocational or higher educational ambitions, are among the factors which may affect such choice. A Welsh medium curriculum may be both difficult to implement and important to foster.

Current Perspective – Policy

While an analysis of the provision for Welsh language teaching in terms of schools, classes and age trends gives an indication of present structure, the policy of the Government, Welsh Office and Local Educational Authorities may provide a complementary picture. The statistics presented provide a picture of the current situation. An examination of Government and LEA policy may portray intended future trends.

Government

"It is recognised that positive support is necessary to enable local education authorities to develop Welsh language policies" (Welsh Office, 1982: 50). Support is supplied in the form of finance to LEA's in respect of expenditure incurred in the teaching of the Welsh language and in teaching using Welsh as the medium of instruction (Welsh Office, 1982). In 1980/81, a half a million pounds was made available by the Government, and in 1982/83 the sum amounted to £866,000. For 1984–85, the Government is to inject 2 million pounds to support Welsh language activity. This money will not only go to the LEA's but will also be used to support Welsh Sunday Schools, the Welsh Books Council, the National Eisteddfod and a large number of other organizations.

Welsh Office

The Secretary of State for Wales is charged with the duty of promoting the education of the people of Wales (Welsh Office, 1982). An Education Department exists within the Welsh office to this end, being assisted by Her Majesty's Inspectors of Education. It is responsible for promoting policies in connection with the Welsh language.

A major policy document, "Welsh in Schools", was published by the Welsh Office in 1981. The Secretary of State notes that it is important to build on the Welsh language provision which is already made in schools in Wales so that the language and the culture which are the nation's heritage are made available to all children. The policy document is of the opinion that all pupils in Wales should be given the opportunity to learn Welsh. The rationale is explicit: "education, especially in schools, is a major factor in safeguarding and developing the language, in extending its use" (p. 9). The goal is also made explicit. For those living in mainly English speaking areas the aim is to acquire sufficient fluency to communicate with mother tongue Welsh speakers. For those living in mixed language areas the aim is "to develop a command of Welsh that allows them to speak, read and write Welsh". Two means to achieve these ends are suggested. First, there should be communication with parents to attract their support. The importance of parental co-operation is acknowledged and some education of parents is tacitly suggested. Second, it is urged that wherever possible, pupils should be encouraged to keep up Welsh until the end of the fifth year (i.e. 16 years of age).

There are two points in particular where this policy is at variance with provision. 13.4% of Secondary schools and 23.6% of Primary schools do not offer children the opportunity to learn Welsh. Next, 74.8% of fifth formers and 73.0% of fourth formers receive no instruction in Welsh. The rhetoric of policy statements is not matched by the reality of provision.

Counties

Legal responsibility for the use of Welsh in the curriculum rests with Local Education Authorities (LEA's) in the first instance and to a certain extent with each school's Board of Governors. H.M. Inspectors of Schools made a comparison of the policy of Gwynedd, Powys and Dyfed counties and primary school bilingual education in 1977. They attribute differences in such policy and primary school practice to differences in the linguistic character of the communities they serve. This point should be borne in mind with the description of county policy which follows.

Gwynedd. At one end of policy dimension is Gwynedd. Since the county contains the highest density of Welsh speakers in Wales and some rural areas where non-Welsh speakers are more the exception than the rule, it might be expected that the Gwynedd Authority could foster a vigorous bilingual policy. The Language Policy dates from 1975. It aims to make "every child in the county thoroughly bilingual". Such bilinguality concerns literacy as well as oracy. The policy includes Welsh being a compulsory subject until the end of the fifth year in the secondary school.

Four justifications for the Language Policy are provided. First, it is stated that "Educationalists of note throughout the world testify to the value of bilingualism. They are unanimous that a bilingual education gives children positive advantages over those who are monoglot. Daily use of two languages helps to develop mental agility, keenness and alertness. The results of external examinations in the bilingual schools of Wales are constantly superior to the national average" (Gwynedd County Council, 1981: 4). While scholars might wish to quibble over some of the terms used and the generalizations made, there is little doubt in the declaration of commitment and the depth of persuasion. Second, bilingual education is justified socially. The belief is that learning Welsh gains access to the life of the community, and that bilingualism promotes sympathy and understanding, co-operation and unity. The missionary zeal of the policy gives no hint that bilingualism can have negative social effects. Rawkins (1979) provides examples of such negative effects within Gwynedd. Third, bilingualism is justified on cultural grounds. "Children and adults who acquire a knowledge of Welsh will inherit and enjoy centuries of prose, poetry, drama and music. They will have the opportunity of taking part in cultural and social activities at local, county and national level – choirs, literary and dramatic societies, eisteddfodau and clubs" (Gwynedd County Council, 1981: 6). The cultural carrot is predominantly high cultural activity. The culture of sport, tavern, chapel and mass media is not mentioned. Fourth, and perhaps most interestingly, a vocational justification is provided. "The ability to speak Welsh is a basic qualification for many posts in education, local government, broadcasting and commerce in Gwynedd and Wales" (Gwynedd County Council, 1981: 7). The list tends to concern professional rather than manual occupations. Is Welsh of no vocational value to the porter, waitress or typist? It would appear that for many non-professional posts, Welsh *is* a desirable asset. Porters, waitresses and typists are also functionally part of the bilingual community. What is also significant in the vocational justification is the reversal from the nineteenth century view that it is English that provides the key for vocational mobility. For the authority, the policy and practice is that Welsh is often essential or at least desirable for local government appointments.

About six out of every ten people in Gwynedd speak Welsh, and approximately seven out of every ten Primary school children are in "Welsh as a first language" class, the remaining three of every ten children being taught Welsh as a second language. The educational policy formulated in 1975 made a difference between traditionally Welsh areas and less Welsh areas. In the former areas, Welsh was to be the main medium of instruction in Primary schools. When English speaking newcomers entered these schools or elected to attend designated Welsh schools in the more anglicized areas, an intensive course in Welsh was to be given so that they adjusted linguistically as soon as possible. In less Welsh areas, equal school time was to be allocated to the Welsh and English languages, and care was to be taken to ensure that suitable provision was made to safeguard and develop the mother tongue of the Welsh speaking minorities in these areas. The appointment of travelling peripatetic teachers (as in Dyfed) aids classroom teachers in the execution of the primary school bilingual policy, particularly in the less Welsh areas.

In early 1984, Gwynedd announced the launching of an experimental centre for immigrant children. This reflects evolution of policy since 1975. One major problem of the LEA with a "strong" bilingual education policy is to assimilate immigrant monoglot English-speaking children. Pupils who at age eight or nine, for example, enter a school where Welsh is the main medium of instruction, pose problems not only for themselves, but also for teachers and for much curriculum activity. Gwynedd's policy is to give such pupils concentrated Welsh tuition for three months in a special centre, where the staff-pupil ratio is very favourable.

At the Secondary school stage, Gwynedd's policy is that all pupils take Welsh as a first or second language up to 16 years of age. At the Headteacher's discretion, Welsh Studies may replace Welsh language at the fourth and fifth form level only. Schools are expected increasingly to provide subjects through the medium of Welsh, three schools in anglicized areas being designated to provide a substantial number of subjects through the medium of Welsh.

Gwent.   A sharp contrast to Gwynedd is the county of Gwent. The 1981 Census returned a Welsh speaking population of 2.5% for Gwent, and in 1982, 0.9% of Primary school pupils were assessed as fluent in Welsh. In 1984, 11 infant classes and four junior classes taught Welsh as a first language out of a combined infant and junior total of 1543 classes. Children of secondary school age who wish to be educated through the medium of Welsh are transported free of charge to Welsh medium Comprehensive schools in the neighbouring county of Mid Glamorgan. The number of such children is about 200, a group apparently not large enough to establish a designated bilingual school within the county. Over 98% of Primary classes provide no tuition in Welsh. As Rawkins (1979) notes, Gwent does not appear to have a formal bilingual educational policy. The county defines its bilingual intentions by practice rather than by policy.

South Glamorgan. Like Gwent, South Glamorgan has a relatively low density of Welsh speakers (5.8%). On the language distribution map in Chapter 1, no wards in South Glamorgan had a density of over 10% of Welsh speakers. The Welsh language policy of the Authority is that instruction in the Welsh language shall be regarded as part of. the curriculum in Primary schools. Two loopholes are provided. Welsh language lessons may be replaced by Welsh Studies, and parents, after consultation with Headteachers, may withdraw their children from Welsh classes. The number of such lessons is to be fixed by the Headteacher.

Structurally, South Glamorgan has one Welsh medium secondary school, eight designated Welsh medium primary schools and nine primary schools containing a bilingual stream where Welsh is the medium of instruction for up to 50% of the timetable. Twenty-five out of the 29 secondary schools have provision for some form of Welsh language teaching.

While the density of Welsh speakers is low in this Authority, there is evidence from Table 7 and policy declarations that provision for Welsh language education has not gone unconsidered. Yet as Table 10 and 11 revealed the percentage of infant and junior classes teaching Welsh has declined in recent years.

Mid Glamorgan. The Authority's policy is that, subject to resources available, every child should have the opportunity to learn and use the Welsh language effectively. Institutional provision is split into two categories. In 23 primary schools the main medium of instruction is Welsh either throughout the school or in a special Welsh Unit attached to the school. In the same category are the three Welsh language secondary schools where Welsh is the medium of instruction for most subjects. The second category of provision is in predominantly English schools where Welsh is taught as a second language. Welsh Office Statistics (1984) show that 204 infant classes (22.1%) and 121 junior classes (11.5%)do not teach Welsh. Of the 42 secondary schools, two have no provision for Welsh language teaching. Mid Glamorgan also shows a recent increase in the percentage of infant and junior classes teaching Welsh.

West Glamorgan. In expressing that the authority "has a significantly responsible role to play in maintaining the Welsh language", West Glamorgan's bilingual education policy provides the reasons for *not* embarking upon a "measure of firm compulsion, planning to introduce every child in its early school patterns to a bilingual approach" (West Glamorgan County Council, undated, p. 3). These constraints may be summarized as:

1. the existence of some communities having no contact with Welsh language and culture

2. the existence of an immigrant population as a result of the increased mobility of labour

3. the European movement imposing a need to consider alternative variants within a bilingual approach

4. the right and liberty of parental choice

5. the cause of bilingualism creating its own momentum rather than LEA created momentum

6. problems in capability of implementation of a scheme

7. the availability of financial and staffing resources.

   The policy documentation suggests that the county's bilingual education should evolve rather than be imposed. It should be responsive, cautious and evolutionary rather than revolutionary and aggressive. Policy is translated into provision by four considerations: to ensure that each District has a Welsh medium Primary school so that parents desiring Welsh medium education for their children have such access; to safeguard Welsh medium education in naturally Welsh areas; to seek a progressive expansion of bilingual education in English speaking areas where there are definite pockets of residual Welsh speakers remaining; and to promote second language teaching of Welsh where there is consent of Headteacher and Managers, where Welsh speaking staff are committed to appropriate techniques and materials, and where there are sufficient supportive resources. Welsh Office Statistics (1984) show that about 7% to 8% of primary school classes teach Welsh as a first language, close to six out of every ten junior classes teach Welsh as a second language, and over three out of every ten junior and five out of every ten infant classes have no Welsh language teaching. Four secondary schools teach Welsh as a first language and 22 schools teach Welsh only as a second language.

Clwyd.   There are some similarities between Clwyd and West Glamorgan. Both have close to the national average in terms of density of Welsh speakers. Both have pockets of Welsh speakers and pockets of English only speakers. Both have areas of industrialization and tourism. Yet Table 7 revealed certain real differences. Almost double the number of Primary school children are assessed as fluent in Welsh in Clwyd compared with West Glamorgan. In Clwyd, 5.5% of infant classes have no Welsh language teaching. In West Glamorgan this figure is 50.9%. In Clwyd 0.4% of junior classes have no Welsh instruction. In West Glamorgan the figure is 34.7%.

Clwyd's Welsh language policy is to ensure that pupils become reasonably fluent in Welsh. To this end "Bilingualism will be introduced at the earliest opportunity" by the provision of bilingual nursery education for those desiring it. The same tense is applied to Primary school policy. "All Clwyd Primary schools *will* be bilingual schools" (Clwyd County Council, undated, p. 1). Children in schools where English is naturally the main teaching medium are to have regular and frequent instruction in Welsh throughout their time in the Infant and Junior Schools (Clwyd County Council, undated). Provision of Welsh as the main medium of instruction is made available by the judicious geographical placement of designated Welsh schools (Ysgolion Cymraeg) and units.

In the secondary schools of Clwyd, children learn Welsh as a first or second language throughout the five compulsory years, although the Head in consultation with parents may allow pupils to follow Welsh Studies as an alternative in the fourth and fifth years. Four designated bilingual secondary schools are available to parents in Clwyd who wish their children to follow much of their timetable in Welsh.

Clwyd's bilingual policy may be more concerned with linguistic engineering than piecemeal evolution. It may not be the policy that explains the differences between Clwyd and West Glamorgan. There are many factors other than policy (e.g. demography, teachers, parental pressure) which may be causes of such inter-county differences. However, Clwyd's bilingual policy cannot be regarded as negative or agnostic.

Powys.   While Powys may, like Clwyd and West Glamorgan, be close to the national average in terms of Welsh language population density (20.2%), its similarity with these counties is little more. As may be seen in the language distribution map in Chapter 1 (Map 2), Welsh speakers are not evenly spread over the county. The map (Chapter 1) shows two heartland areas of Welsh, the north western part of the county in the Montgomery district and the south western part of the Brecknock District. This geographical division is paralleled by the policy of the old Powys counties before Government reorganization. Historically, Montgomery-shire and Breconshire pursued a bilingual education policy while in comparison Radnorshire had no formal policy on the teaching of Welsh (Welsh Education Office, 1977).

Formulated in 1976, Powys' policy attempts to carry over the policies of the former authorities prior to Government re-organization (1972), while moving towards a unified practice in the future (Powys County Council, 1976). In areas where Welsh is the dominant language, school transactions are expected to be predominantly Welsh speaking. In such areas, "Measures would also need to be continued to provide for the education of first-language English-medium groups within the school" (Powys County Council, 1976: 4). This may be compared with Gwynedd, where generally an intensive submersion programme in Welsh has been provided for such English speakers. Powys' policy is that the internal organization of the school needs to adjust to take in both groups. In large primary schools, this may mean parallel streams. In small schools, small groups or individualized learning may allow for such diversity.

In areas where Welsh is the residual or minority language of the community and where few primary school pupils are Welsh speaking, Welsh is to be taught as a second language. Such second language teaching "would probably be appropriate to a greater extent than in wholly and traditionally English-speaking areas" (Powys County Council, 1976: 4).

In English speaking areas, Welsh is to be taught as a second language for the equivalent of approximately 30 minutes a day in junior classes. In Radnor District the teaching of Welsh is not compulsory, and is often provided according to parental choice.

Institutionally, approximately one in ten junior classes are first language Welsh, four secondary schools have a majority or substantial proportion of Welsh speaking pupils, and all secondary schools except one teach Welsh as a first and second language. The most striking statistic is the difference between infant and junior classes in second language teaching and the absence of Welsh lessons. In 48.1% of infant classes there are no Welsh lessons, with 38.9% of infant classes being taught Welsh as a second language. In junior classes, 12.8% have no Welsh lessons and 77.0% have second language Welsh lessons (Welsh Office, 1984). The figures show the relatively low provision of Welsh language activity at the infant stage, although this has increased over recent years. This is a practice common with South Glamorgan in particular and also West Glamorgan. The practice is at variance with Powys' stated policy. In the Director of Education's preface to the language policy document (Powys County Council, 1976), he states "teaching of the second language generally should be introduced at an early stage in the child's school career so giving the pupil the best chance to acquire the language successfully" (p. 1). Later the document states "research and experience have shown the importance of beginning the teaching of a second language very early in the child's education, when the mind is best able to assimilate another language naturally" (p. 2). The mismatch between policy and practice may not necessarily be the fault of the LEA. However, it does provide an issue of policy and practice that will be returned to in the final part of this chapter.

Dyfed.   The linguistic geography of Dyfed is not dissimilar from that of Powys, with wide variations in the population distribution of those able and willing to speak Welsh. Like Powys, it appears unable to develop a uniform policy. While being fully in favour of a bilingual policy in the primary schools, the policy exempts five groups of specified schools in the anglicized areas of Pembroke. The aim of the bilingual policy is to educate pupils so that they have a reasonable facility in the use of both Welsh and English on leaving the primary school, (Dyfed County Council, 1982). 20.5% of infant classes and 13.9% of junior classes have no Welsh instruction, and first language teaching occurs in approximately 45% of all Dyfed Primary school classes. In most (75.7%) of the Secondary schools, Welsh is available as a first language. No Secondary school fails to provide some kind of Welsh lessons. In four major towns there is a designated bilingual Secondary school where much of the curriculum is taught in Welsh.

The health of the language in Dyfed is important. "Dyfed and Gwynedd bear the brunt of responsibility for the national future of the language", (Rawkins, 1979: 104).

Conclusions

From the county by county description of policy and practice, what is immediately apparent is the wide variation. For example, in Gwynedd all Primary classes receive Welsh instruction. In Gwent over 99 classes out of a hundred receive no Welsh instruction.

It is apparent that many of the differences between policy and practice in each county may be attributable to great variations in the everyday use of Welsh, both between and within these counties. However, such differences in the linguistic character of the communities the LEA's serve may not explain all. The comparison made between Clwyd and West Glamorgan in terms of both policy and provision suggests a different approach. If Clwyd's policy and provision take on a missionary appearance, then the West Glamorgan Authority appears to cast itself in a mediation role. The former Authority appears to have a mission, with the preference for a uniform immersion or dip into the Welsh language. The latter Authority appears to take on a different role, mediating between community differences, parental preference, economic realities and alternative ideologies. Ultimately neither is wholly right or wholly wrong. In each LEA there is a different educational reaction to the same issue.

Given that education is just one institution amongst many in the maintenance of the minority language, do county policy and provision suggest that the future of the language is safe and secure? If one in five people say they speak Welsh, then approximately three out of every four children are taught Welsh at some stage in school. That provides a note of optimism. Yet only one in seven children are regarded as fluent in Welsh in the Primary school, even at the completion of Primary schooling.

Most counties appear to have an awareness that immersion into a second language as early as possible is highly preferable. This is well supported by research (Saunders, 1982; Segalowitz, 1977; Cohen, 1976; Miller, 1983). Such awareness is not always translated into practice. Four out of every ten infant classes in Wales have no Welsh language element. This, in itself, may seem worrying to supporters of the Welsh language. At the Junior stage, the picture improves a little with between two and three classes out of every ten not teaching Welsh. However, the small improvement that occurs in Welsh provision between infant and junior classes is at variance with the notion that early second language teaching is preferable.

Age also enters the debate at the secondary school level. Whereas three quarters of school children in Wales are taught Welsh in Form I, by Form III this has dropped to around half the population and by Form V to one quarter. Alongside this age decline, and irrespective of age, is the small number of those speaking Welsh as a first language who take other subjects through the medium of Welsh. About one in three of these pupils take Mathematics through the medium of Welsh in Form III and about one in five take PE/Games through Welsh at the same age. For supporters of the Welsh language, this pattern may induce pessimism as to the future use of the language.

A discrepancy may also be detected between Government policy as expressed in the 1981 policy document, "Welsh in Schools", and actual provision. Welsh Office policy is for the language to be made available to all children. Availability does not imply choice according to the document. The policy is not for parents to be allowed to opt in or opt out of Welsh lessons. Children in English speaking areas are expected to achieve oral fluency in Welsh. 13.4% of Secondary schools and 23.6% of Primary schools have no provision for such aims.

Does the blame for this discrepancy between Welsh Office policy and actual LEA provision rest with county policy and provision, and also with local Headteachers and Managers? Given the ability of Gwynedd to produce a policy aiming to make "every child in the county thoroughly bilingual" and translate this into practice by suitable allocation of re-sources, then some power appears to rest with an authority. As Rawkins (1979) considers, "Despite the increasing responsibility of the Welsh Office and its Department of Education in this field the principal locus of decision-making in regard to the primary and secondary schools remains . . . . . . in the hands of the local education authorities and the head-teachers" (p. 1). That headteachers and School Managers and parents themselves have some power is observable from two opposing movements. The establishment of Ysgolion Cymraeg (designated bilingual schools) in predominantly English areas is often evidence of the power of parental pressure groups. Then, as Rawkins (1979) details, resistance to county language policy in various parts of Wales provides evidence as to the locus of some power in School Managers and headteachers. "Ultimately, it is the headmasters and teaching staffs who will determine the success of both bilingual schools and the teaching of Welsh as a second language" (Rawkins, 1979: 96).

The chapter started with reference to Welsh activists whose recent spotlight has focussed on "Addysg Gymraeg" (Welsh Education). In particular the activists focussed on Government and the Welsh office as targets to be pressurised. So far the conclusion has been that power for change rests with local authorities, Headteachers, managers and parental pressure groups. Rawkins (1979), in a thorough analysis of the imple-mentation of language policy in the schools of Wales (through a Canadian's eyes), provides an alternative or complementary view.

Rawkins (1979) argues that the Government has accepted the legitimacy of bilingualism. Yet the status and position of Welsh depends ultimately not on local authorities or individuals, but on a centralized policy.

"By effectively leaving the initiative in the hands of the LEA's, the government is abdicating its responsibility to Welsh-speakers. While the government fails to co-ordinate the various policy areas relating to the Welsh language, an enormous proportion of the resources allocated to it in a variety of ways must be deemed wasted. To provide a Welsh-medium primary school without enabling the LEA to provide adequate resources for a nursery school; to listen sympathetically to an LEA request to establish a bilingual secondary school without assuring reasonable funding for providing materials or the supply of suitably trained teachers; to preside over an increasing output of graduates from the bilingual school sector without giving serious consideration to the opportunity for Welsh-speakers in further education: all these are indications of the absence of co-ordinated planning." (Rawkins, 1979: 100).

It would appear to be within the capability of government to create and impose an overall long-term policy for the Welsh language which would include bilingual education. The change from a tripartite system of secondary education to comprehensive schools is evidence of such a capability (Betts, 1976). Instead it appears that piecemeal measures in response to short-term political pressures are preferred to a long range co-ordination of policy. Rawkins' (1979) conclusion is a warning, "Without central government leadership and communication emphasizing its commitment to bilingualism, and explaining its meaning and implications, it seems unlikely that bilingualism in Wales can survive as more than an occasional variation on the margins of public institutional life" (p. 101).

The classroom practice of bilingual education depends on provision: provision of suitable institutions, teachers, materials and resources. The provision of bilingual education depends on policy. Doubts exist about whether present policy is long-term, systematic, planned and co-ordinated enough to ensure that bilingual education in Wales can play its part in the survival of the language.

3 "Who Speaks Welsh?" Defining and Measuring Bilingualism

Introduction

To ask somebody, "Are you Welsh?" is ambiguous and imprecise. For some, being Welsh is living in Wales and no more. For others, being Welsh is only possible when the Welsh language is constantly used and when a person identifies with the Welsh culture attached to the language.

To ask somebody, "Can you speak Welsh?" is also imprecise. A person may be able to speak Welsh, but in reality does not use that ability. Just as a person may have the skill to drive a car but doesn't drive, so someone may have the skill to speak Welsh fluently, but fails to use it. The alternative is to ask, "Do you speak Welsh?". Here the concern is about the actual use of Welsh. This alternative is also problematic. A person may use a form of pidgin-Welsh just to one other person. Is that person Welsh speaking?

Defining who can speak or use a minority language is not only important for clarity of meaning and expression. It is also important for measurement. If the Government through a census of the population wishes to establish the proportion and distribution of Welsh speakers, then some kind of question needs to be asked the populace. The problems of such a Census question were considered in Chapter 1. If a county or school wishes to ascertain the ability of children in Welsh then some form of question to teachers or test to children needs to be administered. Such attainment tests may provide, for example, an indication of the effectiveness of an educational bilingual policy. Whatever question or test is used, there will be argument and debate. Since the choice of question or test is very important in defining Welsh speakers, a consideration of the issues in more detail follows.

Language Ability

A variety of definitions of bilingualism and ways of classifying bilingual people are possible. Scholars talk about societal and individual bilingualism, subtractive and additive bilingualism and co-ordinate and compound bilingualism. A good introduction to definitions and classifications may be found in Baetens Beardsmore (1982). One of the most important distinctions is between DEGREE and FUNCTION (Mackey, 1962). Degree is about ability and skill in using language. Function is about actual use made of language.

To measure DEGREE or ability requires more than a simple school-type examination where reading and writing are dominant. All four basic language skills need testing. These may be categorized in a table.

TABLE 14. *Basic Language Skills*

	Oracy	*Literacy*
Receptive	Listening	Reading
Productive	Speaking	Writing

The table issues a warning. Some people can understand Welsh but do not speak it. Others speak and understand Welsh but do not read or write Welsh. So any description or labelling of someone in terms of their ability in Welsh needs an initial consideration of the four basic skills. Unfortunately this is too simple. As Mackey (1962) suggests, there are skills within skills. If a person's ability to speak Welsh is tested, consideration needs to be given to skill in pronunciation, extent of vocabulary, regional variations, correctness of grammar, style, ability to convey exact meanings in different situations. Skills may need to be measured in different contexts. In Wales, there are variations in language usage which need to be taken into account. This is usually referred to as diglossia, where the primary dialect may co-exist with a more formal, grammatical, literary style. There is especially a difference between Cymraeg Llafar/ Cymraeg pob dydd (i.e. oral Welsh, which varies in degrees of "correctness") and Cymraeg Llenyddol (literary Welsh) which is more formalized in structure and vocabulary.

Mackey's (1962) conclusion is that to measure adequately, to validly describe and classify a person's bilingual ability, the framework in Table 15 needs examining with 20 tests for each language.

TABLE 15. *Language Sub-Skills*

	Pronunciation	Grammar	Vocabulary	Meanings	Style
Listening	Test 1	Test 2	Test 3	Test 4	Test 5
Speaking	Test 6	Test 7	Test 8	Test 9	Test 10
Reading	Test 11	Test 12	Test 13	Test 14	Test 15
Writing	Test 16	Test 17	Test 18	Test 19	Test 20

When considering the methodology and technology of such language testing, it becomes apparent that the range and type of sub-skills that can be measured are almost endless, as Lado (1961), Mackey (1965), Oller (1979), Carroll (1980), MacNamara (1969), Williams (1971), Baetens Beardsmore (1982) and Vollmer & Sang (1983) each reveal.

It may be argued that the dimensions and sub-skills tested are mostly measuring the same entity. Children who do well on a Welsh spelling test may also tend to do well on a Welsh reading test or comprehension test. Different language tests tend to correlate moderately well (Oller, 1982). "The evidence now shows that there are both global and componential aspects of language proficiencies. The perfect theory of the right mix of general and specific components, however, has not been found — and probably will never be agreed on" (Oller, 1982: 110).

It is unlikely that all possible dimensions of language need testing (Vollmer & Sang, 1983). Given that there is overlap and communality between sub-skills, then only a sample of sub-skills may need to be tested. However, as Oller (1982) declares, there is little indication yet as to the specification of that sample. In Welsh, there are also very few language tests available. Those that have been in use in the last decade are mostly based on face validity only, without the necessary item analyses needed to refine a scale. The tests developed by the NFER Unit based at Swansea under the direction of Dr Eurwen Price are exceptions (Price & Powell, 1983; Price *et al.*, 1984). These are carefully developed tests of the highest technical standards.

In a Welsh context, there does not exist the range of tests to investigate empirically the most efficient and concise method of portraying language ability and subsequently classifying pupils. In a wider context, there does not exist as yet the knowledge to specify how a condensed description of language skills is to be achieved, although statistical processes such as factor analysis and maximum likelihood provide a basis for identifying groups of tests. While a distinction must be made between classification of abilities and classification of individual people, the former strongly influences the latter.

What has emerged from the discussion so far is a picture of two opposing yet paradoxically necessary ways of describing and classifying bilingual ability. On the one hand there are various categorizations of language ability, first language Welsh (L1) and second language Welsh (L2) being the most popular. Academics trade in compound and co-ordinate bilingualism, primary and secondary bilingualism, receptive and productive bilingualism and preferred language. Classification and categorization is a natural and defensible activity (Everitt, 1974), yet the simplicity of categorization hides the complexity of the reality.

On the other hand there are the multidimensional matrices produced by Mackey (1962) and MacNamara (1969) which suggest that precise description of a person's bilingual ability can only be achieved by a large variety of tests. On the basis of these tests, a complex profile of an individual may be possible. Rather than being simply defined as L1 or L2 a person may be described in a quantitatively accurate manner on a large number of dimensions.

Categorization simplifies unsympathetically. It reduces individual differences to similarities. Categorization is a reduction to black and white, where not only shades of grey are ignored but so is the whole variety of colours that can describe an individual. Yet for the sake of comparability of persons, compatibility of treatment and ease of conceptualization, categorization of both tests and individuals is required. This is the inevitable paradox.

The unsolved problem is that categorization and measurement have not been bedfellows. Those who have produced neat conceptual distinctions and classifications have generally not based them on any empirical foundation. The categorizations tend to be philosophically or theoretically derived, with little or no attempt to test out the validity and replicability of the distinctions in practice. What is particularly disturbing is that the gap between theoretical categorizations and precise multi-faceted descriptions of individual skills in bilingualism is so wide. The result is the practice of labelling children and adults in attractive but simplistic categories, despite the warning from Mackey (1962) and MacNamara (1969) in particular, of the multi-dimensional nature of language ability. Later on in the chapter, a solution will be suggested.

Language Usage

As distinct from ability with language, Mackey (1962) outlines the nature of functional bilingualism. Functional bilingualism concerns when and where and with whom people use their two languages. A person may have great ability in two languages, yet predominantly uses just one language. Another may have simple skills in oracy and not literacy in a minority language, yet use that minority language almost all the time. Skill in, and usage of, a language are not necessarily related.

Compared with measuring language ability, determining a person's use of language might appear to be relatively straightforward. This could be achieved by observation. An anthropological type of study may record details of the range of contexts and contacts where two languages are used. More customarily, use of language has been measured quantitatively. By a short questionnaire it is possible to survey an individual's use of two languages. For example, "Do you speak Welsh to your mother?" may be asked, with replies being Always/Mostly/About half the time/Not often/Never. Or "What language do you speak to your mother?" could alternatively be asked, responses being Always in Welsh/Mostly in Welsh/Sometimes in Welsh, Sometimes in English/Mostly in English/Always in English.

The choice of language targets and situations is both unrestricted and crucial. Baker & Hinde (1984) provide a detailed examination of this issue. The range of people and contexts for a pupil will be a selection of the following.

Family	Significant Others	Contexts/Domains
Mother	Friends at school	Shopping
Father	Teachers at school	Church/Chapel
Brothers	Friends outside school	TV/Video tapes
Sisters	Neighbours	Radio
Grandparents		Books
Other Relations		Newspapers/Magazines/Comics
		Societies and Clubs
		Records/Cassettes
		Microcomputer
		Cinema/Discos
		Correspondence

Further definition and conceptual classification of functional bilingualism is discussed in Weinreich (1953), Ferguson (1959), Mackey (1962), Fishman (1965), Cooper (1969) and Baker & Hinde (1984). Inevitably discussion of what comprises functional bilingualism moves on to measurement. In order to gauge the extent to which a person uses two languages, a Language Background Questionnaire is employed (e.g. Hoffman, 1934; Rees, 1954; Jones, 1966; Weller, 1978; Linguistic Minorities Project, 1983). The most recent published Welsh example is also one of the most inclusive of Language Background Questionnaires. Sharp *et al.* (1973) ask questions about a pupil's use of Welsh and English to parents, brothers and sisters, friends, in church/chapel, mass media, with teachers, various activities (e.g. choir, games, Urdd — The Welsh League of Youth, running errands, other adults, writing and reading).

In Language Background Questionnaires it is also the practice to ask "indirect" questions about a person's language environment. For example, "What language does your mother speak to your father?" The logic of inclusion of such items is that the person being questioned experiences language receptively. There is little apparent difference between mother speaking to "me" directly and mother talking to father when I am listening. Both provide a language background. However, there is an assumption here. The question assumes that "I" am always present, and involved when conversation occurs between other members of the family. This is particularly important as the choice of speaking Welsh or English may change according to who is present. Take a simple example. A mother may speak Welsh to her husband when they are alone. If their child enters and prefers to speak English, the conversation may switch to English. In response to the question "What language does your mother speak to your father?", the child may well answer "Welsh", yet the child's language experience of mother speaking to father is English. In conclusion, such "indirect" language background questions may be misleading.

What appears to be needed is a distinction between the terms functional bilingualism and language background. Language background is the wider concept, referring to indirect as well as direct experience of language. "Bystander" experiences count and may be measured by such questions as "What language does your mother speak to your father when you are present?" Functional bilingualism is a narrower concept, concerning use of language only. Functional bilingualism is restricted to the personal production and reception of language, i.e. speaking, writing, reading and direct listening. Direct listening refers to being directly addressed as opposed to coincidental bystander experience. The distinc tion is essentially between a total language environment and specific use by an individual of language skills.

If there is a choice between a Language Background Questionnaire and a Functional Bilingualism Questionnaire, the former will contain "indirect" language questions, the latter will exclude such items. There is also another choice to be made. How many people and contexts are to be included in the questionnaire? For a pupil, should questions be restricted to the contexts of home, school, mass media and peers? Or should questions be as inclusive as possible, taking in errands, uncles, choirs and letter writing? On the surface it may appear that the more inclusive the questions, the better the scale. There is a problem which an example from Baker & Hinde (1984: 46) will illustrate.

"A person who says she speaks Welsh to her father (mostly away at sea), her grandparents (seen once a year), her friends (but tends to be an isolate), reads Welsh books and newspapers (only occasionally), attends Welsh chapel (marriages and funerals only) but spends most of her time with an English speaking mother and in an English speaking school might gain a fairly high 'Welsh' score."

The example suggests that the "to whom" question needs to be supplemented by a "how often" question. To list a range of situations and people may be to hide the relative extent of usage of Welsh and English. Mackey (1962) and MacNamara (1969) suggest a two dimensional analysis with language contacts representing one continuum and frequency of usage the other. Table 16 illustrates this preferred approach. If "How often do you speak Welsh to these?" is asked, the following table may be completed.

TABLE 16. *A Two Dimensional Analysis of Functional Bilingualism*

Duration in time	Mother	Father	Contacts/Situations Brothers/ Sisters	Mass Media	Friends	School/ Work	Organiza-tional Affiliation
Always							
Often							
Sometimes							
Rarely							
Never							

The final product of a questionnaire to measure language background or functional bilingualism tends to be a single score. A score on a scale seems more refined and sensitive than categorizing people as L1 or L2. It expresses the idea that there are many shades of grey in between the black and the white. But as has been expressed previously, some form of categorization and labelling seems necessary for ease of description. To say that a person uses Welsh at home and school but predominantly speaks English elsewhere and watches large amounts of English language television may be more meaningful than a score of 47 on a questionnaire.

The practice of categorization from such questionnaires is not standard. Jones (1966) reduced scores to three groups: Welsh, English and mixed background. Jones's (1966: 190) method of categorization was as follows:

"Those who score +51 per cent to +100 per cent are Welsh
Those who score −74 per cent to +50 per cent are Mixed
Those who score −75 per cent to −100 per cent are English"

But as Jones (1966) admits, "The exact line of demarcation between these groups in terms of questionnaire scores was largely a matter of personal estimation" (p. 184).

Sharp et al. (1973) reduced scores to four groups:

Group 1: Welsh used more often than English. Scores: 60–100
Group 2: Welsh used as often as English. Scores: 30–59
Group 3: English first language but able to use Welsh. Scores: 1–29
Group 4: English always. Score: 0.

This classification was achieved by a visual inspection of the scores. Classifications from Language Background Questionnaires in Wales have resulted in ten categories (Morgan, 1955) down to two categories (Jones, 1953; Davies, 1957) with little or no comparability or uniformity in categorization. Jones et al. (1957), Jones (1955) and Lewis (1959) each use four categories of language background, bearing imperfect relationship to each other or to Sharp et al's (1973) four categories.

It seems clear that a method other than visual inspection of the distribution of scores is needed to produce categories. A method is needed to establish with some kind of confidence the most appropriate number of categories to be derived from scores on a Language Background Question-naire. A solution to this problem will be offered shortly.

The Problem Stated

From the examination of two issues, the same problem has arisen. In discussing the nature of language skill and ability, it was argued that the categorizations that abound are separate from the measurement proce-dures. To label someone as first language Welsh or second language Welsh is to do an injustice to the wide variety of skills that exist in linguistic ability. It was argued that categorizations and classifications need to be empirically tested or derived. It may be easy to produce a neat distinction between two or more kinds of bilingual ability, but that distinction may not match reality. Such categorizations are capable of investigation by re-search.

In discussing the nature of language usage, a similar but differently derived problem was encountered. With language skill and ability there has been little rapprochement between classification and measurement. With language usage there is a strong tradition of measurement by Language Background Questionnaires and subsequent classification into groups. It was argued that the basis for such categorization was in doubt. With what degree of confidence can we assume when using one set of data that pupils fall into three rather than four or five categories?

The two issues ask the same question. How can measurement of language ability and usage be converted into classification? Having tested bilingual skill with a few or with many tests how many types or groups of people exist? Or after measuring usage of two languages, what major classes of similar individuals exist? A solution lies in a statistical technique called cluster analysis or numerical taxonomy.

A Solution to the Problem

A scaled down and simplified example of the possibilities and process of cluster analysis will be given. Imagine that eight pupils have been measured on language ability or usage. How many skills are tested or how many questions are asked is not a problem in cluster analysis. The aim is to find the number of groups into which the eight pupils fit. Certain cluster analysis techniques start by finding which two pupils are most similar, taking all tests or questions into account. Having joined two pupils together the procedure finds which two pupils are the next most similar to the two "joined" pupils. The fusion process may be represented in a diagram.

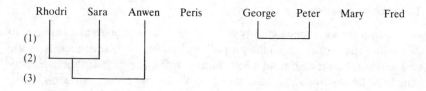

Three fusions are represented. In order they are

1) George and Peter
2) Rhodri and Sara
3) Anwen with Rhodri and Sara

The length of the vertical lines represents the degree of similarity between individuals or groups. The fusion process continues until, for example, a result as follows.

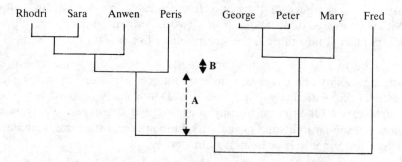

Such a diagram would suggest three groups:

Group 1: Rhodri, Sara, Anwen and Peris
Group 2: George, Peter and Mary
Group 3: Fred

The long dotted line (A) compared with the very short line (B) is one basis in this technique for determining the number of groups. After Peris has been joined to the first group, there is a big distance between the next joining of groups. Fred is in some way idiosyncratic, showing that the technique can recognize exceptions and individual differences.

Cluster analysis is a statistical technique which attempts to sort individuals or any entity into groups. Each individual in a particular group will have more characteristics in common with other members of that group than with individuals residing in other groups. Cluster analysis is an umbrella term for a variety of different specific techniques of calculation (Everitt, 1974).

Having decided on the number of groupings present, then follows the description and profiling of those clusters. Two simplified examples will illustrate.

Ability	Group 1	Group 2	Group 3
Reading Test (Welsh)	good	poor	poor
Reading Test (English)	average	average	good
Composition Test (Welsh)	good	poor	poor
Composition Test (English)	average	average	good
Oral Test (Welsh)	good	good	poor
Oral Test (English)	average	average	good

Group 1 may be portrayed as skilled in Welsh, Group 3 as having ability in English and not Welsh, and Group 2 as having oral but not literary ability in Welsh.

The second example concerns language background.

Language spoken:	Group 1	Group 2	Group 3	Group 4
at home	Welsh	Welsh	English	Mixed
in school	Welsh	English	Mixed	Mixed
with friends	Welsh	Mixed	English	Mixed
mass media	Mixed	English	English	Mixed

Group 1 may be defined as having a Welsh background, Group 3 an English background, and Group 2 having a mixed language environment with Welsh the language of the hearth, but English used at school and in experiencing mass media. Group 4 may be portrayed as the most functionally bilingual, speaking both languages in each of the four contexts.

One example of the classification of a medium sized sample of children using a 26 question Language Background Scale may be found in Baker & Hinde (1984). This study considers the problems and potential of a recent development, latent class analysis, in defining typologies of bilingual background, and the attendant practical difficulties of using cluster analysis. As a result of analysis by the latent class model, the chances (probability) of a person belonging to a group are provided, rather than unambiguous sorting into groups.

A second example is the ongoing production of a Welsh language spelling test for use in Gwynedd schools. To produce a single set of norms (average scores) or spelling ages based on Gwynedd pupils aged 7 to 12 would fail to take into account the existence of variation in language background and language ability. Therefore pupils were given a simple language background questionnaire during the pilot stage. A kind of cluster analysis suggested two major groupings of children and a much smaller third group. As a consequence norms can be produced for two separate groups of pupils, such groupings being defined by the cluster analysis.

Summary and Conclusion

To answer the question "Are you Welsh" is as impossible for the researcher as it is for the respondent. The question is value laden and ambiguous. To answer the question "Are you Welsh speaking?" is also impossible as it is ambiguous. Some can but don't. Others do but with difficulty. Mackey's (1962) distinction between degree and function was regarded as important. However, while it is possible to distinguish between language ability and language usage, it is difficult to define and measure each concept. Language ability concerns speaking and listening, reading and writing, and these four skills can then be broken down into sub-skills, needing to be measured in different contexts and situations. Language usage requires consideration of how many language contacts (e.g. parents, teachers, TV) need to be included in a questionnaire and the balance between direct experience and bystander experience. Usage of two languages has to take into account not only "to whom" but also "how long".

Frequency and duration is one dimension; language contacts a separate dimension.

Both language ability and usage bequeath a problem of the relationship between categorization and measurement. The definition and classification of bilingual skills have tended to occur apart from measurement. Yet it would appear that measurement can confirm, reject or suggest categorizations. The classification of bilingual usage has occurred via the use of appropriate Language Background Questionnaires. However, the categorizations based on scores seem to have little foundation. Different authors have used different ways of grouping pupils and different numbers of groups.

The connection between measurement and categorization seems possible by cluster analysis. Cluster analysis is a statistical process of sorting individuals into groups. Using a variety of tests of linguistic ability, or a variety of questions on language background, it is possible by cluster analysis to establish a foundation for categorization.

4   Does Bilingual Education Work?
A Bilingual Education Model

Introduction

Does bilingual education work? For many Welsh speakers who wish to preserve and protect their language and cultural inheritance, the answer will not be in doubt. For some English speakers, bilingual education is a bone of contention. Where there are separate Welsh-speaking "bilingual" schools or units, English parents may be concerned about, for example, a limited range of subjects being offered in smaller schools, or linguistic divisions being created amongst pupils from the same neighbourhood. Where bilingual education is made almost compulsory, as in the county of Gwynedd, then English speakers may be concerned about the restrictions on freedom of choice. These issues are considered in Rawkins (1979). For a minority of Welsh speakers, bilingual education may also be a bone of contention. To some, bilingual education is a compromise between monoglot Welsh and monoglot English education. Bilingual education is seen by this minority as a stage in the disappearance of the minority language. Irrespective of attitude, bilingual education in Wales is an issue of interest and debate.

Qualitative and Quantitative Approaches

In order to begin to answer the question "Does bilingual education work?" there is a need to suggest how an empirical answer may be achieved. One important approach to answering the question would be to survey parents, teachers, pupils, community leaders, industrialists and other groups interested in the topic. Questions could be asked about their perception of the value and effectiveness of different kinds of bilingual education (Fishman, 1976; Baker & de Kanter, 1983). A large number of different opinions could be obtained, simple or complex, emotive or rational, positive or negative. An anthropological or phenomenological, interpretive approach would examine the assumptions made, the reasons for the views, and through content analysis arrive at some kind of interpretation, theory, or typology. Such a study has yet to be undertaken in Wales. There are pen portraits on a small scale (Rawkins, 1979; Khleif, 1980), but no large scale study. MacDonald *et al.* (1982) have conducted a case study of bilingual education in Boston, USA, providing an example of an in-depth qualitative approach to researching bilingual schooling at a micro level, while at the same time contextualizing the case of terms of United States bilingual education policy.

The question "Does bilingual education work?" is also capable of a different kind of answer. One tradition in social science is the quantitative or statistical approach. Essentially, a problem is reduced to variables and people are measured. For example, an experiment may compare the examination results of a designated bilingual secondary school and a monoglot English school, attempting to take into account such differences as social class and measured intelligence. In this tradition, Baker & de Kanter (1983) provide a meta-analysis of bilingual education in the USA, including the topic of the effectiveness of bilingual schooling. The publication examines measurable components of bilingual schooling on a national scale. Following in the same tradition is Swain & Lapkin's (1982) consideration of Canadian bilingual programmes.

The same question "Does bilingual education work?" can be answered by the two traditions of research, the qualitative and the quantitative. Contentiously, these can be seen as two complementary ways of examining the same issue. This chapter provides a model to examine bilingual education. It is appropriate to both qualitative and quantitative types of research. The model is important in bilingual research because it shows that simple questions necessarily involve complex answers.

The Input-Output Model

The main tradition in research on bilingualism tends to be an examination of a very specific question. For example, Jones (1955) looked at the relationship between Welsh/English language background and English reading ability in 10 and 11 year olds. The assumption is that language background is the cause of more or less attainment in reading in the majority language. This bears a superficial analogy to industrial production. For example, research in a factory may investigate whether the age of the workers affects the volume of production. Do younger workers or older and more experienced workers create higher output? The analogy is used to introduce a model of research, called the input-output model. One input into the factory is the workers; one measurable output is the quantity of production. In terms of reading and language background the input-output model can be pictorially represented in the following way. The arrows show the direction of cause and effect.

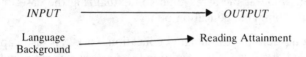

Inputs in Bilingual Education

What are the inputs into bilingual education that may affect outcomes? *First*, there are *teachers*. Troike & Saville-Troike (1982) have suggested the particular qualities needed by bilingual teachers on top of normal qualities expected of all teachers. These are not value-free but may be listed in an abbreviated form as:

Language proficiency. Proficiency may be needed by teachers in two languages. This means proficiency enough to execute normal classroom functions through the majority and minority language. Such bilingual proficiency may be profiled in terms of all the productive and receptive skills as detailed in Table 14 of Chapter 3.

Linguistic knowledge. Knowledge may be needed by teachers of the two languages to teach language acquisition in a rational, purposeful and structured manner. Such knowledge may be divided into two parts. First, a teacher may need to understand something about the methods of teaching language and the developmental sequence in language learning. Pedagogical expertise in teaching both languages as a first language and a second language may be a valued teacher attribute. Second, a teacher may need to understand some of the foundations of linguistics: sociolinguistics, psycholinguistics and syntax, for example.

Cultural knowledge. Awareness may be needed of the bicultural nature of society to enable enculturation to accompany linguistic development. A bilingual teacher may need to be well grounded in the customs, history and traditions of the minority culture or cultures as well as the majority culture. To specify the degree to which a teacher is culturally pluralistic is as elusive as it is to specify the means of properly and fairly imparting both cultures. Awareness of both cultures may be different from the ability to communicate cultural pluralism. A bicultural teacher may not be able to cultivate biculturalism in pupils.

Teaching competencies. The ability may be needed to present lessons in both languages across the curriculum. For example, a Primary school teacher may need to be able to present Science through the minority language. The ability, where necessary, to modify material in a majority language to minority language usage may be an additional requirement of a bilingual teacher.

A *second* input into bilingual education is *pupils*. The sex, social class and personality of pupils are examples of input variables that may have an effect on output (e.g. exam success). In a bilingual educational setting there will be additional and sometimes different inputs from pupils as apart from the inputs of all pupils in all educational settings.

1. What kind of skill and aptitude has a child in the two languages (see Chapter 3)? A pupil may start in school as a nearly balanced bilingual or only be able to speak the majority or minority language. What is the language background of the child both in terms of the home and community? (Mackey, 1977).

2. What attitude has a child to the two languages and two cultures (Sharp *et al.*, 1973)? Attitude and motivation are likely to play a determining part in attainment in the two languages (Gardner & Lambert, 1972). Instrumental and integrative motivation may be important ingredients in a successful bilingual education recipe.

Outputs in Bilingual Education

If the initial ingredients are teacher and pupil characteristics, what are the outputs of bilingual education? These will be contentious and open to addition, but may be listed as:

1. Attainment in two languages (e.g. Swain & Lapkin, 1982).

2. Attitude towards the two languages and culture.

3. Integration into linguistically and culturally different groups.

4. Longer-term effects, e.g. rearing children bilingually, participation in minority language cultural activities throughout life (e.g. Harrison *et al.*, 1981).

5. Short term, intermediate effects, e.g. opting to take Welsh or Welsh Studies to examination level (see Chapter 6), choosing to go to a Bilingual Secondary school after Primary education.

These outcomes are a small but important subset of general educational outcomes, e.g. gaining employment, job satisfaction, affective, moral and personality development, avoidance of criminal activity, examination success and school attendance.

The model outlined so far suggests that a series of questions can be posed by relating inputs to outputs. For example, part of Sharp *et al.*'s (1973) research may be conceptualized in terms of this model.

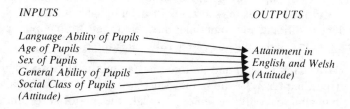

INPUTS

Language Ability of Pupils
Age of Pupils
Sex of Pupils
General Ability of Pupils
Social Class of Pupils
(Attitude)

OUTPUTS

Attainment in
English and Welsh
(Attitude)

It should be noted that attitude to a language can be used as both an input and an output variable. The pupil starts school with attitudes towards two languages and two cultures and these are likely to affect eventual attainment. Simultaneously such attitudes are regarded as an important consequence of bilingual education, possibly containing something which is more long lasting than examination preference. Sharp *et al.* (1973) therefore validly use attitude as both an input an output measure. Similarly ability may be used both as an input and output variable. A pupil's ability may both determine outcome and also be a valued product of the educational experience.

The Context of Bilingual Education

So far the model portrayed has two components, input and output. The full model has four elements (Dunkin & Biddle, 1974; Gage, 1978; Rutter *et al.*, 1979). The need for a third element, context, may be demonstrated by an example. Research has found that language background affects English reading ability (Jones, 1955). This is a very general finding which may need to be refined and constrained by a consideration of intervening variables. Does pupil age or parental social class or the demographical character of the neighbourhood and school catchment area have an effect? Does the type of school matter? Do children in small rural schools, designated bilingual schools in Anglicized areas or large schools in industrial areas follow the same pattern? How does the number of children in a class, the nature of the curriculum, the textbooks or teaching programmes, methods of grouping children, progressive or traditional teaching methods all affect that simplistic relationship between language background and reading ability? A simple relationship between input and output variables in bilingual education may tend to hide a more complex pattern when the reality of the context is added. Input and output variables are like two still figures on a stage. Adding context provides the stage scenery. The figures change in their nature, interaction and importance as the scenery changes.

The context element of the bilingual education model concerns four categories; examples of issues within each category are raised as questions:

(i) *Nature of the Community.* To what extent is the community within which the school is placed bilingual, bicultural, positive or negative towards bilingual education in its various forms? (Sharp, 1973).

(ii) *Nature of the School.* Is the school a designated bilingual school, a school placed in a naturally Welsh area? What is the language of the playground? Mackey (1970) provides a very detailed typology of bilingual schooling.

(iii) *Nature of the Classroom.* Are children linguistically grouped or divided; is there individual instruction in the preferred language? What is the linguistic balance of the classroom? Is there full immersion or partial immersion in the second language? Is the aim transitional bilingual education, submersion, immersion or second language teaching? (e.g. TEFL)

(iv) *Nature of Curriculum Material.* What kind of textbooks, audio visual aids, programmes and projects are used with each language? What approaches does the teacher use in oral work or creative activity? Are technological aids (e.g. microcomputer) used equally in the two languages, or is there a bias towards the majority language in such usage?

While adding a context element to the model allows questions relating input and output to be refined, it also suggests that questions can be asked about the relationship between context and output. For example,

Swain & Lapkin's (1982) evaluation of various French immersion programmes in Canada relates mostly to a context-output model. In part of the research early and late immersion pupils are compared for their proficiency in French. The perceived effects of different bilingual education programmes relates essentially to a context-output research design.

The Process of Bilingual Education

The input-output model and the input-context-output model of bilingual education have dominated bilingual research. The long-running debate on the relationship between bilingualism and "intelligence", the explorations into attitude and motivation as crucial variables in bilingual attainment and cultural identification, and the relationship between bilingualism and school performance (e.g. MacNamara, 1966) are examples of the domination of input-output analysis in research and bilingual literature. The problem with the model is that it is a "black box" model. A researcher and evaluator do not have to enter the classroom to execute such research. W. R. Jones (1966), for example, acknowledges that data for analysis were gained by administrative channels in the Local Authority. Analogously, someone researching on age of workers and production in a factory need not enter the factory door. The term "black box" therefore refers to a researcher being in the dark about what actually goes on in the classroom. A further component to this model is needed. The fourth component of the model is termed PROCESS. Consideration of the processes of a bilingual classroom provides a "glass box" model; one that is open to viewing the second by second interactions between teacher, pupils and the curriculum. Or to change analogies, the figures on stage come alive, they move, develop and change as the play unfolds.

In general, process refers to pupil-pupil interaction, teacher-pupil interaction, pupil-curriculum and teacher-curriculum patterns of activity. In terms specific to bilingual education, examples of questions about process may be:

1. What amount of time does the teacher spend in using each language? What are the variations in this according to the topic or activity or different pupils?

2. How does the teacher interpret and selectively use materials, projects and programmes? How do pupils engage different types of bilingual curriculum? What is their work involvement rate in different languages?

3. What is the distribution of rewards and reinforcements for using each language? What is the nature of encouragement to interact and achieve bilingually?

The methodology and first sightings of such process investigation of bilingual schooling are available in case studies (MacDonald *et al.*, 1982) and in Bilingual Interaction Analysis (Townsend, 1976). However, at the moment process considerations are relatively uncharted territory in bilingual schooling.

An Illustration of the Model

An illustration of the use of the bilingual education model will now be given, demonstrating how a piece of research may use the model. This example will concern only a small subset of variables from each of the four parts of the model in order to provide a relatively simple illustration.

Suppose a hypothetical piece of research examined choice of Secondary school, where pupils have the option of going to a designated Bilingual Secondary school or a more "English" Comprehensive school. The OUPUT variable becomes choice of Secondary education. The research might start by examining the language background of pupils, expecting that language background relates to choice of school. The INPUT variable becomes language background. On finding the predicted pattern between input and output, the researcher may feel concerned that the results were camouflaging an important CONTEXT effect. Suppose a number of pupils of the same language background were found to choose differently. Rural Primary school children may be more keen to attend the Bilingual Secondary school than urban children. The rural or urban nature of the school may intrude significantly in the simple relationship between language background and school choice.

With three parts of the model included, the conclusion may be that a link between language background and school choice is evident, but is affected significantly by attending a rural or urban school. The three parts of the model do not provide a depth interpretation of the causes of the relationship. We have to enter the urban and rural feeder Primary schools to examine potential causes. In looking at PROCESS factors, we may find rural Primary teachers are more positively reinforcing children speaking in the minority language. This may be one factor affecting choice.

The illustration suggests three things in particular. First, that research relating two entities (e.g. input-output) may ignore the complex interactive nature of bilingual education. In reality, there are no simple cause and effects. Variables inter-relate in a complex network of patterns. All research is limited by the selection of variables chosen to examine the complex reality of bilingual education.

Second, while interpretations of relationships can be given from an input-context-output design, such interpretations tend to be relatively superficial until process is examined. To understand process needs an understanding of input, context and output considerations. To understand process is also to move closer to the deeper level of causation in bilingual education.

Third, the illustration could be researched by case study and other interpretive techniques. It could also be examined quantitatively. Each research method has its own ideas about examining causation. Each method has its own techniques of accumulating data or evidence on inputs, outputs, contexts and processes. Both methods can use the model to define and refine analyses.

A Model of Bilingual Education and Some Attendant Problems

The chapter started with the question, "Does bilingual education work?". It has been suggested that the answer could be sought by a poll, case studies or by experimental research. The question can never be answered by a "yes" or a "no". Given the individuality and uniqueness of pupils, teachers, schools and language communities, the best that can be hoped for are some refined generalizations. A model is helpful and necessary to ensure that statements or observations about bilingual education *are* refined. The model encourages great caution and care to be expressed in making pronouncements. Any one observation or research finding is limited by how few factors have been taken into account. This model is presented diagramatically in Table 17.

The model also provides some guidance on making generalizations from research. An illustration may help. To say it will rain in Wales in April next year has a high probability of being correct. At the same time it is of no help to the farmer, fisherman or holiday maker because it is so general as to be imprecise. To say it will rain outside the Castle in Caernarfon at 3.30 p.m., April 23rd next year is to be highly specific, very precise and with much less probability of being correct. If correct, it helps the visitor to Caernarfon Castle, but is of no value to a person elsewhere in Wales.

TABLE 17. *A Bilingual Education Model* [1]

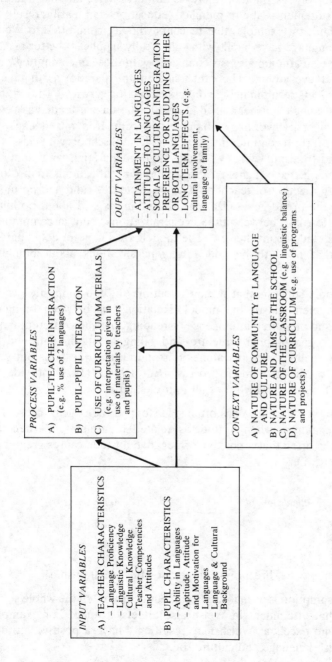

Note 1. This model may be extended to include attributes not specific to bilingual education by reference to Dunkin & Biddle, (1974).

2. Arrows show the most usual connections made by research in relating elements of the model.

In terms of the model, there is a necessary paradox. Making generalized statements about bilingual education can easily result in truisms. To find, for example, that teachers who are committed to Welsh culture and language have pupils with statistically significant better results in terms of Welsh attainment tests compared with those uncommitted says nothing about everything. The other side of the paradox is that very specific statements result in help and reassurance for very few. To find, for example, that female teachers, aged 25 to 30, who have attended a Welsh College or University, working with pupils who come from mixed language homes in Welsh rural communities, teaching in rural schools with class size between 8 and 16, using Cyfres y Ddraig language materials with plenty of open questioning, have higher Welsh attainment with pupils than other complex categorization of teachers, is to be accurate, valid and no more helpful than the broad generalization. Everything is said about nothing. The gauntlet to run is between broad generalizations about large numbers and specific details about the few. The model is valuable in detailing the constraints that need to be added to generalizations about bilingual education.

The model suggests that it may sometimes be too simplistic just to consider two elements of the model. Relationships between bilingual background and measured intelligence or reading, between different types of bilingual organizational structure and bilingual attainment tend to over-simplify reality. Such researches raise important questions but give few answers particularly about process. Rutter *et al.* (1979) provide an illustration of research which uses all four elements.

Bilingual research also has often side-stepped the issue of cause and effect. For example, when attitude is related to attainment, then the presumption is often that a positive or negative attitude causes greater or less attainment, i.e.

Attitude towards   *Attainment*

Welsh   *in Welsh*

(the arrow shows the direction of the cause-effect relationship).

The assumption is probably correct, but does not tell the whole story. It may be that attainment in Welsh also affects attitude. For example, somebody who excels at Welsh may resultingly have a positive attitude towards Welsh language and culture, i.e.

Attitude to Welsh   *Attainment in Welsh*

The arrows in the diagram suggest a reciprocating cause and effect relationship. Attitude to the Welsh language or culture may simultaneously be both a cause and effect of ability in Welsh at school.

A similar though perhaps weaker reciprocation may occur between language background and intelligence or cognitive development. The research examining whether bilingualism has any subtractive or additive effects on "intelligence" or cognitive abilities has often been conceptualized in terms of a simple cause-effect relationship. Peal & Lambert (1962) in their famous research showing cognitive advantages for bilinguals over monoglots were aware of this problem.

> "It is not possible to state from the present study whether the more intelligent child became bilingual or whether bilingualism aided his intellectual development." (p. 20)

The problem of cause and effect highlights a possible illusion in viewing the Bilingual Education Model. It may create the impression of a rather static, deterministic, reductionist education system. An analogy may illustrate. The Model may appear like a still photograph. It may detract from the reality of constantly changing, complex chemical actions and reactions. Reality is more like a film than a snapshot. There is continuity and sequence, there are intended and unintended movements, there is an incalculable mystery of interactions between components. To change analogies, the Model describes the play, actors, scenery, props and gives audience reaction. It may fail to portray the intensity of the drama. Such mystery and drama can be engaged in examining process. In bilingual research, process is all too often ignored.

Summary and Conclusion

In an attempt to answer the question, "Does bilingual education work?" it appears necessary to first of all stipulate the conditions that may make for more or less success. This includes defining what constitutes success. The chapter has suggested that such conditions may be looked at under four headings.

Inputs. Whether bilingual education will be successful or not may vary with the initial ingredients, termed *inputs*. The intial ingredients are pupils

and teachers, and their linguistic and cultural background, bilingual
aptitudes, abilities, attitudes and commitment, all of which may affect the
final product.

Outputs.   Bilingual education may be examined for success or failure by a
number of different products. People will differ as to their expectations of
what these outcomes or *outputs* should be. For some attainment in tests
and examinations in the two languages will be a vital indicator. For others,
attitude to the minority language may be seen as an equal or more
desirable outcome. A favourable attitude to a minority language at the end
of formal education may contain an optimistic promise of a lasting
commitment to that language. If long term products are regarded as
important, then integration into the minority language community culture
may be regarded as a more vital output of bilingual education than
successful performance on tests and examinations.

Context.   Pupils and teachers do not work in a vacuum. There is the
context within which they operate. Similar teachers and pupils may behave
and perform differently according to the type of community ethos which
surrounds them, the atmosphere and aims of the school, the classroom and
the curriculum. The *input-output* relationship is likely to be affected
positively or negatively by the environment that encapsulates the relationship.

Process.   To examine only *input, output* and *context* would not describe the
second by second action of a bilingual classroom. The final element of the
model is *process*, which describes the detailed action of a bilingual
classroom. *Process* concerns interactions, interpretations, rituals, and
activity between teachers, pupils and materials. *Input, output* and *context*
provide still frames of bilingual schooling. *Process* provides a film.

It may never be possible to give a yes or no answer to the question,
"Does bilingual education work?" What the model does is to show what
questions may be asked. It suggests caution in answering questions, by
supplying the constraints needed in an answer. If the answer involves . . .
"it depends on" . . . then the model outlines such dependencies. It provides
a basis for the refinement of answers and analyses.

5 Missionaries and Cells: Curriculum Development in Wales

Prologue

In 1977–1978 the Schools Council Committee for Wales, the body which has been mostly responsible for curriculum development in the Welsh language, floated the possibility of a Project to produce Welsh language curriculum materials and diagnostic tests for children experiencing learning difficulties. Further impetus was gained firstly from the Warnock Report (1978) which emphasized the plight of minority groups whose special needs are not usually met by current curriculum development, and secondly from the Principles and Programmes laid down by the Schools Council in 1979 which included the importance of attending to the needs of individual children with learning difficulties coming from ethnic minorities.

The possibility became reality in the setting up of a large scale curriculum development Project based at the University College of North Wales and the Bangor Normal College (1980–1983). Hereafter this will be termed the Bangor Project. Like previous curriculum development projects in Wales, the team of lecturers, researchers and development officers had a choice. Should the team create what it saw as progressive, enlightened materials and tests? What role should bodies such as HMI and LEA's play in the development and evaluation?

The team appeared to have the choice of three different approaches. These were termed the Missionary, Executive and Broker approaches to development and are discussed in Baker & Griffith (1983) and Baker (1984a). One choice of the Bangor team was to become *Missionaries*. If the team believed they had a preferable vision of what should be, "progressive" and "enlightened" materials could have been developed. Just as Missionaries may take what they see as a preferable religion, even the only

91

true faith to the unconverted, so a Project may consider they have a special revelation of salvation for curriculum practice. A Missionary Project will seek to impose centrally produced curriculum materials based on the assumption of a monopoly of expertise. The Team knows best.

A second choice of an initiating ideal was for the team to become *Executives*. If it is wrong for Project Missionaries to impose grass skirts on naked practitioners, then the direct opposite is to allow teachers to define what educational materials should be produced. Power is placed in the hands of those at grass roots level. The Project team become the Executives of teachers' wants. But how are teachers' wants defined? To talk to small groups of teachers, handpicked or readily available is not enough. What is required in an Executive approach is for the politics of consensus to play a dominant role. All teachers need to be consulted through an opinion poll. The assumption is that teachers know best and can relay this to the Project Team by a survey of wants.

A third approach for a Project is to assume a *Broker* role. The Team acting as Brokers implies that teachers' wants are important, but there are other interest groups which all need to be given the opportunity to state their preferences for development. Teachers' Trade Unions, Advisers and Education Officers in LEA's, Her Majesty's Inspectors of Education, parents, language pressure groups, all may have their own beliefs and wants. Each may be usefully consulted before making a decision about development of the curriculum. The Project Team must question, reconcile, arbitrate, clarify and judge what will be most acceptable to the greatest number of interest groups. The assumption is that everybody knows best. No one party has a monopoly of insight or truth.

These three approaches to fixing the aims, goals and content of developmental work are not mutually exclusive. They are ideal types or caricatures. Because they are models it would be too simplistic to look at Welsh language curriculum developments in the last decade and label them simply as Missionary, Broker or Executive in approach. Yet the developments that will be described shortly tend to be more Missionary than Executive in approach. While each development shows evidence of the Broker approach to a greater or lesser extent, a Missionary ideology has tended to prevail in Wales. What then are the characteristics of these developments and to what extent have they been successful? Has the Missionary tendency changed faith and traditions?

Welsh Language Curriculum Projects – General

The Schools Council Committee for Wales, created in 1964 and dissolved in 1984, was largely responsible for the thrust of Welsh language curriculum development in the 1970's. In 1968, Schools Council initiated a Project to foster experimental "bilingual" primary schools (SCBP). In the same year the Welsh Joint Education Committee established the Welsh National Language Unit which started by producing an audiovisual scheme for Primary schools based on Cymraeg Byw, a form of oral Welsh used in second language teaching (Evans, 1972). In the early 1970's, the Schools Council established two Welsh language curriculum development Projects. One, based at Bangor Normal College, created materials for Primary school pupils whose first language was Welsh (Cynllun y Porth). The other, based at the South Glamorgan Institute of Higher Education, produced a programme to foster reading development in Welsh (Cyfres y Ddraig). Also in the early 1970's, Schools Council commissioned the development of materials, based on initial research into factors such as spelling errors and idiomatic confusions, to aid progress in English of pupils whose first language was Welsh (Sharp *et al.*, 1977). This material was designed with rural children particularly in mind, for, as Chapter 1 revealed, Welsh language heartland areas tend to be rural in nature.

Since the late 1970's the major Welsh language curriculum developments have mostly occurred in a Welsh Office Project. Established in 1978 under the Directorship of Professor Dodson at Aberystwyth, the Project started working in the areas of geography, history and religious education in the Secondary school. In 1979, the Project was extended to create materials and resources in biology, rural sciences, craft, technology and design for Secondary pupils learning these subjects through the medium of Welsh in years one to three. Publication of 40 booklets in History, 19 in Religious Education, 18 in Biology, 27 in Geography and 9 in Craft, Design and Technology was undertaken by a Welsh Joint Education Committee. In March 1983, a new Project was established to prepare Welsh language materials in Geography, History and Religious Education for forms IV and V in Secondary schools. Approximately 70 to 80 booklets are expected to be produced before the end of the current project in March 1986.

Owing to a lack of research evidence and evaluation on a number of these developments, only three Projects have been selected in order to examine the two central questions of this chapter. What kind of curriculum development in the Welsh language may be most effective? Are there more and less preferable paths to Welsh language curriculum development?

Schools Council Bilingual Project (SCBP)

The SCBP combined two changes of direction, one in provision, one in practice. The findings of the Gittins Report (1967) led to the recommendation of the provision of experimental schools where English speaking pupils would use Welsh for about half the day as a medium for instruction. The "Missionary" change invoked by SCBP was to increase greatly the use of Welsh by such pupils, where previously in traditional schools they would mostly have had a half an hour lesson a day of Welsh as a second language.

The "Missionary" change in terms of practice injected into SCBP was the teaching methodology suggested by C. J. Dodson. Dodson (1967) argues for a distinction between medium-oriented and message-oriented communication in language learning. In medium-oriented communication, the focus of teaching and learning is on the language itself. In message-oriented communication the aim is for language to be the tool or means, with the focus on the message. Before SCBP, the dominant tradition in learning Welsh as a second language was by formal exercises in grammar and language with or without some direct oral work. Dodson (1967) criticized these methods for the artificiality and low level of language work. Language teaching was regarded as de-contextualized and language was seen as uncreative.

Dodson's (1967) methodology may be summarized as follows. The mother tongue is used to introduce new concepts and also as a short-cut to meaning when deemed necessary. At the same time each lesson cycle should go beyond a pupil using a second language for its own sake. A pupil needs to be given the opportunity to *make* use of the language for an end other than merely practice itself. For example, language drills or games may be followed by an activity (such as making a collage) which engages use of language learnt from the drill or game sequence. This illustrates one central concept of Dodson's (1967) methodology, that there should be systematic sequencing from medium-oriented to message-oriented communication.

Was and is SCBP successful? Given that a strong Missionary approach was embedded into SCBP by the "experimental school" suggestion of Gittins (1967) and the innovatory ideas of language teaching of

Dodson (1967), has such an approach to second language Welsh instruction been a success?

There are three sources of evidence which suggest that SCBP has met with some success. *First*, the Project started with 60 schools. By 1980, 1047 infant and junior classes in 187 schools were using the approach of the Schools Council Bilingual Project (Welsh Office, 1982). *Second*, in the SCBP quantitative research evaluation by Dr. Eurwen Price (1978), guarded optimism is observable. While amount of lesson time, attitude of teachers, degree of Welshness in a pupil's background all may affect negatively or positively pupil attainment, understanding and speaking were generally well established by the age of seven, with further consolidation and improvement over the next two years. General intellectual development and attainment in other basic subjects did not appear to suffer. Comparing children in the experimental schools with a control group of children revealed no statistically significant differences in English or mathematics attainment. *Third*, the qualitative evaluation report by Dodson (1978) notes a number of Achilles heels in the practical implementation of the ideals. These must not be glossed over, but concerning infant schools Dodson (1978) concludes, "The project can therefore be considered successful in so far as all the work, linguistic and non-linguistic, was by the end of the project superior to that done before and at the beginning of the project, while in many schools progress made was outstanding if compared with work done previously" (p. 53). At the junior school level, the Project was less successful due to four major factors: teachers devoting inadequate time to Welsh lessons; fewer materials and resources available for teaching Welsh; teachers lacking the training to teach Welsh by the method established by SCBP, and the desk-bound, teacher-directed, more academic verbal-written approach being less compatible with the aims and methods of SCBP (Dodson, 1978).

In conclusion, there appears a measure of support for a link between a "Missionary" approach and the success of this Project. Sixty schools became experimental units with a change in aim and teaching methodology, and the result according to Dodson (1978) was "a greatly beneficial impact on a large number of children throughout Wales" (p. 53). It may be argued in opposition to this conclusion that a novel development in education will lead to a "Hawthorne" effect. That is, teachers will be more motivated, more enthusiastic and harder working in a novel experimental situation. SCBP may have been successful because of a novelty effect. In response it may be argued that the project has continued and spread to other schools. Change in approach did not die with the finish of the project. The number of schools using SCBP materials has trebled since the close of the project.

It may also be argued in opposition that Dodson (1978) and Price (1978), the evaluators, had a vested interest in the success of the project which may have affected their evaluation reports. Dodson's methodology for language teaching was on trial in the Project, and Eurwen Price was appointed as a member of an enlarged project team during the life of SCBP. On the surface, it may appear that an agnostic can better evaluate a missionary's effect. A reading of their reports suggests a different picture. No evaluation can be objective. Ideology and a certain degree of subjectivity enter into all educational research (Carr & Kemmis, 1983). Yet Eurwen Price's (1978) psychometric approach is exemplary in that her interpretations rarely go further than the results permit. She constantly expresses caution and treats the findings with reserve and modesty. Similarly, while carrying a missionary's conviction about the correctness of his teaching methodology, Dodson (1978) is perceptively critical of the shortcomings of the project, as well as noting its successes. Comparing the case studies of Dodson (1978) and the "independent" case study of MacDonald et al. (1982), there appears little difference in certain qualities such as critical acumen, interpretivity and detachment.

The conclusion that a link appears to exist between the "Missionary" approach of SCBP and its success seems just. Yet, as will be argued later in the chapter, there are strong grounds for predicting the opposite. A centrally directed new approach imposed on schools with a "Missionary" vision of better practice has been linked with a lack of success in centrally directed projects both in America (Frymier, 1969) and in the U.K. (MacDonald & Walker, 1976; Webster, 1976).

Cyfres y Ddraig – The Teaching of Reading in Welsh

Cyfres y Ddraig is a series title given to a scheme, sponsored by the Schools Council Committee for Wales (1974–1980), to aid the teaching of reading in Welsh. The target age range is four to eight year olds. The reading programme comprises two boxes of materials containing reading books, alphabet cards, flashcards, a song book, cassette tapes and teachers' guides and handbooks.

It would be wrong to portray Cyfres y Ddraig solely as a Missionary project. While it certainly contains such elements, there is also strong evidence of a Broker approach. These two elements will first be examined.

Elen Ogwen (1980), the Director of the research and development project, lists three major origins for the project: the dearth of Welsh reading material; a desire to move away from the tendency in primary schools to teach mechanical reading without comprehension; to base materials on "scientific" research which examines the natural oral vocabulary and interests of the target children. In wishing to change perceived current practices in schools with regard to the teaching of reading, and in wishing to establish such teaching on "scientific" research, there is evidence in this project of the Missionary approach. But in comparison with SCBP, there appears more evidence of a Broker approach. The project team recorded and transcribed the conversations of approximately 1000 children in 30 schools throughout Wales. A computer analysis of the transcriptions provided a word count and a concordance (Ogwen, 1978). These lists for different age groups provided one basis for the creation and modification of the language materials. Simultaneously, the subject-matter for the stories was decided upon after careful examination of the lists of topics initiated by children in their conversations. In basing materials on children's natural language, systematically recorded, there is an element of "brokering" with the children.

Evidence of a Broker approach is also present in the project's formative evaluation. Trial materials were evaluated by individual conversations with teachers in their classrooms, questionnaires completed by class teachers and group discussions with project teachers. "All of the responses were carefully recorded and revision was undertaken during the final weeks of the project, in the light of these responses" (Ogwen, 1980: 319). If the project had taken the Executive approach, such revision would slavishly have followed the responses of the teachers. Grass roots evaluation would take on legally binding status. If the project took a solely Missionary approach, such formative evaluation would be relatively unimportant. It may be interesting, even informative, but never directive. The gospel to be spread cannot be invalidated by the unconverted. This project acted mostly as a Broker in evaluation, asking teachers and a consultative committee for feedback. By retaining the power of final decisions on revisions requested by teachers and the consultative committee, the project retained a measure of the Missionary approach in the formative evaluation.

If it is accepted that Cyfres y Ddraig is part Missionary, part Broker in approach, then the question arises as to the success of the Project. Factual and comparative evidence about its degree of success was obtained by the Schools Council Impact and Take Up Project (1976–1981). Steadman *et al.* (1981) examined the numbers of teachers who had contact or were acquainted with a number of Schools Council and non-Schools Council Projects. This essentially concerns familiarity with a project enough to decide whether to adopt its materials or not. The contact question is a measure of dissemination effectiveness. More important for present purposes was a question on use. This concerns the number of teachers who actually had adopted a project. Table 18 provides selected details of Steadman *et al.*'s (1981) findings.

TABLE 18. *Use and Contact with Projects by Primary School Teachers*

Scheme	% Contact with Teachers	% Use by Teachers
1) Cyfres y Ddraig	97%	93%
2) Breakthrough to Literacy	67%	44%
3) SRA (Non-Schools Council)	56%	39%

TABLE 19. *Use of Schools Council Projects by Primary School Teachers*

Scheme	% Teachers Using
1) Cyfres y Ddraig	93%
2) Communication Skills	16%
3) Environmental Studies	3%
4) Concept 7–9	2%
5) Development of Science & Maths Concepts	3%
6) Cynllun y Porth	69%

Steadman *et al.*'s (1981) findings show that on both contact and use, Cyfres y Ddraig has a higher percentage than two major English language schemes. 93% of teachers who do more than half of their teaching through the Welsh language claim to be using Cyfres y Ddraig materials. This is substantially higher than the most widely used English language primary project "Breakthrough to Literacy" (44% use) and the relatively well known non-Schools Council scheme SRA (39% use). However, where there is a choice, take up is bound to be lower, as is the case with English language schemes. When the 93% usage figure is set against less popular Schools Council Primary school projects, the result appears even more outstanding.

Steadman *et al.* (1981) found that the average use of 13 Schools Council Primary schools projects in the English language was 10%, with a range of 44% to 2% usage. The Welsh language projects were noticeably different. It is not only Cyfres y Ddraig which appears outstanding. Cynllun y Porth (Welsh as a first language at the Primary level) also reaches figures well above English Language projects. 87% of teachers were acquainted with Cynllun y Porth, and although dissemination was still occurring when Steadman *et al.* (1981) carried out their survey, already 69% of teachers who do more than half their teaching through Welsh claim to be using the Cynllun y Porth materials. Why then are these two Welsh Projects successful at least in terms of adoption in the classroom?

There are a number of reasons for the success of these projects developed at the centre and distributed outwards to the periphery. Six major reasons appear to be:

1. Local Educational Authorities involved themselves both in terms of finance and interest. Webster (1976) regards this as of paramount importance.

2. The need for Welsh language material was great. It may be analogous to the provision of a fatted calf when the previous diet consisted of husks of corn. Webster (1976) argues that curriculum innovation often requires a "crisis" situation. The historical circumstances may have produced a "crisis" situation in the 1970's, allowing entry of Welsh language materials.

3. The market for the materials was small in number, and relatively easy to identify and approach for dissemination purposes.

4. Both projects were ably and enthusiastically directed, with motivated and resourceful teams.

5. Particularly with Cyfres y Ddraig, and to a lesser extent with Cynllun y Porth, the curriculum area served has traditionally

been regarded as important and defined in terms of its boundaries with clarity.

6. The dissemination procedure was funded, very active and strategically operated. Nicoll (1982) observed six patterns of dissemination in School Council Projects and describes Cyfres y Ddraig as working with teachers in a supportive way, involving the LEA administrative structure and personnel for in-service training. Nicoll (1982) classifies Cynllun y Porth as providing direct support for teachers where possible. Both patterns are regarded as having their merits.

The major point drawn from Steadman *et al*.'s (1981) "distribution" evaluation of Cyfres y Ddraig and Cynllun y Porth is the difference between the English and Welsh language projects. All projects were centre-periphery in nature. Development was in the hands of a few at the centre, and such developments were then transported outwards to the classroom. The two Welsh language projects, at least partly Missionary in approach, were highly successful in take-up; all English language projects appear less successful. That centre-periphery developments might lack success was forecast by MacDonald & Walker (1976). Their critique of centre-periphery developments will be dealt with later in the chapter. The question that is raised by this section is whether Welsh language curriculum development is a special case. Does it deserve separate theoretical and financial consideration from mainstream British curriculum developments? This will be returned to later in the chapter.

The Bangor Project

At the beginning of the chapter, it was suggested that the Bangor project had an initial choice of whether to be Missionary, Executive or Broker in approach. There existed a tradition. Previous Welsh language projects were at least partly Missionary in approach. The teachers' handbooks with Cynllun y Porth, for example, reveal the desire to make language teaching and learning more progressive, more creative, more child-centred, experiential and experimental. It was also clear that previous Welsh language projects were relatively successful despite, or because of, being at least partly Missionary in approach. However, irrespective of tradition, the choice of approach also needs to consider the dangers of being Missionary, Executive or Broker, and also the general criticisms of the centre-periphery model as a whole.

The danger with the Missionary approach is that a project will deliver material which is unacceptable to teachers. The inherent problem is that the Missionary may carry an ideal and a vision that is impossible to implement given the reality of the classroom. The danger with the Executive approach is that little or no enhancement of current classroom practice will be achieved. The British curriculum has traditionally been evolutionary, piecemeal and uneven in progress. The danger is that if a project responds slavishly to teacher demands, a partly stagnant and self-perpetuating curriculum may be created. To continue classroom practices which have stood the test of time is important. To merely reproduce year after year the same practices without development is indefensible. The danger with the Broker approach is that there will be no unified sense of direction or rational philosophy in the development. The compromises to be made to satisfy and reconcile various interested parties may result in a lack of unity, purpose or cohesion in the materials produced. What is acceptable to a wide spectrum of interests may not constitute what is most valuable in terms of pupil learning.

As a departure from previous Welsh language projects, the Bangor development team initially chose to go to the grass roots level and ask teachers about their preferences. Before the team decided what kind of tests, materials and resources to develop, a national survey of representative teachers was carried out. The results of the survey are reported in Baker & Griffiths (1983). The survey identified the wants of teachers, and had a purely Executive approach been chosen, the project would have necessarily responded to the consensus view as expressed by the survey. To the Broker, a survey of teachers' wants has to be balanced against the preferences of other interested parties. To the Missionary, a survey is unimportant, even irrelevant.

The Bangor project decided to seek advice and information from sources other than teachers. To this end, HMI, Advisers, nominees of Directors of Education in each of the eight counties and peripatetics were interviewed. Also visits were made to key schools and classrooms, resulting in short case studies which tried to portray need in terms of the overall structure and context of the school. Finally a conference was held, where nominated "successful" teachers of the target children talked about their classroom approach and showed the materials and resources they used.

Consideration of the Bangor project alongside that of SCBP and Cyfres y Ddraig shows three alternative points of departure. The SCBP grew out from Gittins' notion of experimental bilingual schools and Dodson's (1967) teaching methodology. Cyfres y Ddraig partly started from a computer analysis of Welsh children's spoken language. The Bangor project started with a poll of teachers and a gathering of grass roots information. The point to be made is not that any one point of departure is preferable to another. Each has its relative merits and dangers. Rather the contrast is that the "educational theory" origin of the SCBP was perhaps the most Missionary of the three projects. The "analytical information" origins of Cyfres y Ddraig tend also to be Missionary in approach but with some effort to become grounded in the experience of pupils. Further along is the Bangor project, ostensibly less Missionary in approach, trying by a "survey approach" to engage some of the strengths of a Broker and Executive approach.

As a result of attempting to take into account the three approaches, the Bangor project produced a variety of courseware. Particularly desired by teachers was a series of graded reading books. Various interested parties were keen for a teachers' handbook to be produced. A Missionary element in the team (and a few interested parties) desired language development activities corresponding to the philosophy behind Cynllun y Porth. Similarly, with test development, a spelling test was produced mostly in response to teacher requests. Little emphasis was given by teachers to the production of a Checklist of Phonic elements. However, a desire to "improve" practice led to the development of such a scale.

While Bangor project materials and tests have been field tested in schools throughout Wales, no summative evaluation can occur until dissemination has been completed. It is therefore too early to assess the degree of success of the project.

The Limitations of the Project Model

From the admittedly sparse research evidence available, Welsh language curriculum development projects investigated appear to have been relatively successful. English projects appear to have been less successful. What then makes for more or less success in a project? In the previous section, the limitations and dangers of the Missionary, Executive and Broker approach were considered. Alongside these may be placed criticisms of centre-periphery projects in general (MacDonald & Walker, 1976). These are basically four in number, although there is overlap and continuity among them.

1. Project materials and aims tend to be adapted and re-defined by teachers. Teachers may use some of the materials in terms of their own philosophy of practice rather than in the manner set out by the designers. Project intentions may fail to be realised in classroom practice. Teachers will need to select, adapt and change project materials to fit customary practice.

2. Teachers cannot be conceived as passive purchasers of goods produced on the project production line. New ideas, new materials, new content, new goals cannot be transplanted into the classroom. The idea that teachers will passively receive and implement innovation is unreal. Rejection of the transplant is as likely as, if not more likely than, acceptance.

3. Schools and their teachers have power to decide what they buy. Projects have to work within a framework of a conservative, professional teaching force. Projects are subordinate to school systems in power.

4. Centre-periphery development is seen by MacDonald & Walker (1976) as the wishes of a minority potentially being imposed on a majority. The individuality and personalization of the classroom may be in danger from the non-democratic control by a few over curriculum content and culture.

There is little doubt that these four limitations of centre-periphery development were experienced by SCBP, Cyfres y Ddraig and Cynllun y Porth. Dodson (1978) found that existing teacher philosophies of practice could not simply be replaced by new methodology. Experience suggests that Cyfres y Ddraig and Cynllun y Porth materials are often adapted in school to suit an individual teacher's preference in classroom practice. New materials are dovetailed selectively into previous approaches.

The project Missionary may feel angry at failure in total conversion. Teachers take aboard parts of the gospel that are acceptable, and reject other parts. To the Missionary, this results in a contortion of project aims and a distortion of proper use of materials. Yet the perspective of the teacher deserves equal if not more weight. A highly trained professional with well tested experience of the reality of the classroom cannot be considered putty in the hands of the Missionary. As Stenhouse (1975, 1983) has eloquently argued, a teacher is a professional educator and can be a researcher, a developer of materials, an agent of classroom change and development.

Criticisms by curriculum theorists, the research of Steadman *et al.* (1981) on the impact and take up of large scale centre-periphery projects, and the demise of the relatively affluent economic conditions that supported the Schools Council projects in the 1960's and 1970's, has recently opened the door to an alternative type of curriculum development often called Action Research (Elliott, 1978; Kemmis, 1982; Carr & Kemmis, 1983; Nixon, 1981). This complementary or alternative method will be briefly outlined, with the underlying suggestion that this is a necessary and important development in the Welsh bilingual teaching context. Even though the centre-periphery model apears to have been comparatively successful in Wales, there is still, on its own merits, a strong argument for teachers to become their own curriculum developers.

Curriculum Development by Teachers

During the "survey" stage of the Bangor project, a conference for nominated teachers was held at Gregynog, Powys. Teachers were asked to show materials they had developed for Welsh speaking pupils with learning difficulties. While the group of teachers may have been an untypical sample, the inventiveness, enthusiasm, thought and loving care given to the production of materials could not be doubted. Rosen & Burgess (1980), researching in a multicultural context in London schools, found a parallel situation. Teachers can and do produce very worthy curriculum developments of their own.

Is it unrealistic to expect teachers to become researchers and developers? Such a function has not been part of the customary role specification of teachers. Yet it is a rare teacher who does not create and develop part of his or her own curriculum. Worksheets, workcards, learning games, structured exercises, are developed by most teachers. Can it therefore be said that teachers are already curriculum developers? In a weak sense this may be the case. In a strong sense, as envisaged by Stenhouse (1975, 1983), Elliott (1978) and Kemmis & McTaggart (1982), such development activity is rare.

The concept of teachers as curriculum developers, in its strong sense, is that such development is constant, systematic, planned and progressive. Localized curriculum development using the "action research" approach will be constant in that there is cyclical activity (Elliott, 1978; Kemmis & McTaggart, 1982). A teacher will not develop materials or a programme of activity once and for all. A problem is pinpointed, defined and classified, a remedy is developed, tried out, evaluated, reflected upon (Baker, 1984a). After evaluation and reflection comes a revised plan of action or new ideas. Development work has no dead end. New avenues and branches constantly seek to refine present practice such that there is progressive evolution.

While such an approach is fairly recent in education, its validity has been demonstrated particularly by Kemmis (1982) in Australia and Elliott (1978) in England. Both have developed a tradition of self-reflective, evaluative, developmental work with interested teachers. The Schools Council Committee for Wales was not slow in recognizing the importance and value of localized development. It funded local groups of teachers who were particularly keen to develop a particular area of the curriculum. The Schools Council Committee for Wales' publication "Quest" contained details of such work. Also this Committee has funded an "Action Research" project (1983–1984) in the schools of North Wales under the leadership of Wilfred Carr. In a bilingual context, teachers from a wide variety of secondary schools developed strategies to cope with mixed ability classes, evaluating these strategies, and progressively developing their philosophy of practice and classroom practice itself.

In such developmental work it is possible to conceive of three types of approach: the teacher as a cell, as a member of a club, and as part of a networked chain. Teachers as *cells* is the traditional approach to teacher based development. Working in relative isolation, a teacher produces changes to previous practice. Although not having the benefit of a critical community or cross-fertilizing ideas with colleagues, there does exist some justification for a cell approach. What works best for one teacher, may not work at all for another. Given the commitment, enthusiasm and partial idiosyncracy behind a teacher's self-produced developments, such developments may be highly effective for that teacher, but for no one else. Another justification for the cell approach is the analogy with a doctor. A doctor will fit the treatment to the patient. Teachers who know their pupils on an individual basis may be the best suited to prescribe and evaluate treatment. A cell approach places power of decision-making in the hands of the individual teacher. This is the direct opposite of the centre-periphery model which vests authority and a certain degree of power in a few.

The teacher as member of a *club* is a fairly normal approach to localized curriculum development. Two, three or more teachers in one school may join together in a team to attempt to find solutions to perceived problems. Constant dialogue, discussion and reflection between participants may provide new directions and progression. Working towards a consensal view may create a more unified momentum in development of the curriculum. Examples of in-school development might be primary teachers in a small rural school working experimentally on team teaching; a subject department in a secondary school producing its own collection of information for a resources-based course; or a variety of teachers in a secondary school producing and revising plans of action to combat absenteeism. Lewis (1982), using her experience of organizational development work with South Wales teachers, outlines how a school based study may effect a problem solving process.

A *club* approach is also possible with teachers from different schools. A group of Welsh history teachers in a local area, or a group of primary teachers experiencing problems using microcomputers in their classrooms, might meet centrally to attack a common problem. Rather than work as cells, a group of teachers creating and debating may lead to stimulation, fresh ideas and an evolution of solutions.

The teacher as part of a networked *chain* is a relatively new and untested idea. The idea may be introduced by reference to University of Wales Faculty of Education projects. These have often drawn together teachers from more than one county who under the project leader and area co-ordinators work together on a common curriculum area. At the University College of North Wales one such project seeks to develop the science curriculum in the junior school and lower secondary school. When a local group or individual teacher produces something outstanding, there can be dissemination while the project lasts. With the finish of the project may come the end of the dispersion of ideas and materials.

The limitation and danger of both the cell and the club type of teacher development work is that the harvest is not shared with a wider community. Individual teachers or groups working in isolation may be duplicating previous work. The concept of a networked chain is to gain input from similar cells or clubs, or share materials, ideas, case studies which would be beneficial to other teachers. The Cambridge Action Research Network of teachers is one solution to this problem of dispersion of teacher development. Teachers are put into contact or may regularly communicate with those of similar interests and problems. A networked chain may operate in a number of ways; through newssheets, exhibitions, computer link-up, a localized teletext system (Astill, 1983), sponsored inter-school visiting, video tapes or membership of an organized association. The essential idea of the networked chain is that developmental work does not stay behind the closed doors of a cell or a club.

Summary and Conclusion

The chapter has attempted to portray two different approaches to curriculum development in Wales. One is well established but decreasing in frequency. The other is new and growing in importance. The first is large scale development with a team of "experts" centrally producing materials or programmes. Such developments are then disseminated to the classroom. Such national developments tend to seek re-directions in the philosophy of practice, or in methods of teaching or in curriculum content. Just as doctors may expect readily available medicines to prescribe, so teachers may expect readily available, glossy materials and directions about how to use such materials.

Large scale project developmental work will have to choose on what basis it develops its materials or programme. Should it consult teachers? Should it consult as wide a variety of opinion as possible? Should it use the educational philosophy of the team? The three approaches have been labelled Executive, Broker and Missionary. A project may execute the wants of teachers, or act as brokers to a variety of interests, or become missionaries with a gospel to proclaim. Each has its own justifications and limitations. No one approach is correct or incorrect.

A review of the Schools Council Bilingual Project, Cyfres y Ddraig and the recent Bangor Project suggested that each contained a missionary element although the Bangor Project tried to contain all three elements. The expectation, particularly in the light of many English centre-periphery projects, tends to be for less success to result from the more missionary approach. Evaluations of SCBP, Cyfres y Ddraig and Cynllun y Porth tended to find relative success. Such success tends to support the idea of the central support and organization of Welsh language or bilingual development projects in education.

It may be argued in opposition that the need for Welsh language curriculum material has and is being fulfilled. Materials in Welsh have been produced for certain primary school and secondary school curriculum areas. Are we at a point where the famine has given way to a time of plenty? This seems very doubtful. But even if this argument has some appeal, it neglects the necessity of re-planting. Curriculum development does not occur once and for all. It has to respond to changes in society. Language becomes dated; story themes become stale and old fashioned. The age of the microcomputer and the information explosion has dawned with far reaching implications for the curriculum. New examinations dictate new curricular approaches and materials. Curriculum development therefore needs to be cyclical. To close the door on central curriculum development in Wales would be to lock out technological progress and culture change.

Despite present economic conditions, despite the limitations and dangers of centre-periphery development, despite the problem of approaches in a large scale project, there is a strong case for the continuation of centre-periphery developmental work in Wales. Despite these limitations, dangers and problems, the evidence available suggests that such work has been a success. The success is both absolute (e.g. programmes and materials have been widely adopted) and relative (the Welsh language development work has gained greater usage than comparative developments in England).

To conclude that further large scale development is all that is needed to support the bilingual curriculum in Wales would be wrong. Partly due to the inherent dangers and limitations of centre-periphery development, but also due to its own rationale and justifications, local teacher based curriculum development is an important accompaniment to centre-periphery development. In teacher based development, local conditions, personal needs, variations in linguistic style and culture throughout Wales may be highlighted. If centre-periphery development seeks to impose uniformity of practice, teacher developmental work can balance this with local initiative and individualism. There is a well established tradition of teachers formulating their own curriculum, sometimes in content, sometimes in approach, sometimes in both. Teacher developmental work capitalizes on this tradition, capturing the commitment, enthusiasm and thought of self creation that often translates into improved teaching and learning. A teacher may become more of a professional and be raised in status by becoming a curriculum developer. Rather than merely implementing the ideas of others, such teachers are invested with the responsibility for initiating and evaluating change and development. The *modus operandi* for such development work is the process and techniques of action research. Such a process should result in teachers constantly reviewing, evaluating and improving classroom practice in a systematic and progressive manner. It may also help to make departments in schools, even schools themselves, more democratic and self-reflective communities through constant dialogue.

Teachers taking on the role of developers may act in a one person cell. They may act as part of an in-school or between-school club. They may become part of a networked chain through which developments are disseminated.

To hard pressed teachers with a paucity of time or resources, the expectation of regularly and systematically developing their own curriculum may seem ill-founded. If the alternatives are a curriculum centrally imposed or a stagnant, self-perpetuating curriculum, then the expectation may have more appeal. Appeal may also come from using the enthusiasm of self-creation and the improved personal and professional relationships that may evolve from democratic dialogue. Best of all, the appeal may come from wanting to serve the best interests of children who will form the future generations of bilinguals in Wales.

6 Who Opts For Welsh?[1]

Prologue: Educational Research in Wales

"A State of Ignorance?" In an important "state of the art" paper reviewing educational research in Wales, Reynolds (1982) perceptively uses this question as his title. The implication is not that Welsh educators are ignorant. Few nations have been so enthusiastic about education. Nor hopefully is the implication that educational researchers in Wales, of whom there are few, are ignorant specimens of the academic community. The judgement is that despite many problems and issues abounding in Welsh education "the volume of clear research evidence which we have available to attempt to resolve the arguments is in general notably deficient" (Reynolds, 1982: 5).

Examples are provided by Reynolds (1982) of gaps in knowledge. There exists little material on the political and historical development of Welsh medium schools, the clientele of designated bilingual schools, the social background of Welsh school parents, their motivations, the ethos and organization of different kinds of schooling, and the rural schools often situated in areas of a high density Welsh speaking population. In the absence of knowledge prejudices, innuendos, false claims and fabrications can flourish.

Five eminent Canadian educationists came to much the same conclusion as Reynolds (1982) after reviewing Welsh education in a comparative light (Beaudoin *et al.*, 1981). Their view was that "there has otherwise been relatively little research conducted on the educational effectiveness of different forms of Welsh language instruction" (p. 507). Beaudoin *et al.* (1981) provide an important reason for research knowledge. Canadian experience shows that research evidence "may be a precondition for the continued expansion of bilingual education for anglophone children in Wales" (p. 507).

In Chapter 2, the necessity of informing and educating parents about bilingual education was stressed. Such information and communication

110

may help create a positive parental attitude towards bilingual education and a desire for their children to become bilingual. Beaudoin *et al.* (1981) argue that such information needs to be empirically obtained. Parents may not be interested in hunches, ideologies and evangelical persuasion. The Canadian experience is that parents, teachers, administrators and politicians require research evidence about the effects and effectiveness of bilingual education. Research evidence is a foundation for the future building of a bilingual schooling system. "It would seem important that parents and educators be made aware of the general educational advantages of full bilingualism and the fact that a very strong emphasis on Welsh throughout school will not detract from children's English skills" (Beaudoin *et al.*, 1981: 507).

A number of factors may have contributed to the state of ignorance about Welsh education.

1. Some educational researchers in Wales have focussed on issues that are contributions to British or international debates.

2. Scotland has its own national research organization, Wales is placed under the umbrella of England.

3. The number of academics in Wales who have the expertise or are available to execute major research is small relative to England or Canada, for example.

4. Well established traditions in bilingual research have terminated with the retirement of their principal proponents (e.g. W. R. Jones's study of bilingualism and intelligence) or departure across the seas (e.g. Nash's study of rural education in Wales). Reynolds (1982) further examines contributory factors.

To conclude that there is total research ignorance about Welsh education would be false. The work of W. R. Jones, Derrick Sharp and co-workers on the Attitudes Project, Carl Dodson, Eurwen Price and the NFER Unit based at Swansea, plus the Curriculum Projects mentioned in Chapter 5 are each examples of valuable research contributions. But however valuable the contributions, there still exists a chasm between need and supply.

The next two chapters contain two pieces of empirical research conducted on bilingual education. Both are the first steps into uncharted territory. Each examines an aspect of Welsh bilingual education.

Introduction

At about 13 or 14 years of age, most pupils in British comprehensive schools can choose to drop some subjects and opt for others. In many areas of Wales, Welsh Language or Welsh Studies is one such option. The research to be presented seeks to locate the relative importance of various factors such as bilingual background and attitude to Welsh in making the decision for or against Welsh as an option choice.

What kind of factors may govern the choice of continuing with Welsh after the first three years in a secondary school? There appear to be four overlapping and inter-dependent factors. First, there are individual factors such as personality, ability, aptitude and sex. Second, there is the influence of significant others, such as parents, peers and relatives. Third, there is the utilitarian need for a future career or a route to higher education. The influence of social and vocational mobility has been historically an important one in Wales, at times working against the preservation of Welsh language and culture (G. E. Jones, 1982). Fourth, there is institutional influence in terms of the school, media and cultural/religious organizations (e.g. chapel, Urdd).

In the Welsh language context, a vote to continue to study Welsh as a language or as a culture is a possible indicator of the future. Opting for Welsh at 13 or 14 years of age may contain some commitment to Welsh culture, values and lifestyle. Of course, this commitment may be neither permanent nor ineradicable. Opting for Welsh may be regarded as one indicator amongst many of the future health of the Welsh language and culture.

The choice to pursue Welsh, or not, may also be an indicator of attitudes to bilingual education. Has the primary school and secondary school system succeeded in inculcating the value of being bilingual and bicultural? While not taking Welsh as an option in the fourth and fifth years of secondary schooling does not necessarily mean a rejection of Welsh, the chances of being a bilingual and bicultural adult may become less likely. The rejection may stand as a symbol or predictor. It may herald future intentions.

The assumption is made that opting for Welsh is an important intermediate outcome (output) in bilingual education. It is also assumed that causally to a limited extent, and symbolically and predictively, opting for Welsh is a desirable outcome of bilingual education in Wales.

Given these assumptions, it appears important to investigate possible causes of this choice, and the relative influence of these causes. This is the aim of the research to be reported.

Choice of Variables

What factors may be linked with, or causally related to, opting for Welsh? Davies (1980) collected data on the following variables:

(i) *The bilingual background of pupils*. This was measured by a Language Background Questionnaire (see Chapter 3). Inclusion of Language Background poses the question: to what extent is the language background of the home and neighbourhood influential in making option choices? Is it crucial or irrelevant? A cluster analysis (see Chapter 3) suggested three groups of pupils. Group one pupils tend to be functionally English speaking. Group two pupils used English at home and mostly Welsh outside the home. Group three contained pupils using Welsh rather than English in and outside the home. These will be referred to as the English (N=364), Mixed (N=26) and Welsh (N=41) groups.

(ii) *The Welsh cultural background of pupils*. This was measured by a short questionnaire and featured questions on use of Welsh language TV, radio, church or chapel, newspapers and comics. The questions were reduced to a single score, the questions being summated in a simple cumulative fashion. The justification for inclusion of cultural background is to examine the relative importance of degrees of immersion in aspects of Welsh language culture on option choice. How much effect does Welsh cultural attachment have on opting for or out of Welsh as a language/Welsh Studies? It was recognized that defining precisely or measuring exactly Welsh cultural immersion is impossible. This variable must therefore be regarded as a measurable part of a large, complex entity.

(iii) *Organizational experience of Welsh as a school subject in the Primary school*. This may be sub-divided into three variables

(a) number of years of Welsh lessons in the Primary school

(b) frequency of Welsh lessons in a week in the Primary school

(c) length of Welsh lessons in the Primary school

It might be expected that Primary school experience provides a foundation for secondary schools to build on with respect to Welsh lessons.

Is this foundation crucial, fairly important, or three years after leaving Primary school has such experience become relatively unimportant? Is the Primary school a more or less potent influence than language background and Welsh cultural attachment?

(iv) *Attitude to the Welsh language.*   The rationale for the inclusion of this variable is the seminal work of Sharp *et al.* (1973). Attitude, as Chapter 4 revealed, may be an important cause and effect of performance and behaviour. Is attitude to the Welsh language an important attribute linked with option choice? Or does such choice depend more on factors other than attitude? Davies' (1980) measurement of attitude was by an abridged version of Sharp *et al.*'s (1973) Likert scale, scored in a cumulative manner.

(v) *Welsh as an option.*   Choice or absence of choice with respect to Welsh as a language or Welsh studies formed the dependent variable.

(vi) *Reasons for choosing or not choosing a Welsh option.*   Each pupil was given a questionnaire listing 11 reasons for choosing and 11 reasons for not choosing Welsh/Welsh Studies as an option. Pupils were asked to tick those reasons which applied to them.

Data were collected by Davies (1980) on 431 pupils from 3 schools within the same county in Wales. 176 pupils chose Welsh as an option, 255 pupils opted out of any kind of Welsh lessons.

Results

The first result which Davies (1980) presents concerns reasons why pupils chose Welsh or Welsh Studies as one of their options. Table 20 provides the details.

The table suggests that close to two-thirds of the sample chose Welsh/Welsh Studies believing that in response to living in Wales, they should learn the Welsh language. Two subsidiary reasons both given by 43% of the sample express instrumental reasons: career prospects and qualifications.

The first result is extended by an analysis of the reasons why 59% of the total sample did not choose Welsh or Welsh Studies (Davies, 1980).

Table 21 suggests that the most frequent reason for not choosing to take Welsh or Welsh studies was a preference for taking another subject available within the option group. The three subsidiary reasons given by over a third of the sample were lack of ability at Welsh, finding the subject difficult, and not needing the Welsh language within the family environment.

TABLE 20. *Reasons for Choosing a Welsh Option*

Reason	% of Total N
Good at Welsh	21.9
Parental advice	22.5
Want a job in Wales	43.3
Want to attend Welsh events	10.1
Teachers' advice	2.8
Friends speak Welsh	11.2
Learn about Wales	34.8
Liking of teacher	12.9
Ought to learn Welsh due to residence in Wales	64.6
To pass an exam in Welsh	43.3
Couldn't do other options	7.3

Total N = 176

TABLE 21. *Reasons for not Choosing a Welsh Option*

Reason	% of Total N
No good at Welsh	47.8
Parental advice	16.6
Didn't want a job in Wales	14.6
No Welsh friends	18.6
Didn't want to attend Welsh events	16.2
Teachers' advice	5.5
Relatives don't speak it	36.4
Don't intend to live in Wales	14.6
Didn't like teacher	23.7
Found Welsh difficult	38.3
Preference for another subject	63.2

N = 255

The second set of results concerns a comparison of two groups: those opting for Welsh/Welsh Studies with those not opting to take Welsh/Welsh Studies. The analyses ask if there are any differences between these two groups in their bilingual background, cultural background, organizational experience of Welsh in the Primary school, and attitude to the Welsh language.

There are two different but complementary ways of examining this issue. First, a profile analysis seeks to locate on which variables there are differences between the two groups.

Table 22 summarizes a series of analyses which suggest that there are differences between pupils who chose a Welsh option and those who did

TABLE 22. *Variables Related to the Choice or Non-choice of a Welsh Option*

	Welsh Option Chosen	*Welsh Option Not Chosen*	*Statistical Test*	*Statistical Significance*
Cultural background	Mean = 4.4	Mean = 1.2	ANOVA F = 121.7	0·0001
Bilingual background	Welsh and Mixed Groups – Less from English Group	Almost all from English Group	CHI SQUARE = 61.3	0·00001
Attitude	Mean = 28.56	Mean = 28.66	ANOVA F = 0.13	n.s.
Number of years of Welsh lessons in primary school	greater number of years	fewer number of years	CHI SQUARE = 49.3	0.00001
Frequency of Welsh lessons in primary school during a week	more days in a week	fewer days in a week	CHI SQUARE = 75.8	0·00001
Length of Welsh lessons in primary school	lessons longer	lessons shorter	CHI SQUARE = 20.7	0·0004

N = 431

not. Those opting for Welsh tended to make greater use of Welsh language, TV, radio, print and church/chapel. Their cultural milieu tends to be more Welsh. The bilingual background of the two groups also differs. Those not opting for a Welsh subject tended to come only from English backgrounds, whereas the Mixed and Welsh groups contained pupils who almost all chose to study Welsh. Attitude to the Welsh language did not discriminate between the two groups, both groups tending towards a neutral stance. A pupil's amount of experience of Welsh as a subject in the Primary school was linked significantly to the choice of Welsh. The greater the number of years, the greater the number of lessons received in a week and the greater the length of each lesson were positively connected to choice of Welsh as an option. Those who did not choose Welsh as an option had less experience of Welsh in the Primary school in terms of years, amount per week and time per lesson. This result is paralleled by the HMI survey (Welsh Office, 1983a). HMI suggest that pupils who have "successfully" learnt Welsh as a second language "refer back to their period in the primary school as well as their experience in the secondary school when asked to explain how they have learned to speak the language" (p. 34).

If these factors are important, the question arises as to which is more important. A Discriminant analysis examines the order of importance of these variables in being able to predict whether a pupil will take up Welsh as an option or not, although no causal relationships may necessarily be implied.

TABLE 23. *Discriminant Analysis of Welsh Option Predictors*

Step	Variable entered	F	Wilks' lambda
1	Cultural Background	56.3	0.81
2	Primary Welsh lessons per week	20.2	0.75
3	No. years Welsh Primary Lessons	5.1	0.73

Variables Not Entered
a) Attitude to Welsh Language
b) Language Background
c) Length of Welsh lesson

Canonical Correlation = 0.53

The Discriminant analysis suggested Cultural background as the variable which best predicted whether a pupil would follow Welsh as an option or not. This was followed by the number of Welsh lessons per week a pupil experienced in the Primary school, and next came the number of years of Welsh lessons in the Primary school. The length of Welsh lessons in the Primary school, attitude to Welsh and bilingual background did not make prediction any better when the three significant discriminating variables were used in conjunction. Using the three variables which were significant in the Discriminant analysis, three-quarters (76.1%) of pupils' choices with regard to taking Welsh or not could be accurately predicted.

The complementary analysis is a cluster analysis. This broadens the analysis and seeks to locate different patterns inside each group. The discriminant analysis assumes that there is homogeneity within the two groups. However, it is possible that this masks varying types of pupil in one group. Within, for example, the group of pupils who chose not to take a Welsh option, there may be identifiable sub-groups with different profiles. Different combinations of variables may exist to reveal different possible "recipes" leading to non-choice of Welsh as an option.

For this analysis, the data was submitted to a cluster analysis, eight clusters of pupils emerged and these may be profiled as follows.

The cluster analysis suggests that those who chose to study Welsh or Welsh Studies follow three different routes (clusters 2, 3, and 4). Cluster 2 contains 51 pupils who have had a fairly constant Welsh environment at home, Primary school, with friends, in using the mass media and attendance at church/chapel. Theirs is a fairly predictable choice of Welsh as a subject given a Welsh milieu. Cluster 4 is identical to Cluster 2 except that the 49 pupils have an English language background (variable 7). While speaking English at home and with friends, the experience of Welsh at Primary school, and in their cultural life, appears to be related to choosing Welsh as a fourth form option. The third cluster, comprising 47 pupils, have a varied bilingual experience, with a home background and primary school experience which is less Welsh than those of clusters 2 and 4. Although choosing to study Welsh, this cluster has a below average attitude to the Welsh language.

Four clusters contained those who had not chosen to study Welsh or Welsh Studies (clusters 1, 6, 7 and 8). The common element among the groups is their English background and below average score on cultural background. The difference among the groups is their varied experience of Welsh in the Primary school. While each group had at least one above

TABLE 24.   Cluster Analysis Table

Cluster	N=66 1	N=51 2	N=47 3	N=49 4	N=48 5	N=83 6	N=40 7	N=47 8
Variable 1	No	Yes	Yes	Yes	Yes/No	No	No	No
Variable 2	Av	+Av	Av	+Av	−Av	−Av	+Av	Av
Variable 3	Av	+Av	+Av	+Av	−Av	−Av	−Av	+Av
Variable 4	+Av	+Av	Av	+Av	+Av	−Av	+Av	Av
Variable 5	−Av	+Av	+Av	+Av	+Av	−Av	−Av	−Av
Variable 6	+Av	+Av	−Av	−Av	+Av	Av	−Av	−Av
Variable 7	Eng	Welsh	Eng/Mixed	Eng/Mixed	Eng/Mixed	Eng	Eng	Eng

Key: Variable 1: Yes = Opting for Welsh/Welsh Studies
   No = Not opting for Welsh/Welsh Studies
   2: Years of Welsh lessons in the Primary School
   3: Number of Welsh lessons per week in the Primary School
   4: Length of Welsh lessons in the Primary School
   5: Cultural Background
   6: Attitude to Welsh language
   7: Bilingual background
   +Av = above average
   Av = average
   −Av = below average

average score on variables 2, 3 or 4 (Primary school experience of Welsh),
no group had above average scores on all three variables, a factor which
appears to separate them from two of the three clusters who chose
Welsh/Welsh Studies.

Discussion and Conclusions

The question was posed, "On what basis do pupils make their choice
with respect to Welsh language/Welsh Studies?" Previous research has
suggested that pupils' subject choice is affected most by an interest in a
subject and its relevance to future employment (Reid *et al.*, 1974).
Utilitarian, instrumental reasons certainly appeared prominent in this
analysis, and affective, integrative reasons a little less prominent. As
Ormerod (1975) found, the teacher had little effect on actual choice. The
difference found with this database is the prominence given to the reason
that because one lives in Wales one ought to learn Welsh. This reason may
contain both instrumental and integrative components (Gardner & Lambert, 1972). It may subsume the wish to follow a career in a bilingual and
bicultural society and also the desire to feel and be Welsh. The prominence
of this reason also demonstrates the argument that society and its culture
not only affect choice of school subjects, but also within that choice may be
a response and commitment to certain values, culture and lifestyle.
Wishing to learn Welsh as a reason for subject choice may suggest both the
effect of the social, cultural and political milieu and also a possible
commitment to such a milieu.

What then is the milieu that may produce such a preference? The
analyses which sought to provide some clues to an answer to this question
suggested that cultural background, experience of Welsh in a Primary
school, bilingual background but not necessarily attitude were all connected to opting to take Welsh/Welsh Studies. This suggests that having a
positive attitude to the Welsh language is not enough. The consistent
experience of Welsh language lessons in the Primary school, in terms of
length of lesson every day over four or more years, appears to be positively
and significantly linked to the choice of Welsh as an option. The importance of consistent and constant experience of Welsh in the Primary School
in its relationship to opting for Welsh is also contained within the cluster
analysis. Examination of these groups who chose not to opt for Welsh
shows that although each had a score above the average in terms of one of
the three Primary school experience variables, none had three above
average scores. Comparison of cluster 3 and cluster 7 suggests that choice

of Welsh is linked to less than "above average" experience in the Primary school only when the cultural background of the pupil is Welsh rather than English. While speaking Welsh at home and with friends was predictably linked with choosing to continue with Welsh, the cluster analysis suggested that it was not an absolute necessity. One group who chose to take Welsh as an option spoke English at home and with friends. This group provides an optimistic note for bilingual education in Wales. Pupils who speak English at home and with friends may still be positive towards Welsh at school. If there is immersion in Welsh culture, a consistent and thorough foundation in Welsh in the Primary school and a positive attitude to the minority language, then Welsh language and culture may have a future in English language areas.

It was neither Primary school experience nor bilingual background that the discriminant analysis highlighted as most important in predicting whether or not a pupil would choose Welsh. The best predictor was cultural background. In the use of Welsh language, mass media and chapels/churches, the pupil may be expressing an affiliation to a cultural milieu. This result also expresses the notion that choice of a subject is linked to the effect of a pupil's culture and a possible wish to extend and reinforce that involvement. Cultural background appears in this analysis to create a context which affects choice of Welsh as an option, and also is furthered by that choice in a mutually reciprocating relationship.

What is it about cultural background that appears to make it such a potent predictor? What are the key components of Welsh cultural activity that are of importance in affecting the outcomes of schooling? Is minority language radio and television vital? Is reading Welsh language comics, magazines, newspapers and books of consequence? Is the integrative Welsh culture symbolized in Welsh chapel attendance of minor or major importance? These are the questions examined in the second research presented in the next chapter.

Notes to Chapter 6
1. The research reported in this chapter is based on an important contribution of research data by Philip Davies.

7 Ur Unig Ateb – The Only Answer?[1] Mass Media, Bilingualism and Education

Introduction

It is common belief that the mass media, television in particular, affect children. The links between TV and violence, racial attitudes, sex stereotyping, while not simple, are well established (Howitt, 1982; Liebert *et al.*, 1982; McQuail, 1977; Hall, 1977). It would not be surprising to find that minority languages and their cultures are also likely to be affected positively or negatively by the mass media. In 1980, Welsh language activists certainly believed this was the case.

In 1975, Goodhardt *et al.* found that the average British family watches around 5 hours of TV a day. Liebert *et al.* (1982) estimated that by 18 years of age an American child will have spent more time watching TV than in any other activity besides sleep, and this includes school. This raises the question, "To what extent is a minority language represented by TV and other media?" Does the Welsh language have sufficient exposure on TV and other media to aid maintenance of the language and its attendant culture?

American research on the effects of television on minority language and culture children attests to its mainly negative effects (Berry & Mitchell-Kernan, 1982). The values, attitudes, cultural stereotypes, political views and cultural patterns that are transmitted by TV affect the socialization of minority language children. To those who wish to assimilate minority groups into mainstream existence, TV provides a potent means of creating change. To those who wish to protect and preserve minority language and culture, TV may be an erosive agent. Such erosion may not only occur at a societal level, but also in individual terms, affecting self-concept, identity formation and social adjustment (Berry & Mitchell-Kernan, 1982). The degree to which an individual identifies with a minority language and culture, and has positive or negative feelings about such a minority, may be determined in part by the viewing of TV.

Welsh Language TV

Through the 1970s, Welsh language activists were certain that the dominance of English-speaking programmes on TV was a major cause in the declining use of the Welsh language. David in 1970 asserted, "Welsh itself is inconspicuous enough to make it inevitable that the predominant cultural influence in every Welsh home has over the last ten years become English" (p. 12). Eleven years later Bedwyr Lewis Jones (1981) reinforced this view: "In every Welsh home television is a voluble and attractive alien presence. The natural domain supports of the language are being cut down by the homogenising aspects of modern mass culture, a culture which by its very nature induces conformity with the norms of a mass market at the expense of the traditional and the particular" (p. 49).

Perhaps the most dramatic picture of the problem was given by Rees (1979) in the form of an analogy. This analogy will be summarized, but deserves reading in full. Rees (1979) invites his reader to imagine being a dictator of a centralized state where regional differences are to be sublimated into a uniform culture. A small country is incorporated within that state, never having been totally absorbed, and with its own historically distinct language spoken by a large minority. Radio and TV are developed as forms of mass communication. "How would you", Rees (1979: 182) asks, "use these new inventions to further your policy of unity and uniformity?". His answer is enlightening. Broadcasting should be monopolized by a central authority responsible to the Government. Most of the programmes would be centrally produced and broadcast uniformly throughout the country. To create an illusion of decentralization, broadcasting regions would be defined, ensuring that the "small country" is part of a larger and more populated area. Because of this, the minority language should not be inflicted upon the larger majority of that region. As a political expedient, occasional minority language programmes would be shown at inconvenient times. Any complaints from this minority would be answered by sympathy and the presence of insuperable technical difficulties. If the small country eventually becomes a separate region, financial constraints and lack of experienced professionals will make the service third-class. Rees (1979) is aware that the analogy imputes premeditated

decision-making rather than piece-meal evolution without deliberate intentions towards the minority language. This is the possible overstatement in
the analogy. Nevertheless, the analogy makes a telling point. The mass
media are agents of influence and control. The locus of power and
authority in mass media is therefore crucial for a minority language and
culture.

The Fourth Channel Debate

In 1974, with the publication of the Crawford Report, central
government appeared to show some awareness of future broadcasting
needs in Wales. The conclusion of the Report was that a fourth TV channel
should be solely devoted to Welsh-medium broadcasting. The conclusion
was generally welcomed by Welsh language activists, although a minority
were concerned that compartmentalizing language to different channels
might result in a proportion of Welsh speakers more or less exclusively
watching English language channels.

Between 1974 and 1980, all that appeared to be needed for an
increase in Welsh language television was for the completion of technical
developments to produce a fourth channel. Early in 1980, debating
replaced waiting. The Government announced that the fourth channel in
Wales would not be devoted to Welsh language programmes. Rather, more
Welsh programmes would be broadcast on existing channels.

The reactions of many Welsh speakers ranged from anxiety to anger.
The reversal in decision was regarded by many as not only concerning
Welsh language TV, but also, and more importantly, the future of the
Welsh language and culture. The event became symbolic for the struggle
for the preservation of a minority language. The fight was personified in
the form of the President of the Welsh Nationalist Party (Plaid Cymru), Dr
Gwynfor Evans, announcing that he would begin fasting to death on 6th
October 1980, unless the Government kept its election promise of a Welsh
speaking fourth channel.

The Welsh language press during the early summer months of 1980
tended to be dominated by the issue. The slogan of the campaign was "YR
UNIG ATEB" ("THE ONLY ANSWER"). The phrase illustrated both
the strong feelings for the preservation of the Welsh language, and the
great importance attached to broadcasting as an influence on language and
culture.

The exact meaning behind the slogan may be illustrated by an extract
from an open letter sent to the Home Secretary in June 1980, signed by 78

very prominent Welsh people drawn from religious, educational and public life.

> "We are concerned about the future of Welsh culture. We support the policy that all Welsh programmes should be transmitted on the fourth channel, since we feel that our culture could best be served in that way. Welsh speakers should be able to watch Welsh language programmes at peak viewing times, and not be forced to accept the inevitability of Welsh programmes being relegated to unsociable times. This means that using a single channel is the only means of forming a uniform pattern, full of Welsh language programmes. And not only that. The Government should ensure enough finance to support such a service. Television is an extremely strong communication medium, and care must be taken to ensure that it is used to strengthen and to enrich the Welsh culture. And all this is a matter of great urgency. The Government should be anxious to ensure that the wishes of the majority of the people of Wales are not ignored. Otherwise, Welsh speakers will be treated as second class citizens, whose principles are of no consequence, even though they are strongly supported by their fellow Welshmen who do not speak Welsh."

The Government caught the strength of the feeling and concern. On September 17th, 1980, it reversed its decision and allocated 22 hours of Welsh language broadcasting to the fourth channel.

Welsh Language TV Programmes

Price-Jones (1982) has shown the degree of imbalance between English language and Welsh language TV provision that existed in a sample week in 1978 and 1981. In 1978, out of a total of 264½ hours of TV on three channels during a sample week, 14 hours 51 minutes were devoted to Welsh language programmes. Thus Welsh language TV represented 5.5% of all TV broadcasts. In 1981 this had risen to 6.5% with a total of 18½ hours of Welsh language programmes. In 1983, with the addition of the fourth channel, in a comparable week 5.7% of all programmes transmitted were in Welsh. Between November 1982 and March 1983 an average of 24.6 hours of programmes were broadcast per week in Welsh (S4C Annual Report, 1983). So while the amount of Welsh language TV had risen between 1978 and 1983, the relative saturation of English and Welsh language programmes had changed little. If we consider the fourth channel (S4C) by itself, a typical week has almost double the amount of English programmes to Welsh programmes although a "peak viewing" time of early evening is mostly given to Welsh programmes.

These figures reflect provision and not usage and do not adjust for the relative use of TV at different times of the day. Nor do these figures allow for the fact that (video recording apart) a person cannot watch all programmes. Normally there is a choice of channel and programme. Despite small provision, it may be that Welsh speakers' actual usage of TV is mostly of Welsh language programmes. This may be unlikely but is not impossible, and will be examined later. However, and contentiously, the statistic that for about every 20 minutes of broadcasting there is 1 minute in Welsh may be set against the statistic that about 1 in 5 people in Wales speak Welsh. In terms of provision, as apart from usage, Welsh language television appears still to be a Cinderella. And despite the advent of S4C, Prince Charming may still not have appeared.

Other Media and the Welsh Language

In contrast with Welsh language media, English language media are in a very dominant position in Wales, although there is considerable variation amongst the different forms of communication.

There is no Welsh language daily paper and an attempt to produce a Sunday paper in Welsh did not succeed. The national Welsh language weekly newspapers have relatively small circulations. Lloyd (1979) estimated that less than a quarter of Welsh speakers read the Welsh language national weeklies. More optimistically, there has been a rise of local Welsh language newspapers called Papurau Bro (Community newspapers). They started in Cardiff in 1973, and much of Wales is covered by these grass-roots efforts. Set against the decline of chapel and church as an institution fostering Welsh language and culture, Papurau Bro have developed as an institution focussing both local and Welsh language activity and some kind of interest in community life, which historically has been very much a feature of Welsh cultural existence.

While there exists the expected imbalance in the number of comics and children's magazines available in the two languages, of 16 Welsh language publications produced since 1967, 10 are still in circulation (Price-Jones, 1982). An even greater imbalance is found with books available, although this very grey and foreboding cloud contains a speck of silver, in that the number of books in Welsh has greatly increased in the last decade. In 1971, 177 new books were published in Welsh; by 1982 this number had doubled (Price-Jones, 1982). A similar recent increase is found with records and cassettes in Welsh. While the traditional production of male voice choir and religious (e.g. soloists and hymn singing festivals) records has continued, popular music of all varieties, especially that aimed at teenagers, has appeared and prospered. Whereas watching a cinema film or commercial video cassette in Welsh would be a unique and even odd experience for many Welsh young people, Welsh records and cassettes are a more accepted and expected cultural experience.

The Problem Stated

At the start of the chapter, two questions were posed. "To what extent is a minority language represented by TV and other media?" "Does the Welsh language have sufficient exposure on TV and other media to aid maintenance of the language and its attendant culture?" The first is a factual question and what little evidence is available suggests two things. First, there is a considerable imbalance. People living in Wales are potentially exposed to a much greater amount of English language and Anglophile culture, although each individual can to some extent control what is experienced. Second, amongst some but not all of the media, the last decade has seen a modest revival in concern for Welsh language media. Records and books are examples of such progress.

If the analogy may suffice, there is awareness of language malnutrition and attendant death. The awareness is amongst those directly experiencing the situation and to a much lesser extent from without. Some effort is being made to produce a better diet and halt death if not malnutrition. Some people believe they have the only answer. No one food is likely to be the sole answer. Other parts of the diet are also receiving attention. It is still uncertain whether the present improving diet is sufficient to stop extinction or successfully fight malnutrition. There may be regional variations in success and failure.

The analogy leads to the second question. It may now be phrased in a different way. "What effect does the media have on the health of the Welsh language?" To produce a definitive answer would be impossible, although Her Majesty's Inspectors are sure of the effect, at least for learners.

"To be commended is the effort of a small number of schools to get pupils to read popular periodicals in the language. It would be valuable to enable as many learners as possible to read

Welsh magazines and newspapers, both local and national, and to partake of the modern literature of a living language which has been, over the centuries, the medium of the oldest continuous tradition of literature in Europe. The learning experience also needs to be extended so that the learner may benefit progressively from the substantial Welsh output on radio and from Welsh developments on television" (Welsh Office, 1983a).

The question posed allows a modest research attempt at least to begin to answer the question. The next part of this chapter looks at some data collected by Price-Jones (1982) on children's use of media and how it may affect attitude to and attainment in Welsh.

Research on Children's Use of TV

Background

Sharp *et al.* (1973) found that "as pupils get older, attitude to Welsh tends to become less favourable, and attitude towards English tends to become more favourable" (p. 155). Sharp *et al.*'s (1973) results concerned a cross-sectional analysis of 10, 12 and 14 year olds. One issue to be tackled is why pupils' attitude to Welsh declines in the early years of secondary schooling. Do mass media have an effect as presupposed in the fourth channel debate? Another issue is how attainment in Welsh is affected by more or less exposure to the mass media.

Sample

192 children from 11 Primary Schools situated in the Llŷn peninsula in Gwynedd were tested by Price-Jones (1982) when in their penultimate year at junior school, and then again, three years later, while in the second year at three different secondary schools. The area is part of the heartland of the Welsh language with approximately 78% of the primary children speaking Welsh as a first language.

Thirteen children out of the original 192 were not tested the second time owing mostly to moving away from the area (11 pupils) or being unobtainable (2 pupils).

Variables

Each child was measured on the following at ten and thirteen years of age. This is a subset of data collected by Price-Jones (1982).

1. Attitude to Welsh (Sharp *et al.*, 1973)

2. Welsh Attainment (Comprehension) Test (Sharp *et al.*, 1973)

3. Welsh Spelling Test (Price-Jones, 1982)

4. Welsh Word Recognition Test (G. J. Evans, undated)

5. Language Background (Baker & Hinde, 1984)

6. Attendance at Welsh speaking Church or Chapel (5 point scale)

7. Use of English newspapers, comics, magazines, books (cumulative scale)

8. Use of Welsh newspapers, comics, magazines, books (cumulative scale)

9. Use of English records and cassettes (5 point scale)

10. Use of Welsh records and cassettes (5 point scale)

11. Amount of time spent watching English and Welsh language TV in one week. (Pupils kept a diary for one week of all TV programmes watched.)

Background Results

Between the ages of ten and thirteen Price-Jones (1982) found that:

a) Attendance at Welsh speaking chapels and churches declined.

b) The reading of English national daily and Sunday papers, comics and books increased as did the reading of Welsh language Papurau Bro, comics and books. English reading was approximately three to four times more than reading in Welsh.

c) The average preference for English programmes was nine times greater than for Welsh language programmes. This was based on a question about favourite programmes on TV. No change in preference for English TV programmes as opposed to Welsh TV was evident over the three years.

d) The average child watched 36 minutes per week of Welsh language programmes at age ten, 51 minutes at age thirteen. The average child watched 16¾ hours of English TV at both ten and thirteen. While there was a definite rise overall in the use of Welsh TV, the imbalance in exposure to the two languages on TV is arguably more striking. Children watched English TV for approximately

95% of time and Welsh language TV for only 5% of time. This result may give a more realistic impression of the language effects of TV than a BBC/IBA survey in 1980 (Bellin, 1984). Using a quota sample of 891 Welsh speakers, the survey found that 64% of the sample watched TV programme(s) in Welsh for five or more days per week. Also it was reported that 55% watched Welsh language TV at least once a day. The figures tend to ignore the likely imbalance in viewing as shown by Price-Jones (1982). However, with the advent of S4C there is evidence to suggest that, in the general population, Welsh language viewing per week is more than Price-Jones (1982) found with children at age ten and thirteen. Although the sample used in this audience viewing research is small in terms of numbers of Welsh speakers and therefore the margin of error is likely to be great, in the first year of operation of S4C the average viewing time for Welsh language programmes in the general Welsh speaking population was approximately 1 hour and 40 minutes (S4C, personal communication).

e) There was an increase in the use made of English language records and cassettes, and a slight statistically non-significant decrease in the use of Welsh language records and cassettes.

f) Parallel to the findings of Sharp *et al.* (1973), attitude to English became more favourable and attitude to Welsh less favourable over the three year span.

In order to test the extent to which mass media affect attitude and attainment, at the simplest level, correlations indicating the strength of this relationship on a scale of 0 to 1 may be calculated. For example, if watching a relatively greater amount of Welsh TV is linked to a positive attitude to Welsh, a moderate correlation may be expected.

The Picture at Age Ten

Attitude. At the age of ten having a more positive attitude to the Welsh language was related to the factors shown in the table opposite.

While a Welsh speaking religious affiliation, consumption of Welsh print, music and TV is linked to having a positive attitude to the Welsh language at age ten, certain other factors appear to have minimal effect (i.e. near zero correlations). These factors are: the amount of use of English TV, English printed material, records and cassettes, and language background.

	correlation (r)	statistical significance (p)
1) Attending Welsh Church or Chapel	0.29	0.0001
2) Reading Welsh newspapers, books etc.	0.26	0.0001
3) Listening to Welsh records & cassettes	0.21	0.003
4) Amount of time watching Welsh TV	0.125	0.05
Multiple R = 0.39		

Attainment. Table 25 summarizes the correlations found between the three indices of Welsh attainment and the independent variables.

All three indices of attainment in Welsh are linked to five Welsh cultural variables. Those whose attainment is relatively good in Welsh spelling, reading and comprehension tend to read more Welsh newspapers, comics, magazines, books, watch more Welsh TV, listen for a greater amount of time to Welsh records and cassettes, are likely to attend more religious services in Welsh and have a more favourable attitude to Welsh. As with attitude it is important to note also those factors which appear relatively non-influential in such attainment: amount of English TV watched, amount of use of English records, cassettes and printed material, and language background.

At age ten, the picture is perhaps predictable but important. Those whose Welsh attainment is higher and attitude to the Welsh language is more favourable are the ones more immersed in a variety of forms of Welsh culture. It is not possible to directly infer from a correlation that one thing causes the other. It would be tempting to argue that, for example, better attainment and attitude is fostered by watching more Welsh TV. To make such a statement requires justification on grounds other than statistical. Logically and psychologically it is possible that the reverse cause-effect relationship also operates. A better attitude to Welsh may cause more watching of Welsh TV, or more use of Welsh printed materials. Similarly attitude to Welsh may be both the cause and the effect of Welsh attainment. For further analyses, a temporal ordering is assumed. While it does not allow for cyclical cause and effect, it provides a more refined analysis of the data (Heise, 1975; Dwyer, 1983).

TABLE 25. *Relationships between Attainment in Welsh and Welsh Cultural Variables*

Relationship	r	p
Welsh Attainment & Reading Welsh newspapers, books, etc.	0.57	0.0001
Welsh Attainment & Attendance at Welsh Chapel/Church	0.45	0.0001
Welsh Attainment & Amount of Welsh TV watched	0.49	0.0001
Welsh Attainment & Attitude to Welsh	0.36	0.0001
Welsh Attainment & Use of Welsh records and cassettes	0.37	0.0001
Multiple R = 0.68		
Welsh Word Recognition & Reading Welsh newspapers, books etc.	0.47	0.0001
Welsh Word Recognition & Attendance at Welsh Chapel/Church	0.38	0.0001
Welsh Word Recognition & Amount of Welsh TV watched	0.30	0.0001
Welsh Word Recognition & Attitude to Welsh	0.23	0.001
Welsh Word Recognition & Use of Welsh records and cassettes	0.25	0.0001
Multiple R = 0.57		
Welsh Spelling & Reading Welsh newspapers, books etc.	0.51	0.0001
Welsh Spelling & Attendance at Welsh Chapel/Church	0.35	0.0001
Welsh Spelling & Amount of Welsh TV watched	0.38	0.0001
Welsh Spelling & Attitude to Welsh	0.28	0.0001
Welsh Spelling & Use of Welsh records and cassettes	0.36	0.0001
Multiple R = 0.60		

A Model. Within these limitations a simple model of cause and effect will be conjectured. It will be assumed that Welsh religious affiliation and use of Welsh media affect, in a causal fashion, attitude to Welsh and attainment in Welsh. It will also be assumed that attitude to Welsh affects attainment in Welsh. In the form of a path diagram, these relationships may be represented thus, with the arrow representing the direction of the postulated cause-effect.

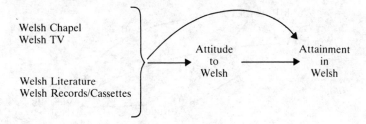

The path diagram poses a question. Does immersion in Welsh culture directly affect attainment, or does such immersion operate through attitude? Take watching Welsh TV as an example. Does such experience directly affect attainment in Welsh? Or does the influence of mass media work by affecting attitude which in turn affects attainment. The statistical method is path analysis (Heise, 1975; Dwyer, 1983).

Figures 8 to 10 show the results of the path analyses.

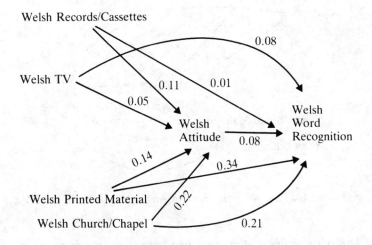

FIGURE 8. *Path Analysis of Welsh Word Recognition Attainment – 10 years old*

The structural coefficients are beta weightings in all path analysis diagrams.

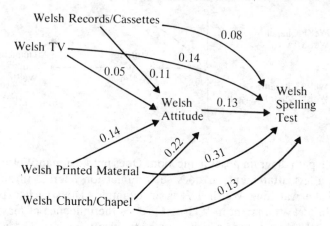

FIGURE 9. *Path Analysis of Welsh Spelling Attainment – 10 years old*

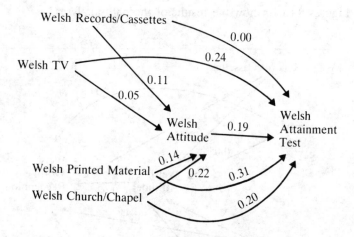

FIGURE 10. *Path Analysis of Welsh Attainment Test – 10 years old*

The path analyses show that two processes appear to be at work. First, attainment seems to be directly affected by use of Welsh printed material in particular and also by Welsh TV and attendance at Welsh Church or Chapel. The direct link between attainment and cultural background is present. At the same time such cultural forms affect attainment indirectly through attitude. For example, TV affects attitude which in turn affects attainment.

However, there are differences. On the one hand television and printed material appear to affect attainment by a direct effect and indirectly through attitude. On the other hand more frequent attendance at Welsh Church/Chapel (in the spelling analysis) has a greater effect on attitude formation (and hence indirectly on attainment through attitude), than on attainment directly. Similarly records and cassettes tend to affect attainment more through their effect on attitude than directly on attainment.

To summarize the findings at age ten: attainment in Welsh is related to mass media. Children who watch more Welsh TV, who read more Welsh books, magazines, comics and newspapers, who listen to Welsh records and cassettes tend to have higher attainment in Welsh spelling, reading (word recognition) and comprehension tests and a more favourable attitude to Welsh. Similar higher attainment was related to a more favourable attitude to Welsh and attending Welsh religious services. A relationship was also found between attitude and religious attachment.

A model was proposed to examine a possible simplified cause and effect pattern. Path analysis of this model suggested that attainment in Welsh was caused by mass media and religious attachment acting directly and indirectly. Watching more Welsh TV and reading more Welsh printed matter appeared to have a direct effect on Welsh attainment. Such TV viewing and reading also appear to affect Welsh attainment through their effect on attitude to Welsh. The effects of Church/Chapel attendance and listening to Welsh records/cassettes on attainment were mainly via influencing attitude to the Welsh language which in turn affected attainment. Here attitude is a mediating influence.

The Picture at Age Thirteen

When the same pupils were tested three years later, they were mostly entering or already embarked upon the adolescent stage. They had made the transition from Primary to Secondary school, and, as reported earlier in the chapter, attitude to the Welsh language had become less favourable.

At thirteen years of age, two pictures are possible, one a snapshot, the other a film. First, a snapshot of the thirteen year old bilingual will assess whether the same patterns occur as occurred three years previously. For example, is watching Welsh TV still linked with Welsh attainment? If so, is the effect direct or indirectly through attitude? Second, a film of development over three years may be presented. Attitude to Welsh declines over the three years. Why? What other factors change over the three years that may cause such a decline? What attributes of individuals may be linked with such a decline? First, the snapshot.

Attitude.   At the age of thirteen, having a more positive attitude to the Welsh language was related to:

	r	p
1) Reading Welsh books, newspapers, etc.	0.35	0.0001
2) Attendance at Welsh Church/Chapel	0.46	0.0001
3) Listening to Welsh records/cassettes	0.25	0.0001
4) Amount of Welsh TV watched	0.04	n.s.

Multiple R = 0.50

The result is the same as at age ten with one exception. Printed material, religious affiliation, consumption of Welsh records and cassettes are each related to a more favourable attitude to the language. The exception is Welsh TV. Watching more Welsh TV is not connected to higher attainment. As at ten years, language background, English records, cassettes, written materials and English TV showed no relationship with attitude to the Welsh language.

Attainment.   Table 26 summarizes the correlations between the three indices of attainment in Welsh and the independent variables.

The results show very much the same pattern as occurred at ten years of age. Welsh attainment is positively linked with reading Welsh literature, listening to Welsh cassettes/records, attending Welsh church or chapel and having a favourable attitude to the Welsh language. However, there is one difference. At ten years of age, watching more Welsh TV was linked with higher attainment in Welsh. At thirteen years of age, no such relationship exists. Welsh TV appears to have no overall effect on attainment in Welsh. A lack of relationship was found between attainment and language background, English language records, cassettes, written matter and English TV.

A Model.   Figures 11 to 13 examine the relationship between attainment and the statistically significant cultural factors in the form of a causal model. Are the same direct and indirect paths between Welsh cultural experience and Welsh attainment the same at thirteen as at ten years of age?

TABLE 26. *Relationships between Welsh Attainment and Welsh Cultural Variables*

Relationship	r	p
Welsh Attainment & Welsh Church/Chapel attendance	0.53	0.0001
Welsh Attainment & Reading Welsh books, newspapers, etc.		
	0.38	0.0001
Welsh Attainment & Amount of Welsh TV watched	0.05	n.s.
Welsh Attainment & Attitude to Welsh	0.33	0.0001
Welsh Attainment & Use of Welsh records/cassettes	0.32	0.0001
Multiple R = 0.58		
Welsh Word Recognition & Reading Welsh books, newspapers, etc.	0.44	0.0001
Welsh Word Recognition & Welsh Church/Chapel attendance		
	0.42	0.0001
Welsh Word Recognition & Amount of Welsh TV watched		
	0.06	n.s.
Welsh Word Recognition & Attitude to Welsh	0.33	0.0001
Welsh Word Recognition & Use of Welsh records/cassettes		
	0.30	0.0001
Multiple R = 0.58		
Welsh Spelling & Reading Welsh books, newspapers, etc.	0.42	0.0001
Welsh Spelling & Welsh Church/Chapel attendance	0.41	0.0001
Welsh Spelling & Amount of Welsh TV watched	0.07	n.s.
Welsh Spelling & Attitude to Welsh	0.33	0.0001
Welsh Spelling & Use of Welsh records/cassettes	0.30	0.0001
Multiple R = 0.57		

As with the previous analyses, the path analyses suggest that attainment in Welsh is affected by reading Welsh printed matter and attending Church/Chapel both directly and also through attitude. Reading Welsh newspapers, books, magazines and comics is more strongly related to attainment compared with Chapel/Church influence which acts more through its effect on attitude, attitude in turn affecting attainment. Listening to Welsh language records and cassettes has relatively little influence on attitude or attainment; amount of viewing of Welsh TV has even less influence.

What is noticeable from a comparison of the ten year old and thirteen year old results is the greater influence at age thirteen of Church/Chapel.

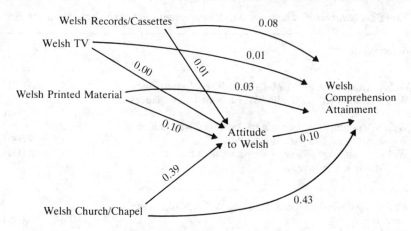

FIGURE 11. *Path Anaysis of Welsh Comprehension Attainment – 13 years old*

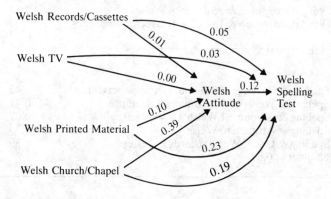

FIGURE 12. *Path Analysis of Welsh Spelling Attainment – 13 years old*

Attending Welsh religious services more frequently is relatively strongly related to both Welsh attitude and attainment.

Change between Ten and Thirteen Years of Age

Two snapshots have been presented: one of the ten year old, the other of the thirteen year old. Since the same pupils were used on both occasions, a film of change may also be presented. Attitude to Welsh over the three years becomes less favourable. Why? What are the possible

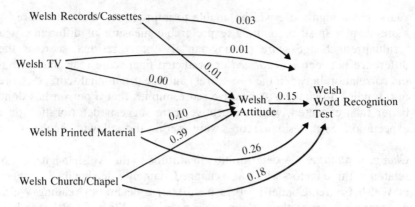

FIGURE 13. *Path Analysis of Welsh Reading (Word Recognition) Test – 13 years old*

causes of someone's attainment in Welsh relatively deteriorating (relative to other pupils) or relatively increasing over the three years? These are the types of questions raised in a longitudinal analysis.

Two technical points first of all. First, taking attitude decline as an example, what kind of factors may influence such decline? Is is possible that other changes over the three years may be related to attitude change. A gradual or sudden decision not to attend Chapel or Church, or watching an increasing amount of English TV may affect attitude. Change in attitude and attainment may be invoked by changes of cultural behaviour. A change in one aspect of life may set up a chain reaction, causing certain other features to change simultaneously or subsequently. It is also possible that change in attitude and attainment may be linked with relatively stable and enduring characteristics. A person who regularly attends chapel over the three years, or who watches a large amount of Welsh TV may have relatively increasing attainment over this period.

It is therefore necessary to build into the analysis changes that have occurred in the three years that may affect attitude and attainment, as well as factors which are relatively stable. This latter potential effect was achieved by calculating an average score for attendance at Welsh Church/Chapel, amount of reading of Welsh print, use of Welsh records/cassettes and Welsh TV using the results at ten and thirteen years of age.

Second, change in attainment and attitude cannot simply be measured by the difference between initial and final scores. A pupil who starts with a low score has ample room to show improvement. A pupil who, at 10 years, has a high score will be unable to improve on his initial score by more than a small amount. The preferable measure of difference is a residualized change score (Youngman, 1979). A residual score is the difference between an *expected* or predicted final score (calculated from the correlation between the two scores) and the *actual* final score. A score of 0 implies no change. A positive score implies that a person has done better than expected, while a negative score suggests deterioration over expectation. Such residual scores were used in the following analyses.

Change in attitude.   A deterioration in attitude to the Welsh language was related to three factors which also changed, namely a decline in attendance at Welsh Church/Chapel (r=0.15 p < 0.02) a decline in reading Welsh newspapers, comics, books and magazines (r=0.13; p < 0.04); and an increase in watching English TV (r=−0.17; p < 0.01). It must be stressed again that the correlations do not imply causation. It may be that a change in attitude to Welsh affects TV viewing, reading and religion, or that a change in reading, religious and TV viewing habits may affect attitude, or both may be operative in a cyclical cause-effect pattern. It is also possible that another factor accounts for both correlations, e.g. a change in attainment in Welsh at school causing a lowering of attitude, reading and religious attendance. Indeed, statistically significant correlations between change in attitude and change in attainment suggest that such an explanation is possible.

A deterioration in attitude did not seem to be affected by a decline in watching Welsh TV or less use of Welsh records and cassettes. The "change" correlations were near zero (0.01 and 0.02 respectively).

Change in attitude over the three years was also linked to more customary, more stable behaviours. This may be listed as correlations:

	r	p
1) Attendance at Welsh Church/Chapel	0.38	0.0001
2) Reading Welsh books, newspapers etc.	0.30	0.0001
3) Listening to Welsh records/cassettes	0.24	0.001
4) Watching English language TV	−0.17	−0.01

Four factors were related to deterioration in Welsh language attitude: relatively less attendance (compared with other pupils) at Welsh religious services, less reading of Welsh printed matter, and less use of Welsh records and cassettes and an increase in English TV viewing. These results may be better stated in a more positive manner. Halting a decline in attitude to Welsh between ten and thirteen years of age is linked to attending Welsh Chapel/Church, reading relatively more Welsh books, newspapers, magazines and comics, and listening to Welsh records and cassettes and watching relatively less English TV.

Certain factors appeared to have no link with a decline in attitude: the amount of Welsh TV watched, language background, consumption of English records, cassettes, books, comics, magazines and newspapers.

To summarize. Between ten and thirteen years of age, attitude to Welsh declined. The results presented suggest that an increase in the amount of English TV watched, a falling off in attendance at Welsh religious services and in consumption of Welsh literature, and the amount of Welsh records and cassettes listened to may be related to such a decline.

The results also suggest that despite pupil consumption of Welsh TV increasing during the longitudinal study, it failed to have any observable effect on deteriorating attitudes. More hours of Welsh TV became available over the three years. The pupils watched more Welsh TV. No consequent effect was observable in the results. However, it is not possible to conclude that TV has no effect on attitude. A deterioration in attitude was linked with an increase in English TV viewing over the three years. It is English television viewing that affects attitude to the Welsh language rather than Welsh television.

Change in attainment. Table 27 summarizes the relationships found between the three change in attainment measures and other behaviour which changed.

On the whole, changes which took place in use of media and in religious attendance had minimal effect on attainment. A relative increase in the Welsh comprehension attainment test was related to an increase in reading Welsh literature. A relative increase in reading skills (word recognition) was related to increased watching of Welsh TV. These statistically significant results were not replicated over the three tests, so their validity and stability must be questioned.

The most stable and strong relationship was between attainment and attitude. A relative decrease in attainment was associated on all three tests

TABLE 27. *Relationships between Change in Welsh Attainment Tests and Change in Cultural Variables, 10 to 13 years*

Relationship	r	p
Change in Welsh Attainment & Welsh Church/Chapel attendance change	0.07	n.s.
Change in Welsh Attainment & Reading Welsh books, newspapers, etc. change	0.15	0.02
Change in Welsh Attainment & Welsh records/cassettes change	0.07	n.s.
Change in Welsh Attainment & English TV change	−0.09	n.s.
Change in Welsh Attainment & Welsh TV change	0.09	n.s.
Change in Welsh Attainment & Attitude to Welsh change	0.22	0.002
Change in Welsh Word Recognition & Welsh Church Chapel attendance change	0.02	n.s.
Change in Welsh Word Recognition & Welsh books, newspapers, etc. change	0.03	n.s.
Change in Welsh Word Recognition & Welsh records/cassettes change	0.03	n.s.
Change in Welsh Word Recognition & English TV change	−0.01	n.s.
Change in Welsh Word Recognition & Welsh TV change	0.13	0.05
Change in Welsh Word Recognition & Attitude to Welsh change	0.19	0.005
Change in Welsh Spelling & Welsh Church/Chapel attendance change	0.05	n.s.
Change in Welsh Spelling & Welsh books, newspapers, etc. change	0.02	n.s.
Change in Welsh Spelling & Welsh records/cassettes change	0.01	n.s.
Change in Welsh Spelling & English TV change	0.01	n.s.
Change in Welsh Spelling & Welsh TV change	0.00	n.s.
Change in Welsh Spelling & Attitude to Welsh change	0.122	0.05

with a deterioration in attitude to the Welsh language. Since few pupils' attitudes became more favourable, the result has to be expressed in this negative fashion. Whether it is attitude deterioration that causes lowering of attainment or attainment deterioration which causes attitude to become less favourable is not inferable directly from these results. It is likely that both are in operation. But since attitude is regarded psychologically as a predisposing, motivating influence, the expectation is more that language attitude influences attainment (Gardner & Lambert, 1972).

So far change in attainment has only been considered in the light of accompanying changes in other variables. It is also possible that change in attainment is affected by the more typical, more stable behaviour of a pupil. Table 28 summarizes such relationships.

TABLE 28. *Relationships between Change in Welsh Attainment Tests and in Cultural Variables*

	r	p
Change in Welsh Attainment & Welsh Church/Chapel Attendance	0.24	0.0001
Change in Welsh Attainment & Welsh books, newspapers, etc.	0.00	n.s.
Change in Welsh Attainment & Welsh records/cassettes	0.03	n.s.
Change in Welsh Attainment & Welsh TV watched	0.11	n.s.
Change in Welsh Attainment & English TV watched	−0.13	0.05
Change in Welsh Attainment & Bilingual Background	0.11	n.s.
Change in Welsh Attainment & Attitude to Welsh	0.11	n.s.
Change in Welsh Word Recognition & Welsh Church/Chapel Attendance	0.08	n.s.
Change in Welsh Word Recognition & Welsh books, newspapers, etc.	0.19	0.01
Change in Welsh Word Recognition & Welsh records/cassettes	0.18	0.01
Change in Welsh Word Recognition & Welsh TV	0.06	n.s.
Change in Welsh Word Recognition & English TV	0.00	n.s.
Change in Welsh Word Recognition & Bilingual Background	0.06	n.s.
Change in Welsh Word Recognition & Attitude to Welsh `	0.122	0.05
Change in Welsh Spelling & Welsh Church/Chapel Attendance	0.13	0.05
Change in Welsh Spelling & Welsh books, newspapers, etc.	0.06	n.s.
Change in Welsh Spelling & Welsh records/cassettes	0.08	n.s.
Change in Welsh Spelling & Welsh TV	0.10	n.s.
Change in Welsh Spelling & English TV	−0.14	0.05
Change in Welsh Spelling & Bilingual Background	0.03	n.s.
Change in Welsh Spelling & Attitude to Welsh	0.10	n.s.

While the correlations are not large, and while there is no factor which is statistically significantly related to all three attainment variables, two relationships are replicated. First, a relatively positive change in Welsh attainment over the three years is associated with watching less English language TV than average. This also means that watching greater than average amounts of English TV is linked to a relative decrease in attainment from age ten to age thirteen. Second, attending Welsh chapel or church is related to a relatively greater increase in attainment over the three years.

A Model.   A Path analysis of the various changes in attitude and attainment both summarizes the findings and assesses the relative direct and indirect influence of the independent variables. Figures 14 to 16 present path analyses of the three attainment measures, restricting the paths to those statistically significant ($p < 0.05$).

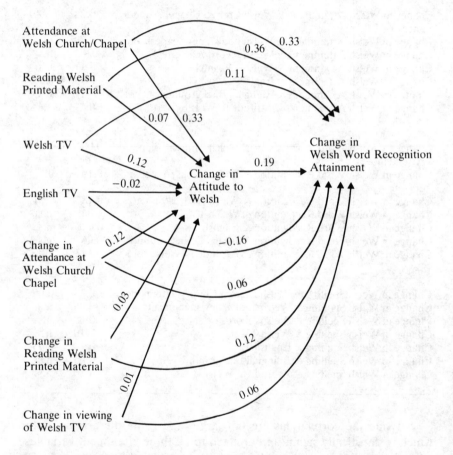

FIGURE 14. *Path Analysis of Change in Welsh Comprehension Attainment*

All the structural coefficients are beta weightings.

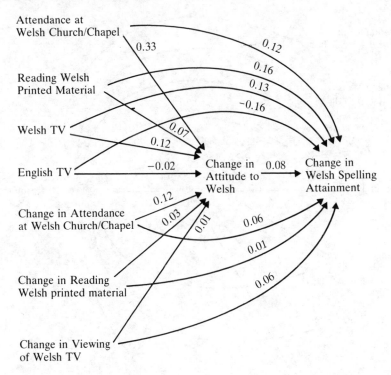

FIGURE 15. *Path Analysis of Change in Welsh Spelling Attainment*

The three path analyses are concerned with one issue. What paths lead more or less strongly to change in attainment? What routes appear to lead to relatively greater or less change in attainment over the three years?

It is apparent that certain factors operate both directly and indirectly. Attendance at a Welsh Chapel/Church affects attainment directly and also through affecting a change in attitude which in turn affects attainment. Similarly, reading Welsh printed matter works directly and indirectly through attitude on attainment. There is a difference in that religious affiliation is comparatively more indirect in its effect, while reading Welsh literature has more of a direct effect on attainment. There is also a difference between the effect of watching Welsh TV and English TV. Watching Welsh TV affects both change in attitude and change in attainment, while watching English TV tends to affect attainment change and not attitude change.

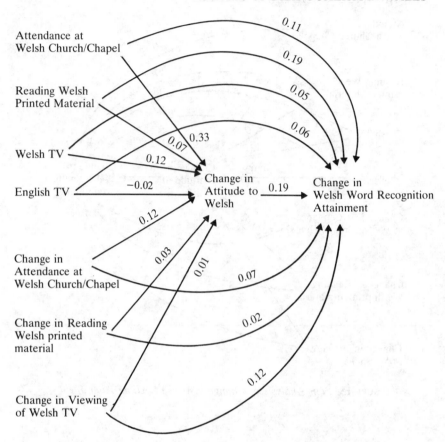

FIGURE 16. *Path Analysis of Change in Welsh Reading (Word Recognition) Attainment*

Three change variables were included in the path analyses. The relationships between these and change in attainment tend not to be so strong as the four variables which reflect more enduring characteristics. Nor are the "change variables" results replicated on all three path analyses. The "change variables" results suggest that a decline in chapel attendance is related to attitude deterioration, and not directly to attainment change. Such a decline appears to have only an indirect effect on attainment through affecting attitude. On the other hand, reading more or less Welsh literature and watching more or less Welsh TV over the three years is connected directly to a change in attainment and relatively little to a change in attitude. However, it should be emphasized that these effects are not strong and not well replicated.

Summary and Conclusions

The theme of this chapter is the relationship between mass media and a minority language. The contemporary history of one aspect of mass communication reveals that Welshmen concerned about their language believe such influence to be a great danger. To Saunders Lewis, television has been the chief destroyer of the Welsh language. The protests of Cymdeithas yr Iaith Gymraeg (Welsh Language Society), in particular, demonstrated the depth of feeling behind this belief. In order to win a Welsh speaking channel, the President of Plaid Cymru, promised a Ghandi-like "fast to the death". The rallying call of "Yr Unig Ateb" was answered by the allocation of 22 hours per week of Welsh language broadcasting to the fourth TV channel.

Since the advent of the fourth channel, the relative saturation of available English and Welsh programmes has changed little. In a week in 1978, Welsh language TV represented just 5.5% of broadcasts. In 1983, with the addition of the Welsh channel, the figure for a representative week was 5.7%. A more healthy picture may be found with other media, records and books in particular. The provision of such media has increased significantly in the last decade.

Yet, clearly, the effect of TV and other media is in terms of usage rather than provision, although the two are related. The chapter looked at the effect of media in terms of two outcomes: attitude and attainment. It is an established research finding that a favourable attitude to Welsh declines as age increases. Do the mass media have an effect on this? Do the mass media also play a part in greater or less attainment at school, especially change in attainment?

The picture painted by the data analysis firstly revealed some static attributes. Children watch Welsh TV for 5% of their total viewing. This suggests that provision and usage are not so dissimilar. Extra provision of Welsh language TV need not result in increased viewing. Preference for different provision tends to be strongly weighted towards the English language. The more a child uses Welsh mass media, the more favourable the attitude to Welsh is likely to be. Both may be the cause and effect of each other. Attendance at a Welsh Church/Chapel tends to appear as more influential than TV or any other individual tool of mass communication in relating to a favourable attitude to Welsh. All these effects occur at ten years and thirteen years of age.

In terms of attainment, reading Welsh literature (books, newspapers, comics, magazines) appears as having the most influence at both ages. What of the influence of TV? Its effect is much greater at ten years of age than at thirteen years, and its effect at ten years is more on attainment than attitude.

The picture painted by the data analysis also reveals change. Attendance at Welsh Church/Chapel declines as does attitude to Welsh. The decline in a favourable attitude to Welsh was not apparently affected by watching less Welsh TV or less use of Welsh records/cassettes, nor with the consumption of English language records and literature. What was related to change in attitude were four factors: the customary degree of Welsh religious attendance, reading Welsh print, listening to Welsh records and cassettes and watching English language TV. With the first three factors, the more involvement in Welsh language activity, the less likelihood of attitude to Welsh becoming unfavourable. Watching a relatively greater amount of English TV is linked with a change towards more negative Welsh attitudes.

What, then, makes for relatively greater or less attainment in Welsh over the years ten to thirteen? Certainly change in attitude to the Welsh language over the three years was connected to change in attainment. What may be uncertain is the causal order. A decline in positive attitude is linked with a relative decline in attainment (relative to the other pupils in the sample). The chicken-egg problem of such a result is that it is difficult to know if a decline in attitude causes a decline in attainment, or a decline in attainment causes a decline in attitude. While it is customary to regard attitude as a predisposing factor affecting performance, it is likely that both operate on each other in a cyclical fashion.

Change in attainment was also related to two customary behaviours: Welsh Church/Chapel attendance and watching English language TV. The path analysis suggested that change in attainment was affected by religious affiliation, partly directly and partly indirectly through the latter's effect on change in attitude. Going to Welsh services is related to maintaining a positive attitude to the Welsh language which in turn may create a positive change in attainment. This also means that those not attending Welsh services tend to be more likely to have a less favourable attitude to the language and are more likely in turn to show a relative deterioration in language attainment.

Although the relationship is not a strong one, the customary amount of English and Welsh TV watched affects attainment, as does the amount of Welsh print read. The larger the amount of Welsh TV watched, the greater the amount of Welsh print read and the less the amount of English TV watched were related to a relative increase in attainment in Welsh over the three years.

It seems fair to argue that mass media do affect attainment and attitude, but not in a strong way. Television viewing and listening to records and cassettes were linked with attainment in Welsh, but the amount of Welsh literature read appeared to have a slightly stronger effect.

Mass media are one kind of cultural influence on attitude and attainment. Welsh Church/Chapel was included to represent another kind of culture. In representing what may be a more traditional form of Welsh culture, it provided a measure of comparison. Against expectation, such religious attendance proved to have the stronger link with attitude and attainment. The effect of such religious enculturation on attitude and attainment was greater than any single item of mass media. Simply stated, having and preserving a favourable attitude to Welsh and relatively favourable attainment in Welsh were most strongly linked to attending Welsh religious services.

It is obviously naive to believe that in order to raise Welsh attainment or improve attitude to the Welsh language, school children need to go to Church or Chapel every Sunday. Entering a beautiful rural parish Church, or singly lustily in Chapel, or listening to prosaic Bible readings and spirited sermons may in itself have but little effect on Welsh attitude and attainment. This variable needs to be regarded as symbolic. It may be a small representation of a larger entity. It is suggested that Welsh Chapel/ Church attendance is one indicator of being immersed in Welsh traditional, rural culture. Such children do not appear to come solely from homes where Welsh is spoken (language background was not strongly linked with Welsh attainment). Their homes are likely to use Welsh *and* be Welsh cultural cells. The milieu of the family may hold close some of the traditional and historical aspects of Welsh life. The results suggest that it is not modern Welsh culture (TV, records and cassettes) that is strongly linked with positive attitude and favourable attainment. The suspicion is that it is the culture surrounding, for example, eisteddfodau, Welsh hymn singing festivals, a community based life where Chapel attendance may provide a community focus, that is linked with a favourable attitude to Welsh and relatively good attainment in Welsh.

If it is this traditional Welsh cultural milieu that provides the breeding ground for a favourable attitude to the Welsh language and relative success at school, then those who wish the Welsh language to be maintained, even restored, may need to re-examine language policy. The tendency has been to believe that language affects culture. One argument against the extinction of the Welsh language is that a distinct and historic cultural form would die at the same time. That is, the Welsh language needs to be safeguarded in order to preserve the attendant culture.

The results of this analysis suggest a different order. Welsh culture needs to be safeguarded in order to preserve the language. At the onset of adolescence, language attitude and attainment flourish particularly when there exists the immersion in traditional Welsh culture. To protect the Welsh language may mean first protecting traditional Welsh culture.

Notes to Chapter 7
1. The research reported in this chapter is based on an important contribution of research data by Emrys Price-Jones.

8   The Microcomputer, The Welsh Language and Education

Introduction

Contemporary historians refer to the present era as the Information Age or as Post Industrial society. It has also been suggested that we are in the midst of the Computer Revolution. Parallels can be drawn between the Industrial Revolution and the ongoing Computer Revolution: a period of rapid advance, progress that cannot be halted, a transformation of the culture and values of society.

One sign of the Computer Revolution is the home computer. It is already fashionable amongst the affluent to aspire to a personal computer for the home. Its versatility as a games player (e.g. space invaders, pac-man, chess, snooker and simulated football), word processor, learning aid and storer of information about tax returns, finance, recipes and addresses, suggests that within a decade the microcomputer will take its place alongside the video recorder, colour television set and hi-fi in the home.

Assuming that there is a revolution in technology that will impinge on the school, the home, as well as on values and culture, then it is likely that there will be consequences for the Welsh language and Welsh culture. It is the aim of this chapter to sketch the changes that are taking place in education as a result of the advent of the microcomputer. The focus of the sketch is the effect of such change on the Welsh language and culture. It will be argued that if the education service and television have been regarded as past threats to the Welsh language and culture, then a present and future threat may be contained within the use of the microcomputer at school and at home. On a more optimistic note it will also be argued that the microcomputer, with foresight, could be used to aid Welsh language and culture.

The Hardware Revolution

Until recently, use of computers by schoolchildren was restricted to secondary schools who owned a telephone link to a central mainframe computer in a University or College. A hardware revolution has taken place. To appreciate the change an analogy is often made with cars. If the car industry had developed at the same pace as computers over the same number of years, then a Rolls Royce would cost a little over £1 (i.e. cost), travel about 3 million miles to the gallon (efficiency) and have enough power to drive the QEII.

All schools can afford a microcomputer. With prices starting at around £70, even the smallest primary school should be able to raise the capital cost. This has been made even more possible by the benevolence of the Department of Industry and the Department of Education and Science. Any primary or secondary school wishing to purchase a micro-computer has been met half-way by the Government. By the end of 1985 it is expected that almost all primary and secondary schools will own at least one microcomputer.

The hardware revolution has been so fast that it appears that microcomputers have solutions to which they are seeking problems. Teachers have not been asked to state their problems for which computer experts go away and create appropriate hardware and software. It is like a chemist contriving a range of medicines for which there are no prior defined diseases. The hardware has entered the classroom and is seeking uses.

It might appear that the Department of Industry, the DES and those Headteachers who respond to the "half-funding" offer are under the illusion that technological advance brought into the classroom will in itself produce progress (Baker, 1983a). Would the subsidizing of complex physical fitness machinery for every home lead automatically to greater health and fitness? Neither educational progress nor curriculum improve-ment is a direct and inevitable consequence of technological advance. "A piece of equipment does not a revolution make" (Sheingold et al., 1983: 413).

There is little American or British evidence as yet to suggest the computer has led to any significant improvement in terms of pupil achievement. Might, then, the Government subsidy and the eagerness of many Headteachers to purchase a microcomputer be mistaken? Might the money be better spent on increasing manpower in the schools or in the purchase of books and other curriculum materials? Are the Welsh language and culture served more by the Government subsidizing the computer or by further subsidizing necessary Welsh language curriculum materials? Are the language and culture best served by Headteachers and PTA's investing in a microcomputer or in Welsh curriculum materials?

Consider a practical example. At Bangor, the University School of Education and the Normal College were funded by the Schools Council in Wales to produce Welsh language diagnostic materials and tests suitable for pupils with learning difficulties (see Chapter 5). The target group forms a minority of a minority. In the many small rural primary schools of Wales, the materials may be suitable, of necessity, for only one or two children. At the moment the materials available for such children are almost non-existent. However educationally vital these materials may be for such children, there is an inbuilt high cost per pupil. Examples of needed Welsh language materials in other curriculum areas could have been used. The question is one of priorities. For primary schools in particular, the value of the microcomputer has yet to be proved. In this context of alternatives, there is a risk of the Welsh language and culture not being best served by a capital investment in hardware and the recurrent need to purchase software and maintain and update the hardware, until evaluation of the value of installing hardware in schools is available. At present there is an experiment which uses almost all schools. Would it not have been preferable to experiment in a small number of schools? In education, tape recorders, films, teaching machines and television were all expected in their infancy to change teaching and learning. Yet blackboard and chalk, exercise books and exposition are still the major elements of most classrooms. In the past, new technology has had only a marginal impact on the pattern of classroom education. Will the silicon chip have a similar marginal impact on the school? Because of the versatility, portability, cheapness and availability of microtechnology developments for education, there are grounds for believing that the impact will be more than marginal. Could this impact be used positively to aid Welsh language and culture?

Computer Aided Instruction (CAI)

Possibly the most common use of computers as a learning aid in the classroom and home is for drill and practice. For example, computer software may be written to take a child sequentially through multiplication. At the start a child will be given instruction in the most simple of tasks, progressing step by step to complex multiplication. At each stage the pupil is given plenty of practice, and when competency is shown the child progresses to the next stage. Drill and practice software are not only to be found in Mathematics but also in Music, Economics, Geography, Physics, Chemistry, Biology, Business Studies, History, French and German. Modern language software gives structured drill and practice in grammar, vocabulary, verb formation and translation. The pupil is not restricted to "speaking" to the computer by the QWERTY "typewriter" keyboard. Input may be by a microphone, a light pen that touches the display on a "television" screen, a graphics tablet used for writing, or by a "joystick" particularly useful for entering graphical displays.

"Drill and practice" is alternatively called computer aided instruction (CAI) and the concept of instruction contains the idea of the computer acting as a teacher substitute. In instructing and providing limitless examples, CAI attempts to replace the teacher.

The advantages customarily listed for CAI make it appear very attractive. The program can be adjusted to the ability and achievement of the pupil; the pupil controls the speed at which the lesson advances; there is immediate feedback. The teacher is necessarily slow in marking calculations, or checking translation and written answers of 30 different pupils. Learning theory suggests that greater learning occurs when feedback is immediate. This the microcomputer can give. Not only can right and wrong answers immediately be indicated but some kind of stereotyped encouragement is normally provided. Given such individual instruction, it is to be expected that pupils will be more involved and more active. Instead of the teacher asking a question to one pupil at a time, leaving most pupils to sit passively until their turn, the microcomputer appears to keep pupils on their toes. If there are benefits for the pupil, there may also be benefits for the teacher. Use of such software may free the teacher to provide more individual tuition and personal contact.

Such CAI programs may be very attractive to the teacher in bilingual schools. However, there are educational dangers which also have to be recognized (Baker, 1983a & b; Sheingold et al., 1983). Apart from general educational limitations, there are dangers in a bilingual situation. The software produced in Britain and that imported from America is almost without exception in the majority language. Maths and Science software uses literacy skills as well as mathematical language while the arts subjects naturally involve considerable reading and some language input via a keyboard. The proliferation of CAI programs in the English language potentially poses a threat to Welsh as a medium of instruction in schools. Will the invasion of cassette tapes and floppy discs into the classroom tilt the balance of language more towards English and less towards Welsh? Is this another, new and different form of increased pressure for children to use English at the cost of Welsh?

Some CAI programs come from commercial software houses. Except for French and German programs, this software is totally in English. The government since 1980, through the Micro-electronics Education Programme (MEP), has invested £18 million in developing micro-electronics-based education. While Wales has a Regional Information Centre based in Cardiff, and a sub-centre based in Wrexham, its £1 million budget (1980–1986) has been slow to produce software specifically for the Welsh language situation. Whether this is through ignorance or indifference on the part of the MEP or of Welsh educators is open to debate (Hansard, 1984: 51–53). It is somewhat paradoxical that the excellent MEP word processing software for Britain written in English was produced in North Wales.

Computer Assisted Learning (CAL)

With drill and practice software the desire is to act as teacher substitute. The microcomputer acts as an instructor. In Computer Assisted Learning, computer software attempts to act as a tutor. The model of learning changes from drill and practice to discovery learning. One well-known piece of CAL software manipulates the ecology of a pond. The pupil can vary the number of fishermen, the length of the close season, how often the pool is fished, and whether the fishermen return the catch or not. The consequent effect on the remaining stock of fish, on phytoplankton and herbivores may be studied. Other CAL examples include manipulating a complex economic model of demand and supply (e.g. with car production), recreating an archeological expedition and simulating a dangerous chemical experiment. The common denominator is that the CAL program holds a model; a model of conservation in ponds, a model of elasticity, an experimental model, a model of archaeological excavation.

There are doubtless advantages in using CAL software and their introduction into the curriculum may provide enhancement and progress. It saves time, energy, organization and labour to run an experiment or simulation on the computer. Many of the advantages previously listed for computer aided instruction are also applicable to CAL. There are also dangers, limitations and criticisms of computer assisted learning. The limited range of experience provided by a computer, the implications for discipline and control, the restricted development of language, the danger of the pupil being programmed by the computer and the legitimation of authoritative knowledge, are all issues which need to be examined before the chip is swallowed too quickly with consequent indigestion. These issues are explored in Baker (1983 a & b).

The issue in this chapter is the possible effect of CAL on bilingualism and bilingual education. As with CAI, there is a large and ever-increasing amount of CAL software on the market. Almost without exception, such software is in English. Bilingual education is in danger from increased use of the majority language. If maths, physics, biology, chemistry, geography, history, economics, English, music and art teachers in bilingual areas wish to use CAL software, the medium of instruction between computer and pupil becomes English. If the primary teacher wishes to use the generous gift of a microcomputer, it is English language software that is usually provided *gratis* with the machine and may be subsequently purchased. The Micro-electronics Education Programme provided schools and colleges with a free introductory pack of computer based learning software. Welsh speaking schools were given English speaking software. At one level this is generosity. At another level it is insensitivity to the role of language in the classroom. Possibly unconsciously or through ignorance, the English language finds another Trojan horse to enter the sparse breeding grounds of the minority language. At this level, CAL may accidentally be a factor in minority language decay.

CAL software may not only be a potential threat to the minority language. Welsh culture may also be facing another small invasion. In the curriculum areas where the indigenous culture is likely to be most manifestly or latently transmitted. CAL programs tend to be English. In History, for example, there is some interesting and valuable software on English history: the Norman conquest, Early English castles, the development of a Saxon Village. One first class piece of software comprises a simulation of the discovery and excavation of the Mary Rose, King Henry VIII's flagship which sank in the Solent in 1545 while defending Portsmouth against a French invasion (Whittington, 1984). In 1982, the remains of the warship were raised from the sea-bed off Portsmouth. The sophisticated software and accompanying written and visual materials engage children in a simulation, searching for a wreck by navigation, diving, scanning and surveying. "Systematic investigation simulates for the children the long process which leads finally to the rediscovery of the hull and enables them to experience the satisfaction and excitement of a famous and successful piece of archaeological research" (Cambridgeshire Software House, 1982: 3). While not doubting the historical and educational value of this software, for the Welsh pupil, the danger is that the history curriculum will become a little more biased towards culture not indigenously Welsh. The great value and attractiveness of such a program may unintentionally move the Welsh curriculum further away from minority cultural forms. In geography, English, European and World topics have been reduced to CAL software (Forer, 1983: Shepherd *et al.*, 1980). This is to be applauded and welcomed. What diet does the geography teacher in Wales provide when keen to use CAL software? The inherent danger is that the cultural balance in the classroom will tilt slightly more towards non-Welsh culture.

The previous two chapters reported research which suggested the primacy of Welsh culture as protector of the language. The final chapter examines this issue in more depth. Given that the transmission of Welsh culture in schools is of great importance in supporting the Welsh language and given that CAL materials are a permanent and increasing feature of education, the creation of Welsh cultural CAL materials becomes essential.

Computer Managed Learning (CML)

Computer Managed Learning is a means of helping the teacher to administrate rather than teach. Instead of giving a description of its operation, an example of where it may be useful is first provided.

Take a primary school containing about 20 to 40 pupils with two or three teachers. The classes have a large age range, the teacher coping with three or four different age groups. In each class, half the pupils speak Welsh as a first language, the other half speak English. Add to the linguistic and age difference in the school the normal wide spread of ability, aptitude, interests, motivation, past achievement and sex differences, and the result is a highly complex, almost impossible, management task for the teacher.

Management of a full curriculum to provide the full range of educational experiences, management of both the teacher's and pupils' time, results in problems of great magnitude.

How do such teachers cope? The Welsh Office Education Survey (1978a: 24) reports that:

"Most of the (small school) teachers claimed that, whatever groupings they adopted in their classes, they regarded the individual child as the main focus of their attention and curricular planning. They declared that they aimed to assign to each individual child particular and progressive tasks in all areas of the curriculum and particularly in the basic skills of language and mathematics, according to his/her age, aptitude and ability. This claim has validity in practice and in most of the schools. About half of these teachers, however, are unconvinced that they do, in fact, fulfil this aim satisfactorily. Many stress the complex problems presented by the wide age and ability ranges, and, in many schools, the widely differing linguistic backgrounds of their pupils".

In summary,.such teachers cope with their complex management task by individualized learning. Computer managed learning is based on learning cycles and individualized learning with the simple aim of reducing the management role of teachers, relieving them for more individual teaching contact with pupils. CML will certainly be no panacea for the small rural primary school, but it could help with the management of the curriculum. CML has been previously used in Wales (South Glamorgan) to aid management of remedial reading. One example of its present use on microcomputers is in Hertfordshire Secondary schools, to manage a mixed ability mathematics course.

Computer Managed Learning has three main functions:

1. *Routing*. Teachers in small schools using individualized learning latently or manifestly have a route through the curriculum which pupils follow. There will be an order, a sequence through which pupils travel. Some pupils may be allowed to take short cuts. Other pupils will follow remedial branches before returning to the main trunk road. Such routes, if they are capable of being made explicit and represented in a logical sequence, can be translated into a computer program. The program instead of a teacher tells the pupil what is the next activity: which book to read, which page of arithmetic problems to tackle, which map to draw, or a request to go and see the teacher.

2. *Testing*. Routing partly depends on testing. A test of present pupil competence will aid a decision by the teacher on which route the pupil next takes. The test may be given by the computer, by the teacher or be taken independently by the pupil who then feeds the result into the computer. The test is likely to reveal the extent to which a pupil has mastered a previous task. The test is less likely to compare one pupil with another. That is, the test is likely to be criterion-referenced and diagnostic rather than normative.

While testing aids routing, which route a child takes may be decided by the inclusion of more factors than mere testing. A child's interests, aptitude, and typical level of achievement may also be included in the routing decision. This may result in variation for pupils in their rate of learning, objectives pursued and the method of learning (e.g. working independently, use of audio-visual materials, amount of interaction with the teacher).

3. *Record keeping and Reporting*. The CML program can store and record how well pupils are doing and what ground they have previously covered. The computer record of a pupil will indicate achievement in the various tests and precisely what components of the curriculum a pupil has tackled. This may provide up-to-date, cumulative information for the teacher, and also feedback to the pupil and reports for parents. A detailed and comprehensive pupil profile may be retained by the microcomputer for immediate access. The reporting ability of CML also provides information to aid decision making, administration and curriculum development by the teacher (McMahon, 1983).

The idea of computer managed learning has been introduced to suggest a positive use for microcomputers in Wales. The small schools of Wales are mostly to be found in the rural Welsh language heartland areas. Recent reports have highlighted the special difficulties faced by such schools (Welsh Office, 1978b: Schools Council Committee for Wales, 1983). The introduction of computer managed learning may help alleviate some of those special difficulties.

Computer managed learning has attendant practical and theoretical limitations. The practical implementation of CML in small schools requires an initial large expenditure of money to provide appropriate hardware and software. The introduction of CML tends to carry with it an objectives — type, atomistic, individualized curriculum. But while there are limitations, the benefits for hard pressed one-teacher, two-teacher and three-teacher schools may be great enough to require detailed evaluation of CML as a future aid to small bilingual schools, and also to other bilingual classroom settings where the teacher faces management problems.

Information Retrieval

Start with five apparently unrelated facts and events. (1) A daily newspaper can be stored on a silicon chip less than a centimetre square and a millimetre thick. (2) Via teletext, news, recipes, computer programs, travel information and weather (for example) can be brought instantaneously into the classroom or living room. (3) Within seconds, a Californian computer can be accessed from anywhere in Wales and asked to print out a list of all known books and articles on bilingual eduction. (4) A video conference is held and the conference report is distributed around the world by satellite. (5) The family breadwinner has an office at home and transmits and receives all communications to the central office by a microcomputer coupled to a G.P.O. line. Letters are replaced by electronic mail. By high speed data lines and satellite links, the same message is sent simultaneously to 500 people.

The significance of each fact or event is not only that each is real and possible. Each example demonstrates that small or vast amounts of information can be stored permanently, retrieved instantly and communicated universally with ease. Knowledge is now so easy to obtain instantly. The days of hunting tediously through encyclopedias, waiting days for post, missing the rugby and football results are almost past. Instant information is available at the press of a button.

One of the most attractive uses of a computer is its ability to store massive quantities of data. Census data, police files, encyclopedias, dictionaries, names and addresses of car drivers, premium bond data, the list of information that can be stored is endless. In certain Clwyd schools, pupils may access a database of local nineteenth century Census returns. The idea is that pupils can examine local history by manipulating the database, making and testing hypotheses. For example, a pupil may look at particular extended families and occupations. A pupil does not have to spend wasted time searching slowly through pages of Census returns. There is an immediate retrieval of information. Similarly a pupil does not have to find slowly the right page in the right volume of a large encyclopedia. The computer, at the input of a keyword, can instantly present the required information on a screen or on paper.

The wider notion of information retrieval also includes another idea. It is easy, and becoming more easy, to access information from a distance. For example, all books, articles and reports connected with education are indexed in a large database called ERIC held on a Californian computer. It is possible to access ERIC by computer terminal and acoustic coupler from any part of Britain. Should a teacher or researcher require a listing of all books, articles and reports on learning difficulties with bilingual children written in English from the year 1976 onwards, by entering a few keywords immediate details can be provided. As part of the Bangor Project (see Chapter 5) this was achieved at minimal cost.

In Britain, a Council for Educational Technology project has evaluated the automatic distribution of CAL software to schools and colleges by PRESTEL. By simply owning a suitable microcomputer and telephone, teachers can obtain copies of computer software written for their classrooms by PRESTEL. It is not necessary to spend time visiting and searching a library for a list of software available or news of this telesoftware project. The information is available instantly by accessing PRESTEL. It is similarly easy to download software via TELETEXT to the home or school microcomputer. Such software can be stored on tape or disc and used any time in the future.

Join together the information explosion with the technological revolution and the resulting Information Society promises likely cultural change. If educational software can be sent via the telephone or teletext or television or by satellites and ocean cables, then the nature of education may change. Will more education occur by using the microcomputer in the home? Will classroom education become more based on centrally developed and distributed CBL software? The exponential progress of microcomputers in the last five years makes prediction both difficult and dangerous. The soothsayers of the information society suggest great social, economic and educational changes (e.g. Large, 1980; Evans, 1980). International colour newspapers and electronic post sent directly to the home microcomputer; people working at home linking to the office via their micro; direct computer access to library databases, banks, shops, diagnostic medical programs, legal and horticultural advice databases and voting on many issues by an interactive TV system have all been forecast. The introduction of just a small proportion of these is likey to create simultaneous cultural change. Such cultural change will affect the Welsh language and its attendant culture.

The language of such information is English. Whether it is accessing ERIC in America, or downloading a flood risk settlement database from London by PRESTEL, the language of the majority will be used by the minority in Welsh speaking Wales. If in the future newspapers, medical databases or vast encyclopedic databases are accessed, the language of communication is unlikely to be Welsh. The universal progress of microelectronics means the increasing importance attached to universal languages. Widespread, standard use of microcomputers means the wider spread of standard international languages. The Industrial Revolution ensured the decline of the Welsh language by urbanization and the desire for greater affluence. The Computer Revolution may instigate further decline by language standardization and the desire to possess information.

Research Evidence

Consideration of the relationship between the Welsh language and the Computer Revolution has been necessarily predictive of the future. One piece of research tells a little about the present. In 1984, the Economic and Social Research Council commissioned a survey of microcomputer usage and attitude in Welsh speaking schools in Wales (Baker, 1984b). A postal questionnaire was sent to all Secondary schools where Welsh is taught as a first language (N=92) and a systematic random sample of 1 in 3 Primary schools where Welsh is the sole, main or part medium of instruction (N=182). The survey revealed that the microcomputer was being used almost totally in English. Secondary schools reported 97% usage in English; Primary schools 86%. Bearing in mind that these are "Welsh language" schools, it may appear of concern that 70% of secondary schools and 55% of primary schools used the facility solely in English. What is apparent is the mismatch between the language balance of various types of Welsh speaking schools and the language balance when these schools use their microcomputer(s). In classrooms where Welsh is the dominant medium of communication, English is the dominant language in using the microcomputer.

At the outset of the survey, such an imbalance was expected. What was not expected was the response by teachers to the question "What effect, if any, do you think the microcomputer has had, and will have on the Welsh language?" The expectation was that responses would be negative and pessimistic. Not so. Only 10% of all comments were negative, as opposed to 28% of comments that were unconditionally positive. A further 25% of responses suggested that there would be little or no effect on the Welsh language. The remainder either suggested that a positive effect was conditional on the provision of good Welsh software (26%) or that Welsh must become a technological language, a language of the microcomputer, otherwise attitude to and the status of the language would become less favourable (11%).

In a second part of the survey, where non-teachers and organizations were invited to comment, one respondent argued that "Welsh" schools must benefit equally from every kind of technological progress, and that "Welsh" education must not become inferior by the absence of technology.

Yet at the same time, "Welsh" schools need to be provided with quality software in the Welsh language.

The evidence of the survey suggests that at present, when Welsh is dominant in the classroom, English is dominant when using the micro-computer. If such a situation continues, the result may be as one teacher responded "un hoelen arch arall iddo" (one more nail in its (Welsh language) coffin). Yet teachers are optimistic about the future. The provision of Welsh software may help preserve the language.

Towards the Future

Must there be decline in the use of Welsh due to the Computer Revolution? There is no escaping that the majority language will be essential to those who wish to take part in technological advance in the future. That is to be expected in a bilingual country containing a universal language. At the same time, it is possible to ensure that Welsh is a "computer" language of the future and not just the traditional language of eisteddfodau, chapel and "y werin" (the folk people). There are five ways in which such might be achieved.

1. Software could be developed to aid the teaching of Welsh as both a first and second language. Such software will never replace teachers, but may provide a useful addition and extension. Such software may be useful in the classroom and at home, with schoolchildren and adult learners. Software to help learn French and German already exists as sources to copy and improve. Such Welsh software may aid spelling, vocabulary, grammar and comprehension. The simultaneous and inter-connected use of a tape recorder may provide the necessary oral accompaniment. Language games in Welsh, such as Hangman or the Executioner complete with sound, animation and colour graphics, may be easily created (G. Roberts, 1983). The use of Welsh word processing programs to create and edit prose or poetry could be a valuable compositional activity for Welsh learners and first language pupils alike. The production of such software may provide one more piece of armour in the struggle to defend the language.

2. There is no insurmountable problem in translating English language CAI, CAL or CML software into Welsh. Given the consent of the author, changes in language may be relatively cheap, quick and simple (Baker, 1984b). This possibility also extends, although at a higher level of difficulty, to altering the language used in programming a computer (e.g. BASIC, FORTRAN).

Gwynedd Education Department have launched a scheme which selects software and then translates the language from English to Welsh so that the pupil inputs in Welsh and receives output in Welsh. Such a scheme is essential in combating the importation of English into "Welsh" classrooms brought about by advances in computer based learning. Such a scheme has to be continuous to keep pace with development and advances in Computer Based Learning. There is also a strong case to ensure that word processing software is available in the minority language. While the creation and production of Welsh software may never be great, there are already examples of such software available from, for example, Swyddfa'r Graig (Newcastle Emlyn), Trinity College, Carmarthen, and Philip Davies' team based at the North East Wales Institute of Higher Education.

3. A case has already been made for the exploration of the relevance in a bilingual situation of Computer Managed Learning. Such a tool may be of particular help to Welsh speaking areas. Such areas tend to contain many small schools. The teachers in these schools often have difficult management problems. CML may partially relieve these problems.

4. The presence of many English language databases is natural. Much information accessed by Welsh speakers will of necessity be in the majority language. Particularly valuable for Welsh schools would be the availability of Welsh language databases and Welsh cultural databases. For example, a database containing Welsh language Census figures at a local level, both from past Censuses and from the most recent Census, may be useful in History and Welsh and Geography lessons. Children may become aware of their linguistic roots, more aware of language change, more aware of the nature of the local community. There are two issues here. First, databases may be created that can be accessed and manipulated using the Welsh language. A database for local historical social reconstruction or databases on Welsh literature, poetry or music are all feasible. The second issue is that, possibly irrespective of language, Welsh cultural databases may be important. In order for Welsh cultural transmission to occur, it is Welsh data that need to be stored. Traditions in Welsh history, music, literature, religion, science and education may each create a database. The alternative is that information retrieval will be solely in a universal language and concern English culture. A balance is needed where at present there exists total imbalance.

5. Apart from Welsh language education, there are possibly positive benefits in the Computer revolution for Welsh society in terms of rural and home life. It is likely that more people will be able to work from home in

the future. Human word processors, programmers, teachers in distance learning services, journalists and directors of companies may all work via a microcomputer and telecommunications. If certain occupations become less centralized in towns and cities in the future, rural life may be both more stable and more attractive. As Chapter 1 showed, Welsh language heartlands tend to be rural in nature. Rural existence and the minority language and culture may be encouraged by present and future microtechnology developments, and their effect on employment.

It is not only future employment patterns that may affect Welsh society. Education at home and leisure may also change in the future, and in turn create changes in culture and society. If high quality software is produced that will assist pupil learning in a variety of curriculum areas, some school activity may be transferred to the home. There is an ever-increasing amount of software being marketed for the education of children at home. With the advent of cable television, interactive videodisk and Teletext/Prestel, home based education is likely to increase (Sage & Smith, 1983; Boyd-Barrett, 1983; Hawkridge, 1983). Rural children may potentially benefit from such developments both in the home and in their small, rural schools. Communication, the sharing of certain resources between relatively isolated rural schools, is increasingly possible with the Computer Revolution (Sage & Smith, 1983). This may strengthen the rural educational breeding grounds where the Welsh language and culture have traditionally been strong.

Owing to levels of unemployment, a shorter working week, earlier retirement and longer holidays, there is ever-increasing time for leisure activity. While the origins of increasing leisure time are complex, the Computer Revolution is one of a number of catalysts of more time for home life and cultural and leisure activity. Potentially this extra time could be used to strengthen Welsh language and cultural activity. Increased time for home, community, societies, sport and music is potentially increased time to foster forms of existence which utilize the minority language and cement and develop the various forms of Welsh culture. Harnessing leisure time to support the minority language and culture may require planning and foresight. The dividends from such advanced planning may play an important part in the survival of the language and culture.

Conclusions

Industrial and technological change has been a constant threat to the minority language in Wales. Provision of roads, trains, cars, wireless and television are just a few examples of sources of Anglicization in this

century. Progress and affluence have sometimes brought language deterioration. In Chapter 7, the threat of the 1970's was perceived by many to
be television. One threat to Welsh in the 1980's and 1990's is likely to be
the Computer Revolution and the Information Society.

The investment in microcomputer hardware by schools, particularly,
but also increasingly by affluent homes, has provided an accidental Trojan
horse. The horse holds anglophone language and culture. The great
quantity of software available to teachers, parents and pupils is in English.
Much of the software contains a universal culture. Much software is also a
vestibule of English culture.

The information society increasingly feeds from instant information
retrieval available through micro-electronic developments. Again the
language of communication is English, and where there are cultural
trappings they are not Welsh.

The Trojan horse cannot be stopped. With the Trojan horse comes
powerful developments that prophesy progress, affluence, less drudgery,
more pleasure in learning and leisure. What may be needed in Wales is the
foresight to harness the horse and use it for Welsh language and Welsh
cultural purposes. It may not be the horse that will win the race against
time to save the Welsh language. But it may be a necessary horse to help
work in the field of Welsh language education.

9 A Future for the Welsh Language?

Introduction

The concluding chapter must of necessity look to the future. Welsh is a minority language set in an engulfing ocean of a majority, international language. Welsh culture is similarly fighting for survival in the jungle of English, American and European mainstream culture. Can the Welsh language and culture survive?

As an inexact but important and irreplaceable barometer of the condition of the Welsh language, the decennial Government Census has shown a constant decline in the percentage of the population in Wales who are Welsh speaking. In the most recent ten year span (1971 to 1981) the decline was appreciably less than previously. But decline there was. Given the same rate of decline in that ten year period, the language would become extinct in approximately one hundred years. Taking the last nine Censuses into account, the statistical prediction is of extinction in the year 2026. While to make a prediction of the year of extinction from such figures is very simplistic, a point is made. The present trend *is* towards extinction. There can be no real optimism until the Census figures show a levelling or an upturn.

There is no such barometer of the health of Welsh culture. With the variety of definitions of culture (Hall, 1977) and the difference of opinions about what is and is not Welsh culture, it is impossible to put a percentage figure on the state of Welsh culture. A barometer could not operate by a simple question in an opinion poll. It requires the talents of historian, sociologist and philosopher, the evaluations of poets, musicians, communication experts and folklorists, and a detailed study of home, social and economic life in rural and urban communities. It may be found on the one hand that eisteddfodau continue to flourish, but Welsh chapel attendance declines. Welsh hymns may be sung more heartily in the tavern than the chapel. Male voice choirs and Cerdd Dant may still be of high

167

standards, but gone are the days of noson lawen (social evenings with singing and reciting). A cultural balance sheet is as impossible to total as it is to define its components. Yet it is clear that the health of language and culture are inseparably linked. Just as the heart and brain are interdependent in the functioning of a healthy body, so are culture and language in the health of the Welsh language and indigenous Welsh culture.

Welsh Culture

What is Welsh culture? Raymond Williams (1981) proposes three particular meanings for culture: (i) a developed state of mind as in "a cultured person"; (ii) a developmental process as in "cultural activities", and (iii) the means of this process, which is the anthropological and sociological use, indicating a "whole way of life" of a distinct group of people.

The crowned bard at the National Eisteddfod may represent a cultured Welsh person. The activities of eisteddfodau may represent one kind of Welsh cultural process. However, the preferred notion of Welsh culture is a whole way of life. Welsh culture then concerns language, ways of perceiving and organizing experience, ways of anticipating the world, forms of social interaction, rules and conventions about behaviour, moral values and ideals, technology and material culture as well as poetry, music and history.

If Welsh culture is regarded as a whole way of life, it appears more rational to talk in the plural, in terms of Welsh cultures. Rather than trying to describe a culturally stereotyped indigenous Welsh person, it seems more sensible to allow for a kaleidoscope of Welsh cultures. The Welsh pop culture becomes as relevant as the culture of Welsh poetry and penillion singing. The culture of Welsh rugby, rural life and radio, the experience of the hearth and the harp are each contributing colours in the kaleidoscope. The edges of the kaleidoscope of Welsh culture will be blurred. Where a "Welsh way of life" is mixed with other British and non-British cultures, sharp definitions will fade. Towards the centre, there will be ways of life unique to Wales.

Despite the availability of a kaleidoscope of Welsh cultures, to be bilingual is not necessarily to be bicultural. To use two languages or especially to have the ability to speak Welsh and English is not to become, de facto, bicultural (Grosjean, 1982). For example, do some of those who

become fluent in Welsh at school never participate in Welsh cu
activity? It is probable that at the heart of the kaleidoscope, certain f(
of Welsh culture can be properly experienced only through the Welsh
language. Yet speaking that language need not lead to such experience.
Bedwyr Lewis Jones (1981) reflects this distance between the presence of
the Welsh language and its use in a variety of cultural domains. "Welsh,"
he argues, "although functioning as an ethnic language, occupies for a
growing number of people a partial if not a marginal place in the overall
picture" (p. 49).

It appears axiomatic that, for the Welsh language to survive, it needs
to penetrate an individual's whole way of life. For the language to be
relegated to the eisteddfod field, the chapel, Welsh language lessons in
school, to one channel on television and radio is to provide a badly
balanced diet that will inevitably lead to malnutrition and attendant death.
Welsh speech events in every kind of cultural activity need to become more
possible. The Welsh Language Act of 1967 attempted this at an institutional level. The Welsh language was formally recognized by this Act as a
legitimate language in legal and administrative contexts.

As Williams & Roberts (1983) argue, such official recognition is an
important event, for two reasons. First, allowing the Welsh language to
have "equal validity" in law and administration opens the door for further
claims in the public sector. Second, such recognition, however narrow,
may help create greater awareness among the populace of the minority
language and its legitimate place in society. A status that is ascribed by
government to a language clearly does not lead to the achievement of that
status in the eyes of the populace. It may be, nevertheless, an important
provision in the cultural diet of the nation.

In 1978, the Council for the Welsh Language, critical of the 1967
Welsh Language Act, argued for a more positive and comprehensive
approach to the language "in all walks of life" (p. 49). The Council's
criticism mirrored the Canadian federal policy of having two official
languages but no official culture (McLeod, 1984). This 1967 Act made
Welsh an official language, but disregarded the cultural context of Welsh.
Yet it is Welsh cultural forms that may need more status and more support
at a governmental level. Governmental decisions about housing, employment, media, public administration all affect Welsh culture. Institutions of
Welsh cultural transmission such as bilingual schools and Yr Urdd (see
p. 172) may need extensive financial support, if Welsh cultural activity is of
the essence in the struggle to save the Welsh language.

The Primacy of Culture

Quite unexpectedly, the two chapters which examined aspects of education by statistical research, pointed to the crucial nature of certain aspects from the kaleidoscope of Welsh culture. For pupils at school, it was the culture symbolized in Welsh chapel/church life rather than television, records and the printed word which was more closely linked to a positive attitude to Welsh and relative success in Welsh attainment tests. In analysing the possible reasons for opting for Welsh in the secondary school, it was the cultural background rather than being taught Welsh in the primary school that was most imp_____ _____. While the two researches used a different conception of Welsh cult_____ _____ Both suggested the primacy of Welsh cul_____

It appears that Welsh culture _____ _____ f the Welsh language. It may be that it is _____ _____ ld be fostered in order to preserve Welsh _____ _____ at the culture must be fostered to preser_____ _____ h are entwined in an inseparable way. H_____ _____ earch suggests that in terms of finance, e_____ _____, it is Welsh culture that needs support. To support a language without support- ing its attendant culture is to fund an expensive life-support machine attached to someone culturally dead or dying. To support Welsh culture may be to give a life-saving injection to the language.

Supporting what culture? The chapter on mass media suggested that the symbolic notion of chapel culture was more important in Welsh attitude and attainment than Welsh TV or Welsh records or the printed word. Initially this makes some sense. Television, literature, records are relatively passive, non-participatory media. If it be allowed that chapel culture extends to participating in eisteddfodau as well as chapel, in general Welsh music as well as hymn singing, then the culture is more active. While values, beliefs, attitudes are transmitted by the mass media, through the personal relationships built up by immersion in an active, participatory culture, more pervading and lasting values and attitudes may be transmitted. It seems possible that active participatory involvement in Welsh culture rather than sampling the passive culture of Welsh TV, literature and records, may be more influential in the preservation of the Welsh language.

It is with younger people, particularly those in the education process, that much of the future of the language rests. Young people are the pliable putty who may mould themselves, or be moulded into protectors or unconscious destroyers of the Welsh language and culture. To hope that young people will attend chapel and thereby be inculcated with Welsh culture is unrealistic. Gone are the days of packed pews, chapel conformity and the power of the preacher. If culture is the bedrock of the language, it makes it essential to provide the opportunity to engage that culture. If chapel is no longer the main transmitter of Welsh culture, what institutions may be vital in the present and future?

Bilingual Schooling

The education system has its part to play in cultural transmission. Chapter 6 revealed that being taught Welsh in Primary school may be not enough to carry on taking Welsh to the end of Secondary school. It is clearly possible to teach somebody Welsh without their becoming cultural-ly Welsh. To learn the language is not to learn to be Welsh. The choice of topics in Music, History and Geography, the choice of literature in English as well as Welsh lessons, as well as the language used to transmit science, sport and religious education may each contribute in a small but important way to a child's cultural identification and values. The culture of the hidden curriculum of the school is equally important in Welsh cultural transmis-sion and reproduction.

Sociologists regard education in Wales as a key form of cultural reproduction, and the cultural transmission that occurs tends to be that of the dominant society (Williams & Roberts, 1983; C. Roberts, 1983). The comment of Khan (1978) regarding minorities in English schools is also true of many schools in Wales.

"The mainstream school is essentially mono-cultural and mono-lingual. It does not recognize or accord value to the culture and language of children of minorities, and this does not fulfil the aim of developing the overall educational potential of the child" (Khan, 1978: 1).

Transmission of Welsh culture by education depends on educational policy, provision and practice. As Chapter 2 revealed, there is a gap between policy and provision, between rhetoric and practice in bilingual education. The legitimacy of bilingual schools is not doubted at govern-ment or LEA level. No centralized leadership is given to the development of bilingual education; few resources are provided for LEA implementa-tion of bilingual schooling. The Council for the Welsh Language (1978) called for a planned system of unbroken bilingual education, with no response. It argued that education authorities tended to respond to, rather than generate, public demand for bilingual education. This has not changed since 1978.

Five Canadian educationalists summed up the importance of bilingual schooling in Wales in terms of the trend towards the extinction of the Welsh language and culture:

> "Although Welsh language schools by themselves may be insufficient to reverse this trend, they are clearly necessary if Welsh is to have any hopes of survival" (Beaudoin *et al.*, 1981: 508).

Yr Urdd

Cultural transmission is also heavily invested in Yr Urdd. Urdd Gobaith Cymru (The Welsh League of Youth – or literally, The League of the Hope of Wales), founded in 1922 by Syr Ifan ab Owen Edwards, is "the first large-scale movement of any kind to have found in the Welsh language its initial inspiration and the ultimate end of its endeavours" (D. G. Jones, 1979: 311). Yr Urdd is a non-political and non-sectarian movement with a three-fold aim: to serve Wales, fellow man and Christ. With a financial turn-over of approximately a million pounds and a membership of about sixty thousand, Yr Urdd's *raison d'etre* is the fostering of the Welsh language and culture both with learners and Welsh speakers (Japheth, 1983). Through its 1,129 branches throughout Wales, through local, county and national eisteddfodau, summer camps, magazines, with limited government aid and extensive voluntary contributions, it provides an important, and a possibly underestimated force, in the preservation of the Welsh language and culture. It serves Welsh speaking children and learners alike in a widely accepted and successful movement (D. G. Jones, 1979). The type of residential courses it provides were particularly highly valued by HMI (Welsh Office, 1983a) in furthering the Welsh language.

If it is accepted that tranmission of Welsh culture to children is crucial and essential for the preservation of the language, then D. G. Jones (1979) has rightly located one pivot on which much of the weight of the future of the language balances. Referring to Urdd Gobaith Cymru, Jones (1979) considers that "it shoulders a cultural responsibility probably greater than that of any other Welsh movement" (p. 311).

Welsh Heartlands

The importance of Welsh cultural preservation does not only raise issues about children. Cultural preservation also relates to the debate about heartland areas and territorial language planning. This issue was examined in Chapter 1. The maps in that chapter pointed to two things in particular: the decreasing size of those heartland areas and the fragmentation and separation of such areas in South West Wales. Also the age trends and oracy-literacy trends suggest that further diminution and separation may occur in the future. There is evidence of the language being safeguarded in Gwynedd, but less so in Dyfed, Powys and West Glamorgan.

In the light of the existence and decline of heartland areas, one solution is for such areas to receive special designation and status. Centrally directed policy may attempt to preserve such heartland areas in terms of the use of Welsh language and culture by consideration of, for example, education, administration, housing and building policy. The technology to identify such areas in terms of their cultural as well as linguistic properties has been developed. The public and political debate about the value of designating heartland areas has started. It may be timely for the debate to move to the Welsh Office, Whitehall and Westminster.

The case for language zoning might be weaker if county with county comparisons were not so different. Chapter 2, in particular, located differences between counties in educational policy and provision. Some of these differences result naturally from differing densities of Welsh speakers. Gwynedd and Gwent are comparative examples. However, when such density differences are taken into account, there still exist differences of policy and provision between counties. The difference in policy between Clwyd and West Glamorgan was detailed as an example. Similarly provision of Welsh lessons to infants varies among counties in a way that relates to policy. County bilingual educational policy is clearly influential in promoting or otherwise the Welsh language in schools. Gwynedd is a case where a strong bilingual policy appears to be linked with the maintenance of Gwynedd as a language stronghold as found in the 1981 Census.

In the education policy of the eight Welsh counties, there is, therefore, evidence of language zoning already in operation. Gwynedd's policy is designed to safeguard the county as a heartland of Welsh language. In this sense, territorial language planning is already in operation across Wales. But such planning tends to concern educational policy rather than other local government policy (e.g. housing, employment, economic and cultural development).

The case for territorial language planning is not a simple one. If such planning operated, contiguous communities might become split. Vocational and geographical mobility involved in changes in patterns of employment and industry may quickly alter the nature of a community. Those urban areas which would fall outside heartland status often contain thriving cells of Welsh language and cultural activity. Such urban areas often contain seats of power and influence. It is there Welsh TV, radio and publishing are to be found. It is there that those who wish to exercise leadership tend to· gravitate (e.g. Lewis, 1978). It is there that large numbers as opposed to high densities of Welsh speakers are to be found.

The heartland issue is important because it generates debate and awareness. Recognition of a diminishing and fragmenting heartland may lead to recognition of the plight of the Welsh language and culture. Shrinking heartlands are a tangible and easily expressed symbol of a declining language. If the argument about heartlands should wilt, it is a likely sign that the language is in the valley of the shadow of death.

The Need for Government Policy

While a county's bilingual educational policy is important, Rawkins (1979) has argued strongly that the status and position of Welsh ultimately depend on centralized government policy. A long-term policy rather than piecemeal, reactive decisions may be needed. If central government had not acted in the past there would be no compulsory education, no comprehensive schools, no national health service. In terms of the computer revolution central government has acted, with a multi-million pound investment in placing micro-computers in secondary and primary schools as well as teacher training establishments. It has also invested heavily in the MEP project, mostly aimed at microcomputer software production. Such a policy is not short-term, myopic or piecemeal. It demonstrates the power of central government to impose a policy which plans for the future and which also may be a threat to the maintenance of Welsh language and culture.

When faced with new developments that will affect the culture of the 21st century, the government has been quick to move. Their consideration of cable television and advanced information technology bears witness to forward planning that has cultural effects (Boyd-Barrett, 1983). When faced with language decline and associated cultural effects that will affect the culture of people in Wales in the 21st century, the government has been slow to move.

Cannot there be long-term, strategic planning for the future of the Welsh language and culture? Cannot there be systematic and co-ordinated action by government to protect the pools of water in the dried up lake, to secure the crumbling castle against invasion, to ensure a fitting and balanced diet in the face of malnutrition and starvation?

This is not to suggest that government has ignored the Welsh language. The Welsh Office grant aid to the Welsh Books Council and support of bilingual projects and schemes is evidence of its awareness of the plight of the Welsh language and culture. The problem is the absence of an overall, synthesized long-term strategy. The same principle is to be found in the charitable giving of money to a starving tribe in danger of extinction. There is great goodness in such charity. The money is likely to be used for immediate purposes. The money may be injected into relieving the present problem. A long-term view may be preferable. Feeding the starving does not solve the long-term problem. A co-ordinated policy to ensure that the conditions causing starvation are not repeated is necessary. Such a policy has to be centrally derived and directed. Giving money is not enough. Investing foresight and supervision, having the vision to create a future for the language and culture is also needed.

Should a long-term, strategic policy be evolved, there already exist some institutions of excellence to implement that policy. A good example was the Schools Council Committee for Wales. The take-up of its Welsh language projects has, as Chapter 5 details, been very high. Despite centre/periphery projects being relatively less successful in England and America, the Welsh language projects have been widely accepted into classroom practice. Yet this institution was dissolved in March 1984 after Government consideration of the Trenaman Report. As Brace (1982) commented, Mrs Trenaman, in her review of Schools Council, saw little or no difference between the schools of Wales and those of England. Wales was regarded as "an extension of England, and only recommended a stay of execution for the Schools Council Committee for Wales because of that eccentricity that refuses to go away, the Welsh language" (Brace, 1982: 68). In the event, a smaller Committee with smaller funding was created to replace the Schools Council Committee for Wales. Labelled the Schools Curriculum Development Committee its dozen members chosen by the Welsh Office represent headteachers, WJEC, LEA's and Industry. Universities and Colleges, whence much of the large scale curriculum development in Wales has stemmed, are noticeable for their absence.

A long-term, strategic policy by central government may include consideration of territorial language planning and fostering curriculum development at a national and a local teacher-based level. Increased support of a voluntary institution of excellence, Yr Urdd, may also be considered. Each of these topics has been previously considered. Four further considerations, not previously examined, may also need to be a part of such a centralized directed policy.

Ysgolion Meithrin

To spread the language to children from English speaking homes, it is vital, as Chapter 2 suggested, for second language teaching to commence as early as possible. Chapter 2 revealed that infant provision of Welsh language teaching tended to fall short of junior provision and Welsh Office policy. An increase in infant provision is clearly desirable, since second language teaching best occurs early. Welsh language nursery school provision also may be a key feature in the future preservation or restoration of the Welsh language. Mudiad Ysgolion Meithrin (Welsh Medium Nursery Schools and Playgroups Association) is an important focus in early immersion in the language. While the language of these playgroups is Welsh, approximately 65% of children come from non-Welsh speaking homes. When handling water and sand, singing and listening to stories, children acquire language relatively easily. Such a pattern exemplifies Dodson's (1983) belief that medium-oriented activity is vital in early bilingual development. The movement has around 550 groups, providing for about six thousand children and is very active in anglicized areas as well as the Welsh heartlands. The Welsh Office provides a degree of financial help (£305,000 in 1984). Much more money is raised by voluntary efforts (approximately £650,000 in 1984). As with Yr Urdd, its success has been great. Like Yr Urdd, Mudiad Ysgolion Meithrin shoulders a good deal of responsibility for the future of the language. That may require far greater resources than are at present being made available.

Welsh In-Service Courses

Second, the quality of bilingual educational provision ultimately rests with the skills, dedication and enthusiasm of bilingual teachers. Supportive government and county policy, well equipped schools, eager pupils and parents count for little if the quality of teachers and teaching is low. For teachers already in service, continuing education is important. Baker & Terry (1982), in a survey of in-service education needs within Gwynedd, found that teachers' greatest overall want was for courses in existing and new Welsh language curriculum approaches. 75% of Primary teachers requested courses to help them teach Welsh as a second language. 70% of Primary teachers and 46% of Secondary teachers requested in-service education on teaching general subjects through the medium of Welsh. The wants of teachers may influence in a small way the provision of in-service courses. The present and future needs of the planning agencies, particularly Local Education Authorities, may be more influential in the definition of such provision. Even more influential may be the providing institutions which create and design courses mostly according to their competencies. There is minimal research in Wales evaluating the short term or long term effect of these in-service courses, whether needs and wants are being met, and whether the courses are of a sufficient standard and relevance to help the bilingual teachers. Research by HMI (Welsh Office, 1983) suggests that in over a third of Welsh Departments in Secondary schools surveyed, no member of the Department had attended a course. Indeed, HMI found the position even less encouraging, reporting that there no longer existed a sufficient number of Welsh teachers whose mother-tongue is Welsh to sustain Welsh language teaching for first or second language speakers. What may be needed is a co-ordinated survey of pre-service provision and in-service need across Wales that results in a more centralized policy for Welsh language pre-service and in-service provision. It may be increasingly important in the bilingual context that such provision is given inspiration and motivation at a national level.

Salary and Qualifications of Bilingual Teachers

Third, however excellent the topping-up exercise of in-service education, however excellent the initial training of bilingual teachers, unless people of quality, dedication, enthusiasm and ability choose to teach in schools, the education system is less likely to serve as an agency for Welsh cultural transmission and the promotion of the Welsh language. O. M. Edwards at the turn of the century asked "Pwy yw'r dynion pwysicaf yn y wlad?" Who are the most important people in the country (of Wales)? His answer would be confirmed by many today. "Ar lawer cyfrif mentraf ateb – athrawon ein hysgolion elfennol." On many counts I would answer – elementary school teachers (quoted in G. E. Jones, 1982: 18). It may be that parents are more important than teachers in promoting the language and culture. But teachers are very important. Most children spend approximately 15,000 hours at school. Teachers therefore have ample time to make the experience of Welsh language and culture anything from a tedious necessity to an enjoyable and essential experience. At present there appears little recognition for the essential service given by bilingual teachers.

Bilingual teachers need to have special skills, different qualifications, extra abilities as Chapter 4 considered. Troike & Saville-Troike (1982) have portrayed the extra qualities needed by bilingual teachers on top of qualities expected of all teachers. Being proficient in two languages, being able to teach Welsh as a first language as well as a second language within the same classroom often simultaneously, being aware of the bicultural nature of society and enabling an enculturation process to occur, being able to modify curriculum material for dual language purposes, being able to present lessons in both languages, particularly when there is the need to use the technical jargon of both languages (e.g. science), all represent considerable skills not required of ordinary teachers.

There exists the need to train primary and secondary teachers for such a difficult, demanding and skilful role. The tendency is for initial training courses to polarize towards English language situations or Welsh language situations. There are good training facilities available for Welsh medium or English medium courses. While not absent, far less effort and expertise exists to produce primary and secondary teachers for bilingual situations. To teach in a bilingual classroom is radically different from teaching Welsh as a second language. It involves far more than the teacher being merely proficient in two languages. Bilingual teaching requires management skills as well as language skills, a grounding in bilingual theory and practice as well as biculturalism. It would appear that an initiative to promote skilled bilingual teaching at both pre-service and in-service training levels is urgently required in Wales.

There also appears to be an argument for financial recognition to be given to bilingual teachers. As important as it is to induce the best quality teachers into bilingual classrooms, this is a weak argument for such financial recognition. All children need the best quality teachers. Financial recognition needs to be given because of the definite extra skills and qualities needed by bilingual teachers. Teachers with special skills in counselling, administration and organizing extra-curricular activities often are given higher salary scales. Teachers with degrees and higher qualifications usually obtain increments in their salary scale. Bilingual teachers have special skills over and above that required of all teachers. Bilingual teachers need special extra training to teach in a bilingual classroom which should be recognized in formal qualifications. It is on the basis of extra skills and qualifications that there appears to be a strong argument for financial reward. Teachers in special schools, teachers in educational priority areas, teachers in inner and outer London all receive extra financial reward. Why not bilingual teachers? Such financial reward should not only include bilingual teachers in Wales, but also bilingual teachers in immigrant areas (e.g. London, Bradford, Birmingham). It should not include teachers who use Welsh almost exclusively. The idea of financial reward is for bilingual situations and not for a predominantly monoglot context. It has to be conceded that the definition of what constitutes a bilingual teacher is complex. The practical implementation would generate debate and argument. Modern language teachers of French and German are an example where definition is difficult. However, the difficulties of practical implementation should not affect or deter the establishment or rejection of the principle. It is the principle which first needs establishing. Thereafter the complexity of the practice of the principle needs untangling.

The idea of specific qualifications for bilingual teachers, specification of needed extra skills and financial reward is not a flight of fancy. In specific areas of America it exists (Carpenter-Huffman & Samulon, 1983). The USA Bilingual Education Act (1968) defines precisely the qualities necessary for a person to be regarded as a qualified bilingual teacher. This includes having successfully completed a course of study in the use of classroom materials and instructional practices for bilingual education. Eighteen States and the District of Columbia specify the necessary components of such bilingual education courses (Carpenter-Huffman & Samulon, 1983). These will comprise components selected from: language proficiency, linguistics, culture, ability to use, adapt and develop instructional methods and materials, assessment, school-community relations, nature of bilingualism and supervised bilingual teaching experience. Carpenter-Huffman & Samulon (1983) also report the existence of bilingual teachers receiving an increment of a thousand dollars in at least one large school system. Admittedly this is justified on the grounds of attracting appropriate teachers. Nevertheless, the financial precedent does exist.

Educational Research

Fourth, particularly in bilingual education in Wales, there is a great paucity of evaluative effort and research work. In Chapter 6, the prologue suggested the range of ignorance on bilingual issues in Wales. Little is known about what makes a bilingual school more or less effective. Little is known about the factors that facilitate or constrain the development of lifelong bilingualism. Little is known about the functioning of rural primary and secondary schools situated in the Welsh heartlands. As Webster (1982) argues, "There is patently much research that requires to be done on rural education in Wales. The educational, linguistic and social effects of area schools need detailed study, as do the curriculum and organization of small rural secondary schools and especially those serving bilingual communities" (p. 210).

In 1968, the Welsh Committee of the Schools Council lamented the fact that comparatively little educational research had been carried out in Wales. They pointed to financial resources for research work being so small. Comparison may be made with Scotland. For almost sixty years, the Scottish Council for Research in Education (SCRE) has provided research evidence to aid educational evolution in Scotland. In 1983 it composed a Director, Deputy Director, Assistant Director, 16 Research Staff, five Technical Staff, three Information and Library Staff, two Finance and Administration Staff, and 10 Clerical and Secretarial Staff. In 1983, SCRE had 19 projects in progress with funding of approximately half a million pounds. There is no comparable body in Wales. The National Foundation for Educational Research has a small Welsh extension based at Swansea. It has a total of four staff, is currently concerned with four projects, and is under the auspices of the parent body based outside London. Despite the excellence of its activity, the Unit is dwarfed by SCRE. No blame can be given to the Social Science Research Council (now called the Economic and Social Research Council) who have generally been responsive to Welsh research projects. Is a modest Welsh Council for Research in Education not just desirable but essential? Bilingual education in Wales needs to be supported with enquiry and evaluation. Such research may in turn provide the information to Local Education Authorities and the Welsh Office to help with planning and policy. Such research may provide information to parents and teachers to help make rational choices and decisions. A modest Welsh Council for Research in Education may be one essential facet of progressive bilingual education in Wales.

Educational policy and practice need to be informed by evaluation and research. At present in Wales, bilingual policy and practice often has to draw on hunches, best guesses, evangelical persuasion. As Chapters 3 and 4 have demonstrated, there are never simple answers. Simple questions hide complex issues. While research and evaluation can rarely definitively answer the questions or perfectly order the complex issues, it can provide a kind of knowledge that is preferable to prejudice, innuendos, fabrications and false claims. The Canadian experience is that parents, teachers, administrators and politicians require research evidence about the effects and effectiveness of bilingual education. The experience goes to the point of believing that research evidence is a precondition for the expansion of bilingual education.

The Future

The preservation of the Welsh language and culture is safe for the remainder of the 20th century. Whether it will still exist in any healthy form by the end of the 21st century seems in doubt. Maintenance of the *status quo* is a likely cause of extinction. So is a simple faith that everything will work out fine in the end. A short-sighted view by government and a cheerful indifference by ordinary Welsh folk are roads to decline and fall.

R. Tudur Jones (1979) quotes from a letter of Griffith Jones written on the 11th October, 1739.

> "Thus. . . .appears the loving-kindness of God, in his confounding the languages and dispersing the people, by giving them different tongues; and if the goodness and wisdom of God must be acknowledged to run through the whole in general, how can it be denied in any particular branch thereof. . . .when we attempt to abolish a language. . . .we fight against the decree of Heaven, and seek to undermine the disposals of divine providence." (p. 69).

An act of God is in danger of being destroyed by a lack of acts by man.

Appendices

Appendix 1
Wards within the 70% Isopleth 1981 Census Welsh Language Figures

A List of Wards with 70% or over inhabitants speaking Welsh. Census 1981.

Spellings of place names are in accordance with 'Rhestr O Enwau Lleoedd', University of Wales, 1958.

Clwyd
(a)   Colwyn District
            Ward 13 Llanfair Talhaearn and Llanefydd
            Ward 14 Llansannan and Bylchau
            Ward 16 Cerrigydrudion
            Ward 17 Gwytherin and Llangernyw

(b)   Glyndwr District
            Ward 9 Betws Gwerful Goch and Gwyddelwern
            Ward 11 Llandrillo

Dyfed
(a)   Carmarthen District
            Ward 4 Cenarth and Newcastle Emlyn (Castellnewydd Emlyn)
            Ward 5 Llanfihangel-ar-Arth
            Ward 6 Llangeler
            Ward 7 Llanllwni, Llanybydder (part) and Pencarreg
            Ward 12 Llanarthne and Llanddarog
            Ward 14 Cilymaenllwyd, Llandysilio East and Grondre
            Ward 15 Llangyndeyrn
            Ward 20 Abernant, Llanwinio and Trelech a'r Betws

(b)   Ceredigion District
            Ward 5 Lampeter (Llanbedr Pont Steffan)
            Ward 6 Aberaeron
            Ward 8 Ciliau Aeron, Hefynyw Upper and Llanddewi, Aber-arth
                    Upper
            Ward 12 Llanwenog
            Ward 13 Dihewyd, Llanfihangel Ystrad and Trefilan
            Ward 23 **Llanafan, Llanilar, Llanfihangel-y-Creuddyn and Upper
                    Llanbadarn-y-Creuddyn**
            Ward 24 Llandeiniol, Llangwyryfon, Llanrhystud Anhuniog and
                    Llanrhystud Mefenydd
            Ward 25 Llandysul (part)
            Ward 26 Llandysul (part)
            Ward 27 Bron-gwyn, Llandyfriog and Orllwyn Teifi
            Ward 32 Betws Eraw, Llangynllo and Troed-yr-aur
            Ward 33 Betws Leucu, Gartheli, Gwynfil, Llanddewibrefi and
                    Nancwnlle

Ward 34 Caron-Is-Clawdd, Llanbadarn Odwyn and Llangeitho
Ward 35 Blaenpennal, Caron-Uwch-Clawdd, Gwnnws Isaf, Lled-
         rod Isaf, Gwnnws Uchaf, Lledrod Uchaf and Ysbyty
         Ystwyth

(c)   Dinefwr District
Ward 2 Llandovery (Part) (Llanymddyfri)
Ward 4 Ammanford (part) (Rhydaman)
Ward 5 Ammanford (part) (Rhydaman)
Ward 6 Ammanford (part) (Rhydaman)
Ward 7 Cwm Aman
Ward 12 Llandeilo-Fawr-Rural (part)
Ward 14 Llandybie (part)
Ward 15 Llandybie (part)
Ward 16 Llandybie (part)
Ward 20 Llansawel and Talyllychau
Ward 22 Quarter Bach (part) (Cwarter Bach)
Ward 23 Quarter Bach (part) (Cwarter Bach)
Ward 24 Quarter Bach (part) (Cwarter Bach)

(d)   Llanelli District
Ward 8 Llanelli Rural (part) Pemberton, Felinfoel, Gelligaled

(e)   Preseli District
Ward 9 Cilgerran and Manordeifi
Ward 10 Capel Colman, Castellau, Penrhydd, Clydau, West Cil-
         rhedyn and Llanfyrnach
Ward 11 Monington (Eglwys Wythwr), Llantood, Bridell,
         Eglwyswrw, Llanfair-Nant-gwyn, Llanfihangel Penbedw
         and Whitechurch (Eglwys Wen)

West Glamorgan
(a)   Lliw Valley District
Ward 8 Ystalyfera, Cwmllynfell/Llangiwg

Powys
(a)   Brecknock District
Ward 30 Cwm-twrch Uchaf

(b)   Montgomery District
Ward 21 Garthbeibio
Ward 23 Llanwddyn, Hirnant, and Llangynog
Ward 28 Pennant
Ward 30 Llanbryn-mair
Ward 31 Caereinion Fechan
Ward 32 Isygarreg, Uwchygarreg, Darowen and Penegoes

Gwynedd

(a)   Aberconwy District
                      Ward 17 Llanrwst Rural
                      Ward 21 Penmachno and Dolwyddelan

(b)   Arfon District
All the district *except*:
                      Ward 1 Bangor (part)
                      Ward 2 Bangor (part
                      Ward 3 Bangor (part)
                      Ward 4 Bangor (part)
                      Ward 6 Bangor (part)
                      Ward 7 Bangor (part)
                      Ward 32 Vaynol (Bangor)
                      Ward 33 Llandygai/Tregarth (part) and Bryn Eglwys

(c)   Dwyfor District
All the district *except*:
                      Ward 4 Porthmadog (part)
                      Ward 9 Beddgelert
                      Ward 19 Llanbedrog
                      Ward 20 Abersoch

(d)   Meirionydd District
                      Ward 1 Bala
                      Ward 3 Dolgellau
                      Ward 4 Ffestiniog
                      Ward 5 Blaenau Ffestiniog (part)
                      Ward 6 Blaenau Ffestiniog (part)
                      Ward 9 Llanfrothen
                      Ward 10 Llandecwyn
                      Ward 11 Trawsfynydd
                      Ward 14 Tal-y-llyn
                      Ward 18 Llanymawddwy and Mallwyd
                      Ward 19 Llanycil and Llandderfel
                      Ward 20 Llanuwchllyn

(e)   Anglesey District
                      Ward 4 Amlwch (part)
                      Ward 5 Amlwch (part)
                      Ward 14 Llangefni (part)
                      Ward 15 Llangefni (part)
                      Ward 16 Llangefni (part)
                      Ward 19 Newborough (Niwbwrch) and Llangaffo
                      Ward 20 Llanfihangel Ysgeifiog
                      Ward 24 Llanidan
                      Ward 25 Penmynydd and Llanddaniel-fab
                      Ward 27 Trefdraeth, Llangadwaladr and Llangristiolus
                      Ward 29 Llanerchymedd

Ward 30 Llangwyllog, Tregaean, Coedana, Llanfihangel, Llan-
           dyfrydog, Llanddyfnan
Ward 35 Llanfechell, Llanbabo and Llanfair-yng-Nghornwy
Ward 38 Llanfachraeth, Llanfaethlu and Llanrhyddlad
Ward 41 Trewalchmai and Llechylched
Ward 42 Heneglwys, Bodwrog and Cerrigceinwen
Ward 43 Aberffraw

Appendix 2
Wards containing a difference between Oracy and Literacy of greater than plus one standard deviation, 1981 Census Welsh Language Figures

The following wards contain a higher proportion of people speaking but not reading or writing in Welsh. Higher proportion refers to greater than plus one standard deviation (i.e. over 11.8% difference)

Clwyd
(a)   Alyn and Deeside District
               Ward 23 Treuddyn

(b)   Delyn District
               Ward   6 Whelston/Flint Trelawnyd

(c)   Glyndwr District
               Ward   1 Denbigh (Dinbych) Henllan
               Ward   2 Denbigh (Dinbych) Llanrhaeadr
               Ward   8 Llanarmon Mynydd Mawr, Llangedwyn and Llanrhaeadr
                         ym Mochnant

(d)   Wrexham District
               Ward 17 Pen-y-cae
               Ward 20 Rhosllannerchrugog Ponciau
               Ward 21 Rhosllannerchrugog Pant
               Ward 22 Rhosllannerchrugog Johnstown

Dyfed
(a)   Carmarthen District
               Ward   1 Carmarthen (part) (Caerfyrddin)
               Ward   2 Carmarthen (part) (Caerfyrddin)
               Ward   3 Carmarthen (part) (Caerfyrddin)
               Ward 12 Llanarthne and Llanddarog
               Ward 15 Llangyndeyrn
               Ward 16 Llangynnwr and Newchurch (Llannewydd)
               Ward 17 Llan-gain, Llangynog and Llansteffan
               Ward 18 Meidrim and St. Clears (Sancler)
               Ward 19 Llandyfaelog and St. Ishmael (Llanismel)
               Ward 21 Eglwys Gymyn (part) and Whitland (Hendy-gwyn)

(b)   Ceredigion District
Ward   4 Cardigan (Ceredigion)
Ward   5 Lampeter (Llanbedr Pont Steffan)
Ward   7 New Quay (Ceinewydd)
Ward 18 Llangorwen and Tirymynach
Ward 30 Llangoedmor

(c)   Dinefwr District
All the district *except*:
Ward 10 Cynwyl Gaeo and Llanwrda
Ward 11 Cil-y-cwm and Llanfair-ar-y-bryn
Ward 17 Llanegwad and Llanfynydd
Ward 18 Llangathen, Llandyfeisant and Llanfihangel Aberbythych
Ward 19 Llansadwrn and Llangadog
Ward 20 Llansawel and Talley (Talyllychau)
Ward 21 Llandingad Without, Myddfai and Llanddeusant

(d)   Llanelli District
All wards within the Llanelli District

(e)   Preseli District
Ward   3 Fishguard (Abergwaun)
Ward   4 Goodwick (Wdig)
Ward 13 Newport – Dinas (Trefdraeth Dinas)
Ward 14 Llandudoch Rural and Trewyddel
Ward 15 Treletert, St. Edrens, St. Lawrence, Llantydewi, Caslai,
         Treamled and Trefgarn
Ward 18 Llanllawer, Llanfair-Nant-y-Gof, Llanychar, Y Bont-
         faen, Mervil, Casnewydd-bach, Cas-mael, Cas-fuwch and
         Castellhenri
Ward 21 Llanwnda, Tremarchog, Fishguard South (De Aber-
         gwaun), Manorowen, Treopert, Trefwrdan and Llanstinan
Ward 23 St. David's Cathedral Close
Ward 29 Llanrhian, Llanhywel, Whitchurch (Tre-groes) and St.
         Elvis (Llaneilfyw)

West Glamorgan
(a)   Afan District
Ward   5 Cwmafon

(b)   Lliw Valley District
All the district *except*:
Ward   3 Llwchwr/Gowerton (Tre-gwyr) and Llangyfelach

(c)   Neath District
Ward   4 Michaelston Higher (Llanfihangel-ynys-Afan Uchaf)
Ward 11 Dyffryn Cellwen
Ward 12 Dulais Uchaf
Ward 13 Dulais Isaf (part)/Crynant

Powys

(a)   Brecknock District

Ward   6 Llanwrtyd Wells
Ward 13 Traean-mawr and Traean-glas, Glyntawe
Ward 14 Llanfihangel Nant Bran and Llandeilo'r Fan
Ward 15 Crai and Senni (Senny Bridge)
Ward 19 Gwarafog, Llanfechan, Llanllywenfel, Penbuallt and Treflys
Ward 28 Ystradfellte
Ward 29 Ystradgynlais Uchaf
Ward 30 Cwm-twrch Uchaf
Ward 31 Ystradgynlais Isaf
Ward 32 Pen-rhos (Ystradgynlais)
Ward 33 Glanrhyd (Ystradgynlais)

(b)   Montgomery District

Ward   1 Newtown East and South (Y Drenewydd)
Ward   9 Machynlleth North
Ward 10 Machynlleth South and West
Ward 23 Llanwddyn, Hirnant and Llangynog
Ward 38 Llanidloes Without

Gwynedd

(a)   Aberconwy District

Ward   4 Conwy
Ward 13 Llanfairfechan South
Ward 14 Llanrwst
Ward 15 Penmaenmawr
Ward 19 Dolgarrog, Llanbedrycennin and Talybont
Ward 20 Llanrhychwyn and Trefriw

(b)   Arfon District

Ward   3 Bangor (part)
Ward   4 Bangor (part)
Ward   5 Bangor (part)
Ward   6 Bangor (part)
Ward   7 Bangor (part)
Ward 10 Caernarfon (part)
Ward 11 Caernarfon (part)
Ward 12 Caernarfon (part)

(c)   Dwyfor District

Ward   2 Pwllheli

(d)   Meirionydd District

Ward   3 Dolgellau

(e)   Anglesey District

Ward   1 Beaumaris West
Ward   6 Holyhead (part) (Caergybi)

Ward   7 Holyhead (part)   "
Ward   8 Holyhead (part)   "
Ward   9 Holyhead (part)   "
Ward 10 Holyhead (part)   "
Ward 11 Holyhead (part)   "
Ward 12 Holyhead (part)   "
Ward 13 Holyhead (part)   "
Ward 18 Menai Bridge (part) (Porthaethwy)
Ward 36 Holyhead Rural (Caergybi)

Appendix 3
Wards containing a difference between 5 and 24 years and 25 and 65+ years of greater than plus one standard deviation, 1981 Welsh Language Census Figures

The following wards contain a higher proportion of 'younger' than 'older' people speaking Welsh. Higher proportion refers to greater than plus one standard deviation above the mean (i.e. over 8.5% difference).

Clwyd

(a)   **Alyn and Deeside District**
Ward   9 Northop Hall/Connah's Quay South (Llaneurgain/De Cei Cona)
Ward 15 Llanfynydd

(b)   **Colwyn District**
Ward 14 Llansannan and Bylchau
Ward 16 Cerrigydrudion
Ward 17 Gwytherin and Llangernyw

(c)   **Delyn District**
Ward 15 Mold Rural (Y Wyddgrug), (Gwernaffield, Gwernymynydd, Broncoed)

(d)   **Glyndwr District**
Ward   9 Betws Gwerful Goch and Gwyddelwern
Ward 11 Llandrillo
Ward 15 Llanelidan and Llanfair Dyffryn Clwyd
Ward 18 Y Gyffylliog and Llanynys Rural
Ward 19 Clocaenog, Derwen, Efenechtyd and Llanfwrog

(e)   **Ruddlan District**
Ward   2 Prestatyn North/North West

Dyfed

(a)   Ceredigion District

Ward 8 Ciliau Aeron, Hefynyw Uchaf and Llanddewi, Aberarth Uchaf

Ward 9 Cilcennin, Llanbadarn Trefeglywys and Llansantffraid

Ward 10 Llandysiliogogo, Llanina and Llanllwchaearn

Ward 11 Llanarth

Ward 12 Llanwenog

Ward 14 Cellan, Lampeter Rural (Llanbedr Pont Steffan), Llanfair Clydogau, Llangybi, Llanwnnen and Siliau

Ward 16 Ceulan-y-maes-mawr, Llangynfelyn and Ysgubor-y-coed

Ward 23 Llanafan, Llanilar, Llanfihangel-y-Creuddyn Isaf and Llanbadarn-y-Creuddyn Uchaf

Ward 24 Llanddeiniol, Llangwyryfon, Llanrhystud Anhuniog and Llanrhystud Mefenydd

Ward 26 Llandysul (part)

(b)   Dinefwr District

Ward 20 Llansawel and Talyllychau

Powys

(a)   Montgomery District

Ward 23 Llanwddyn, Hirnant and Llangynog

Ward 30 Llanbrynmair

Ward 31 Caereinion Fechan

Ward 32 Isygarreg, Uwchygarreg, Darowen and Penegoes

(b)   Radnor District

Ward 16 Bochrwyd, Y Clas-ar-Wy and Llansteffan

Gwynedd

(a)   Aberconwy District

Ward 5 Capel Curig and Betws-y-Coed

Ward 17 Llanrwst Rural

Ward 18 Caerhun, Henryd, Rowen, Tyn-y-groes

Ward 20 Llanrhychwyn and Trefriw

Ward 21 Penmachno and Dolwyddelan

(b)   Arfon District

Ward 8 Caernarfon East

Ward 9 Caernarfon North

Ward 14 Gerlan (Bethesda)

Ward 15 Bethesda (north)/Rachub

Ward 16 Tal-y-sarn (Dyffryn Nantlle)

Ward 18 Llanllyfni

Ward 19 Carmel

Ward 20 Groeslon

Ward 21 Bethel and Rhiwlas

Ward 22 Waunfawr, Betws Garmon and Ceunant

Ward 23 Bontnewydd and Caeathro
Ward 24 Llanwnda
Ward 25 Deiniolen and Dinorwig
Ward 26 Llanddeiniolen, Bryn'refail and Penisarwaun
Ward 27 Llanberis and Cwm-y-glo
Ward 28 Llanrug
Ward 31 St. Anne's, Llandygai, Glasinfryn and Pentir

(c)   Dwyfor District
All wards *except*:
Ward 11 Llanaelhaearn
Ward 16 Abererch/Y Ffor
Ward 24 Aberdaron

(d)   Meirionydd District
All wards *except*:
Ward 2 Barmouth (Abermo)
Ward 3 Dolgellau
Ward 5 Blaenau Ffestiniog (part)
Ward 7 Tywyn
Ward 8 Aberdyfi
Ward 17 Llanfachreth
Ward 20 Llanuwchllyn

(e)   Anglesey District
Ward 3 Amlwch Rural
Ward 19 Newborough (Niwbwrch) and Llangaffo
Ward 20 Llanfihangel Ysceifiog
Ward 24 Llanidan
Ward 25 Penmynydd and Llanddaniel-fab
Ward 26 Pentraeth
Ward 27 Trefdraeth, Llangadwaladr and Llangristiolus
Ward 29 Llanerchymedd
Ward 30 Llangwyllog, Tregaean, Coedana, Llanfihangel, Llan-
          dyfrydog, Llanddyfnan
Ward 31 Llanallgo, Llaneugrad and Penrhoslligwy
Ward 32 Rhosybol and Llaneilian
Ward 33 Benllech (part)
Ward 34 Benllech (part)
Ward 35 Llanfechell, Llanbabo and Llanfair-yng-Nghornwy
Ward 38 Llanfachraeth, Llanfaethlu and Llanrhuddlad
Ward 39 Llechgynfarwy, Llantrisant, Llanddeusant and Llandry-
          garn
Ward 41 Trewalchmai and Llechylched
Ward 43 Aberffraw
Ward 44 Llanfaelog

Appendix 4
Wards containing a difference between 5 and 24 years and 25 and 65+ years of greater than minus one standard deviation, 1981 Welsh Language Census Figures

The following wards contain a higher proportion of 'older' than 'younger' people speaking Welsh. A higher proportion refers to greater than minus one standard deviation below the mean (i.e. under −10.7% difference).

Clwyd

(a)   Colwyn District
         Ward   8 Colwyn Bay (Bae Colwyn)

(b)   Delyn District
         Ward   6 Whelston/Fflint, Trelawnyd
         Ward 23 Whitford (Chwitffordd)

(c)   Glyndwr District
         Ward   1 Denbigh (Dinbych)
         Ward   2 Denbigh (Dinbych)
         Ward   3 Rhuthun
         Ward   6 Glyntraean and Llansanffraid Glynceiriog
         Ward   8 Llanarmon Mynydd Mawr, Llangedwyn and Llan-
                  rhaeadr-ym-Mochnant
         Ward 20 Trefor Isa
         Ward 21 Llangollen Rural Llandysilio

(d)   Wrexham District
         Ward 17 Pen-y-cae
         Ward 20 Rhosllanerchrugog Ponciau
         Ward 21 Rhosllanerchrugog Pant
         Ward 22 Rhosllanerchrugog Johnstown
         Ward 27 Esclushan Above and Minera (Mwynglawdd)
         Ward 28 Brymbo
         Ward 29 Coed-poeth
         Ward 30 Bersham (Bers)

Dyfed

(a)   Carmarthen District (Caerfyrddin)
         Ward   1 Carmarthen (part) (Caerfyrddin)
         Ward   2 Carmarthen (part) (Caerfyrddin)
         Ward   3 Carmarthen (part) (Caerfyrddin)
         Ward 16 Llangynnwr (part) and Whitland (Hendy-gwyn)
         Ward 21 Eglwys Gymun (part) and Whitland (Hendy-gwyn)

(b)   Ceredigion District
         Ward   1 Aberystwyth (part)

     Ward 7 New Quay (Ceinewydd)
     Ward 20 Upper Vaenor (Y Faenor Uchaf)

(c)   Dinefwr District
     Ward 1 Llandovery (part) (Llanymddyfri)
     Ward 3 Ammanford (part) (Rhydaman)
     Ward 5 Ammanford (part) (Rhydaman)
     Ward 8 Llandeilo
     Ward 16 Llandybie (part)

(d)   Llanelli District
All wards *except*:
     Ward 5 Kidwelly (Cydweli) and Pen-bre (part)
     Ward 11 Llannon and Pontyberem

(e)   Preseli District
     Ward 2 Haverfordwest (part) (Hwlffordd)
     Ward 3 Fishguard (Abergwaun)
     Ward 15 Treletert, St. Edrens, St. Lawrence, Llantydewi, Cas-lai,
          Treamlod, and Trefgarn
     Ward 22 Mathri, Lland-lwy, Llanrheithan and Breudeth
     Ward 23 St. David's Cathedral Close

(f)   South Pembroke District
     Ward 8 Arberth
     Ward 10 Llanddewi Felffre, Crynwedd and Llanbedr Felffre

Mid Glamorgan
(a)   Cynon Valley District
     Ward 1 Llwytgoed
     Ward 2 Aberdar Gadlys
     Ward 3 Aberdar Town

(b)   Rhondda District
     Ward 8 Treorci

West Glamorgan
(a)   Afan District
     Ward 5 Cwmafan
     Ward 7 Port Talbot Rural/Margam

(b)   Lliw Valley District
All wards *except*:
     Ward 6 Mawr/Felindre, Garn-swllt

(c)   Neath District
     Ward 4 Llanfihangel-ynys-Afan-Uchaf
     Ward 10 Blaen-gwrach
     Ward 11 Dyffryn Cellwen

Ward 12 Dulais Uchaf
Ward 13 Dulais Isaf (part)/Crynant
Ward 14 Dulais Isaf (part)/Cilfrew
Ward 15 Blaenrhondda

(d)   Swansea District
Ward 3 Swansea (part) (Abertawe)
Ward 5 Swansea (part) (Abertawe)
Ward 6 Swansea (part) (Abertawe)
Ward 7 Morriston (Treforus)
Ward 18 Llanrhidian Uchaf

Powys
(a)   Brecknock District
Ward 6 Llanwrtyd Wells
Ward 13 Traean-mawr and Traean-glas, Glyntawe
Ward 14 Llanfihangel Nant Bran and Landeilo'r-fan
Ward 15 Crai and Senni (Senny Bridge)
Ward 18 Llanfihangel Abergwesyn, Llanddulas, Llanwrtyd
          Without
Ward 19 Gwarafog, Llanfechan, Llanllywenfel, Penbuallt and
          Treflys
Ward 28 Ystradfellte
Ward 29 Ystradgynlais Uchaf
Ward 30 Cwmtwrch Uchaf
Ward 31 Ystradgynlais Isaf
Ward 32 Pen-rhos (Ystradgynlais)
Ward 33 Glan-rhyd (Ystradgynlais)

(b)   Montgomery District
Ward 1 Newtown East and South (Y Drenewydd)
Ward 3 Llanidloes West
Ward 9 Machynlleth North
Ward 10 Machynlleth South and West
Ward 26 Llanfechain
Ward 29 Meifod
Ward 33 Aberhafesp
Ward 37 Llangurig
Ward 28 Llanidloes Without
Ward 29 Llanwnnog

Gwynedd
(a)   Aberconwy District
Ward 3 Llandudno South
Ward 14 Llanrwst

(b)   Arfon District
Ward 1 Bangor (part)
Ward 3 Bangor (part)

        Ward 5 Bangor (part)
        Ward 7 Bangor (part)

(c)   Anglesey District

        Ward 6 Holyhead (part) (Caergybi)
        Ward 7 Holyhead (part)   ″
        Ward 8 Holyhead (part)   ″
        Ward 9 Holyhead (part)   ″
        Ward 10 Holyhead (part)   ″
        Ward 11 Holyhead (part)   ″
        Ward 12 Holyhead (part)   ″
        Ward 13 Holyhead (part)   ″
        Ward 17 Menai Bridge (part) (Porthaethwy)
        Ward 40 Bodedern and Llanfair-yn-neubwll/RAF Valley

Bibliography

AMBROSE, J.E., & WILLIAMS, C.H., 1981, On the Spatial Definition of Minority. In E. HAUGEN, J.D. McCLURE & D. THOMSON (eds), *Minority Languages Today*. Edinburgh: Edinburgh University Press.

ASTILL, W.M., 1983, EDFAX – a teletext emulator *CAL NEWS*, August 1983, 11.

BAETENS BEARDSMORE, H., 1982, *Bilingualism: Basic Principles*. Clevedon: Multilingual Matters.

BAKER, C., 1983a, A Critical Examination of the Effect of the Microcomputer on the Curriculum. In C. TERRY (ed.), *Using Microcomputers in Schools*, London: Croom Helm.

—1983b, The Microcomputer and the Curriculum, *Journal of Curriculum Studies*, 15, (2), 207–10.

—1984a, Two models for curriculum development in minority languages. In P. WILLIAMS (ed.), *Special Education in Minority Communities*. Milton Keynes: Open University Press.

—1984b, *A survey of Microcomputer Usage in Primary & Secondary Schools in Welsh Speaking Schools in Wales*. Report to the Economic & Social Research Council, April 1984. London: ESRC.

BAKER, C. & DAVIES, P., 1982, Factors affecting the Guidance of Welsh as an Option Choice in the Comprehensive School, *The Counsellor*, 3 (6), 13–21.

BAKER, C. & GRIFFITH, C.L., 1983, Provision of Materials and Tests for Welsh Speaking Pupils with Learning Difficulties: a National Survey, *Educational Research*, 25, (1), 60–70.

BAKER, C. & HINDE, J., 1984, Language Background Classification, *Journal of Multilingual and Multicultural Development*, 5, (1), 43–56.

BAKER, C. & TERRY, C., 1982, Teachers' Preferences for In-Service Education in North Wales, *British Journal of In-Service Education*, 8 (3), 144–50.

BAKER, K.A., & DE KANTER, A.A., 1983, *Bilingual Education*. Lexington, Mass.: Lexington.

BEAUDOIN, M., CUMMINS, J., DUNLOP, H., GENESEE, F. & OBADIA, A., 1981, Bilingual Education: A Comparison of Welsh and Canadian Experiences. *Canadian Modern Language Review*, 37, 498–509.

BELLIN, W., 1984, Welsh and English in Wales. In P. TRUDGILL (ed.), *Language in the British Isles*. Cambridge: Cambridge University Press.

BERRY, G.L., & MITCHELL-KERNAN, C. 1982, *Television and the Socialization of the Minority Child*. New York: Academic Press.

BETTS, C., 1976, *Culture in Crisis, The Future of the Welsh Language*. Wirral: Ffynnon Press.

BOARD OF EDUCATION, 1927, *Welsh in Education and Life*. London: HMSO.

197

BOWEN, E.G., 1959, Le Pays de Galles. *Transactions of the Institute of British Geographers*, 26, 1–23.

BOWEN, E.G. & CARTER, H., 1974, Preliminary Observations on the Distribution of the Welsh Language at the 1971 Census, *Geographical Journal*, 140, (3), 432-40.

—1975, The Distribution of the Welsh Language in 1971: An Analysis, *Geography*, 60, (1), 1–15.

BOYD-BARRETT, J.O., 1983, The Educational Potential of Cable Television Networks in the U.K., *Educational Studies*, 9,3, 221–32.

BRACE, J., 1982, The Educational State of Wales: The Debate Reviewed, *Education for Development*, 7,2, 63–72.

CAMBRIDGE SOFTWARE HOUSE, 1982, *The Mary Rose Manual*, Aylesbury: Ginn.

CARPENTER-HUFFMAN, M. & SAMULON, M.K., 1983, Case Studies of Delivery and Cost of Bilingual Education. In K.A. BAKER & A.A. DE KANTER (eds), *Bilingual Education*. Lexington, Mass.: Lexington.

CARR, W. & KEMMIS, S., 1983, *Becoming Critical: Knowing Through Action Research*. Deakin: Deakin University Press.

CARROLL, B., 1980, *Testing Communicative Performance*. Oxford: Pergamon Press.

CARTER, H. & THOMAS, J.G., 1969, The Referendum on the Sunday opening of Licensed Premises in Wales as a criterion of a culture region, *Regional Studies*, 3, 61–71.

CARTER, H. & WILLIAMS, S., 1978, Aggregate Studies of Language and Culture Change in Wales. In G. WILLIAMS (ed.), *Social and Cultural Change in Contemporary Wales*. London: Routledge and Kegan Paul.

CLWYD COUNTY COUNCIL, undated, *Welsh Language Policy*, Mold: Clwyd C.C.

COHEN, A.D., 1976, The Case for Partial Total Immersion Education. In A. SIMOES (ed.), *The Bilingual Child*. N. York: Academic Press.

COOPER, R., 1969, Two Contextualized Measures of Degree of Bilingualism, *Modern Language Review*, 53, 166–72.

COUNCIL FOR THE WELSH LANGUAGE, 1978, *A Future for the Welsh Language*. Cardiff: HMSO.

DAVID, R., 1970, The Future of Broadcasting. A Symposium. *Planet*, 2, 12–13.

DAVIES, B.L., 1981, Anglesey and the Reports of the Commissioners of Inquiry into the State of Education in Wales in 1847. *Transactions of the Anglesey Antiquarian Society*, 83–112.

DAVIES, D.L., 1957, A Comparative Study of some of the Intellectual, Social and Emotional Characteristics of Bilingual and Monoglot Students at a Welsh University College. Unpublished M.A. thesis, University of Wales.

DAVIES, J.P., 1980, Ymagweddiad disgyblion trydydd dosbarth Ysgolion Uwchradd yng Nghlwyd tuag at y Gymraeg. Unpublished M.Ed. thesis. University of Wales.

DENHAM, C. & RHIND, D., 1983, The 1981 Census and its results. In D. RHIND (ed.), *A Census User's Handbook*. London: Methuen.

DODSON, C.J., 1967, *Language Teaching and the Bilingual Method*. London: Pitman.

—1978, The Independent Evaluator's Report. In C.J. DODSON & E. PRICE (eds), *Bilingual Education in Wales*, 5–11. London: Evans/Methuen.

—1983, Living with Two Languages, *Journal of Multilingual and Multicultural Development*, 4, 6, 401–14.

DUNKIN, M. & BIDDLE, B.J., 1974, *The Study of Teaching*. New York: Holt, Rinehart & Winston.

DWYER, J.H., 1983, Statistical Models for the Social and Behavioural Sciences. Oxford: Oxford University Press.

DYFED COUNTY COUNCIL, 1982, *General Information for Parents about Dyfed Schools*. Carmarthen: Dyfed County Council.

ELLIOTT, J., 1978, What is Action Research in Schools? *Journal of Curriculum Studies*, 10, 355–57.

EVANS, C., 1980, *The Mighty Micro*. London: Coronet.

EVANS, E., 1972, Welsh as a Second Language in the Junior School. In M. CHAZAN (ed.), *Aspects of Primary Education*. Cardiff: University of Wales Press.

EVANS, G.J., undated, *Prawf Geiriau Darllen*. Caernarfon, G. Evans.

EVERITT, B., 1974, *Cluster Analysis*. London: Heinemann/SSRC.

FERGUSON, C., 1959, Diglossia, *Word*, 15, 325–40.

FISHMAN, J.A., 1965, Who Speaks What Language to Whom and When? *La Linguistique*, 67–68.

—1976, *Bilingual Education: An International Sociological Perspective*. Rowley, Massachusetts: Newbury House.

FORER, P., 1983, Software and geography teaching in New Zealand. In J. MEGARRY, D.F.R. WALKER et al. (eds), *World Yearbook of Education 1982/83* (Computers and Education). London: Kogan Page.

FRYMIER, J.R., 1969, *Fostering Educational Change*. Columbus, Ohio: Merrill.

GAGE, N.L., 1978, *The Scientific Basis of the Art of Teaching*. Columbia: Teachers College Press.

GARDNER, R.C. & LAMBERT, W.E., 1972, *Attitudes and Motivation in Second Language Learning*. Rowley, Mass.: Newbury House.

GITTINS REPORT, 1967, *Primary Educaton in Wales*. A Central Advisory Council Education Report. Cardiff: HMSO.

GOODHARDT, G.J., EHRENBURG, A.S.C. & COLLINS, M.A., 1975, *The Television Audience: Patterns of Viewing*. Farnborough: Saxon House.

GREENE, D., 1981, The Atlantic Group: Neo Celtic & Faroese. In E. HAUGEN, J.D. McCLURE & D. THOMSON (eds), *Minority Languages Today*. Edinburgh: Edinburgh University Press.

GROSJEAN, F., 1982, *Life with Two languages: An Introduction to Bilingualism*. Cambridge, Massachusetts: Harvard University Press.

GWYNEDD COUNTY COUNCIL, 1975, *Language Policy*, Caernarfon: Gwynedd County Council.

—1981, *Your Children in their New Schools: An Introduction to the Bilingual Policy in Gwynedd's Schools*. Caernarfon: Gwynedd County Council.

HALL, S., 1977, Culture, the Media and the 'Ideological Effect'. In J. CURRAN, M. CUREVITCH & J. WOLLACOTT (eds), *Mass Communication and Society*. London: Edward Arnold.

HANSARD, 1984, Written Answers to Questions, 16th January to 20th January, No. 1295, pp. 51–53. London: HMSO.

HARRISON, G., BELLIN, W., & PIETTE, B., 1981, *Bilingual Mothers in Wales and the Language of their Children*. Cardiff: University of Wales Press.

HAWKRIDGE, D., 1983, *New Information Technology in Education*. London: Croom Helm.

HEISE, D.R., 1975, *Causal Analysis*, New York: Wiley.
HOFFMAN, N., 1934, *The Measurement of Bilingual Background*. New York: Columbia University Teachers College.
HOWITT, D., 1982, *Mass Media and Social Problems*. Oxford: Pergamon.
ISAAC, N., 1972, *Ifan ab Owen Edwards: 1895–1970*. Cardiff: University of Wales Press.
JAPHETH, J., 1983, Urdd Gobaith Cymru, *Education for Development*, 7, 4, 37–44.
JONES, B.L., 1981, Welsh: Linguistic Conservation and Shifting Bilingualism. In E. HAUGEN, J.D. McCLURE & D. THOMSON (eds), *Minority Languages Today*. Edinburgh: Edinburgh University Press.
JONES, D.G., 1979, The Welsh Language Movement. In M. STEPHENS (ed.), *The Welsh Language Today*. Llandysul: Gomer Press (2nd. edition).
JONES, E. & GRIFFITHS, I.L., 1963, A Linguistic Map of Wales: 1961, *Geographical Journal*, 129, (2), 192–96.
JONES, G.E., 1982, *Controls and Conflicts in Welsh Secondary Education, 1889–1944*. Cardiff: University of Wales Press.
JONES, R. TUDUR, 1979, The Welsh Language and Religion. In M. STEPHENS (ed.), *The Welsh Language Today*. Llandysul: Gomer Press, (2nd. edition).
JONES, W.R., 1953, The Influence of Reading Ability in English on Intelligence Test Scores of Welsh-speaking Children. *British Journal of Educational Psychology*, 23, 114–20.
—1955, *Bilingualism and Reading Ability in English*. Cardiff: University of Wales Press.
—1966, *Bilingualism in Welsh Education*. Cardiff: University of Wales Press.
JONES, W.R., MORRISON, J.R., ROGERS, J. & SAER, H., 1957, *The Educational Attainment of Bilingual Children in relation to their Intelligence and Linguistic Background*. Cardiff: University of Wales Press.
KEMMIS, S., (ed.) 1982, *The Action Research Reader*. Deakin: Deakin University Press.
KEMMIS, S., & McTAGGART, R., 1982, *The Action Research Planner*. Deakin: Deakin University Press.
KHAN, V., 1978, *Mother Tongue Teaching and the Asian Community*, SCOPE Communications, Occasional Paper 2, Southall, Middlesex: SCOPE.
KHLEIF, B.B., 1980, *Language, Ethnicity and Education in Wales*. New York: Mouton.
KLINE, P., 1983, *Personality, Measurement and Theory*. London: Hutchinson.
LADO, R., 1961, *Language Testing*. London: Longmans.
LARGE, P., 1980, *The Micro Revolution*. London: Pan.
LEWIS, D.G., 1959, Bilingualism and Non-Verbal Intelligence: A further study of test results. *British Journal of Educational Psychology*, 29, 17–22.
LEWIS, E.G., 1978, Review of Culture in Crisis; C. Betts, *Language Planning Newsletter*, 4, 3, 2–3.
—1981, *Bilingualism and Bilingual Education*. Oxford: Pergamon.
—1983, Modernization & Language Maintenance. In G. WILLIAMS (ed.), *Crisis of Economy and Ideology*. Bangor: UCNW.
LEWIS, J., 1982, Helping Schools Change. *Education for Development,* 7, (2), 49–62.
LIEBERT, R.M., SPRAFKIN, J.N. & DAVIDSON, E.S., 1982, *The Early Window. Effects of Television on Children and Youth*. Oxford: Pergamon.
LINGUISTIC MINORITIES PROJECT, 1983, *A Short Report on the Linguistic*

Minorities Project/Pupil Questionnaire. London: University of London Institute of Education.

LLOYD, D.T., 1979, The Welsh Language in Journalism. In M. STEPHENS (ed.), *The Welsh Language Today*. Llandysul: Gomer.

MACDONALD, B., ADELMAN, C., KUSHNER, S. & WALKER, R., 1982, *Bread and Dreams. A Case Study of Bilingual Schooling in the U.S.A.* Norwich: CARE Occasional Publications, No. 12.

MACDONALD, B. & WALKER, R., 1976, *Changing the Curriculum*. London: Open Books.

MACKEY, W.F., 1962, The Description of Bilingualism, *Canadian Journal of Linguistics*, 7, 51–85.

—1965, *Language Teaching Analysis*. London: Longmans.

—1970, A Typology of Bilingual Education. *Foreign Language Annuals*, 3, 596–603.

—1977, The Evaluation of Bilingual Education. In B. SPOLSKY & R. COOPER (eds), *Frontiers of Bilingual Education*. Rowley, Massachusetts: Newbury House.

MACNAMARA, J., 1966, *Bilingualism and Primary Education*. Edinburgh: University Press.

—1969, How Can One Measure the Extent of a Person's Bilingual Proficiency? In L.G. KELLY (ed.), *The Description and Measurement of Bilingualism*. Toronto: University of Toronto Press.

McLEOD, K.A., 1984, Multiculturalism and Multicultural Education: Policy and Practice. In R.J. SAMUDA et al. (eds), *Multiculturalism in Canada: Social and Education Perspectives*. London: Allyn & Bacon.

McMAHON, H., 1983, Computer roles in the management of learning. In J. MECARRY, D.F.R. WALKER et al. (eds), *World Yearbook of Education 1982/83* (Computers and Education). London: Kogan Page.

McQUAIL, D., 1977, The Influence and Effects of Mass Media. In J. CURRAN, M. GUREVITCH & J. WOOLLACOTT (eds), *Mass Communication and Society*. London: Edward Arnold.

MILLER, J., 1983, *Many Voices. Bilingualism Culture and Education*. London: Routledge and Kegan Paul.

MORGAN, E.R., 1955. A Comparative Study of the Effect of Varying Degrees of Bilingualism. Unpublished M.A. thesis, University of Wales.

NICOLL, J., 1982, *Patterns of Project Dissemination*. London: Schools Council.

NIXON, J., 1981, *A Teachers' Guide to Action Research*. London: McIntyre.

OFFICE OF POPULATION CENSUSES AND SURVEYS, 1983, *Census, 1981: Welsh Language in Wales*. London: HMSO.

OGWEN, E., 1978, *Cyfres y Ddraig. (The Teaching of Reading in Welsh)*, Basingstoke: MacMillan.

—1980, Learning to Read in a Bilingual Situation in Wales. *Journal of Multilingual and Multicultural Development*, 1, (4) 313–20.

OLLER, J.W., 1979, *Language Tests at School*. London: Longmans.

—1982, Evaluation and Testing. In B. HARTFORD, A. VALDMAN & C. FOSTER (eds), *Issues in International Bilingual Education*. New York: Plenum.

ORMEROD, M.B., 1975, Subject Preference and Choice, *British Journal of Educational Psychology*. 45, 257–67.

PEAL, E., & LAMBERT, W.E., 1962, The Relationship of Bilingualism to Intelligence. *Psychological Monographs*, 76.

POWYS COUNTY COUNCIL, 1976, *The Welsh Language in Education: Powys.* Llandrindod Wells: Powys County Council.

PRICE, E., 1978, Report. In C.J. DODSON & E. PRICE (eds), *Bilingual Education in Wales 5–11.* London: Evans/Methuen.

PRICE, E., & POWELL, R., 1983, *Listening, Understanding and Speaking.* Cardiff: Welsh Office.

PRICE, E., *et al.*, 1984, *Survey of Writing among 10–11 Year Old First Language Welsh Pupils.* Cardiff: Welsh Office.

PRICE-JONES, E., 1982, A Study of some of the factors which determine the degree of Bilingualism of a Welsh child between 10 and 13 years of age. Unpublished Ph.D. thesis, University of Wales.

RAWKINS, P.M., 1979, *The Implementation of Language Policy in the Schools of Wales.* Centre for the Study of Public Policy, University of Strathclyde.

REES, A.D., 1979, The Welsh Language in Broadcasting. In M. STEPHENS (ed.), *The Welsh Language Today,* Llandysul: Gomer.

REES, M.E., 1954, *A Welsh Linguistic Background Scale.* Pamphlet No. 2. Aberystwyth: Faculty of Education, University College of Wales.

REID, M.I., BARNETT, B.R. & ROSENBERG, H.A., 1974, *A Matter of Choice.* Slough: NFER.

REYNOLDS, D., 1982, A State of Ignorance? *Education for Development,* 7, (2), 4–35.

REYNOLDS, D. *et al.*, 1976, Schools do make a Difference, *New Society,* 29th July, 223–25.

RHIND, D., 1983, Mapping Census Data. In D. RHIND, (ed.), *A Census User's Handbook.* London: Methuen.

ROBERTS, C., 1983, The Sociology of Education and Wales. In G. WILLIAMS, (ed.), *Crisis of Economy and Ideology: Essays on Welsh Society 1840–1980.* Bangor: UCNW.

ROBERTS, G., 1983, Computers and Second Language Learning. In C. TERRY (ed.), *Using Microcomputers in Schools.* London: Croom Helm.

ROSEN, H. & BURGESS, T., 1980, *Languages and Dialects of London Schoolchildren: An Investigation.* London: Ward Lock.

RUTTER, M., MAUGHAN, B., MORTIMORE, P. & OUSTON, J., 1979, *Fifteen Thousand Hours.* London: Open Books.

SAGE, M. & SMITH, D.J., 1983, *Microcomputers in Education. A Framework for Research.* London: SSRC.

SAUNDERS, G., 1982, *Bilingual Children: Guidance for the Family.* Clevedon: Multilingual Matters.

SCHOOLS COUNCIL COMMITTEE FOR WALES, 1983, *Small Schools in Concert.* Cardiff: Schools Council.

SEGALOWITZ, N., 1977, Psychological perspectives on Bilingual Education. In B. SPOLSKY & R. COOPER (eds), *Frontiers of Bilingual Education.* Rowley, Massachusetts: Newbury House.

SHARP, D., 1973, *Language in Bilingual Communities.* London: Edward Arnold.

SHARP, D., BENNETT, G., & TREHARNE, C., 1977, *English in Wales.* London: Schools Council.

SHARP, D., THOMAS, B., PRICE, E., FRANCIS, G. & DAVIES, I., 1973, *Attitudes to Welsh and English in the Schools of Wales.* Basingstoke/Cardiff: MacMillan/University of Wales Press.

SHEINGOLD, K., KANE, J.H., & ENDREWEIT, M.E., 1983, Microcomputer

Use in Schools: Developing a Research Agenda. *Harvard Educational Review*, 53, 4, 412–32.

SHEPHERD, I.D., COOPER, Z.A., & WALKER, D.R., 1980, *Computer Assisted Learning in Geography*. London: Council for Educational Technology.

SIANEL PEDWAR CYMRU (S4C), 1983, *Annual Report*. Cardiff: S4C.

SOUTHALL, J.E., 1895, *The Welsh Language Census of 1891*. Newport: Southall.

STEADMAN, S., PARSONS, C., LILLAS, K. & SALTER, B., 1981, *The Schools Council. Its Take-Up in Schools and General Impact, Final Report*. London: Schools Council.

STENHOUSE, L., 1975, *An Introduction to Curriculum Research and Development*. London: Heinemann.

—1983, *Authority, Education and Emancipation*. London: Heinemann.

SWAIN, M. & LAPKIN, S., 1982, *Evaluating Bilingual Education: A Canadian Case Study*. Clevedon: Multilingual Matters.

THOMAS, C. & WILLIAMS, C., 1978, Linguistic Decline and Nationalist Resurgence in Wales. In G. WILLIAMS (ed.), *Social and Cultural Change in Contemporary Wales*. London: Routledge and Kegan Paul.

THOMAS, J.G., 1956, The Geographical Distribution of the Welsh Language. *Geographical Journal*, 122, 71–79.

TOWNSEND, D.R., 1976, Bilingual Interaction Analysis: Development and Status. In A. SIMOES (ed.), *The Bilingual Child*. New York: Academic Press.

TROIKE, R.C. & SAVILLE-TROIKE,M., 1982, Teacher Training for Bilingual Education: An International perspective. In B. HARTFORD, A. VALDMAN & C. FOSTER (eds), *Issues in International Bilingual Education*. New York: Plenum.

VOLLMER, H.J., & SANG, F., 1983, Competing hypotheses about second language ability: a plea for caution. In J.W. OLLER (ed.), *Issues in Language Testing Research*. Rowley, Massachusetts: Newbury House.

WARNOCK REPORT, 1978, *Special Educational Needs*. A Department of Education and Science Report. London: HMSO.

WEBSTER, J.R., 1976, Curriculum Change and 'Crisis', *British Journal of Educational Studies*, 24, 3, 203–18.

—1982, Education in Wales. In L. COHEN, J. THOMAS & L. MANION (eds), *Educational Research and Development in Britain 1970–1980*. Slough: NFER-Nelson.

WEINREICH, V., 1953, *Languages in Contact*. Hague: Mouton.

WELLER, G., 1978, *Measurement of the Degree of Bilingualism and Biculturalism*. Sociolinguistic Working Paper No. 48. Texas: South West Educational Development Laboratory.

WELSH EDUCATION OFFICE, 1977, *Welsh in the Primary Schools of Gwynedd, Powys and Dyfed*. Survey No. 5. Cardiff: Welsh Education Office.

WELSH OFFICE, 1978a, *Primary Education in Rural Wales*, Education Survey No. 6. Cardiff: Welsh Office.

—1978b, *Statistics of Education in Wales*, No. 3. Cardiff: Welsh Office.

—1980, *Statistics of Education in Wales*, No. 4. Cardiff: Welsh Office.

—1981a, *Welsh in Schools*. Cardiff: Welsh Office.

—1981b, *Statistics of Education in Wales*, No. 5. Cardiff: Welsh Office.

—1982, *Statistics of Education in Wales*, No. 6. Cardiff: Welsh Office.

—1983a, *Welsh in the Secondary Schools of Wales*. Cardiff: Welsh Office.

—1983b, *Statistics of Education in Wales,* No. 7. Cardiff: Welsh Office.

—1984, *Statistics of Education in Wales,* No. 8. Cardiff: Welsh Office.

WEST GLAMORGAN COUNTY COUNCIL, undated, *Report on Bilingualism.* Swansea: W. Glamorgan County Council.

WHITTINGTON, I., 1984, Problem Structuring and Solving Skills 2: Simulations. In R. JONES (ed.), *Micros in the Primary Classroom.* London: Edward Arnold.

WILLIAMS, C.H., 1977, Cynllunio ar Gyfer yr Iaith yng Nghymru, *Barn,* 179, 392–93 (Part 1) and *Barn,* 180, 2–5 (Part 2).

—1978, Some spatial considerations in Welsh language planning, *Cambria,* 5, (2) 173–81.

—1979, An Ecological and Behavioural Analysis of Ethnolinguistic Change in Wales. In H. GILES & B. SAINT-JACQUES (eds), *Language and Ethnic Relations.* Oxford: Pergamon.

—1981, The Territorial Dimension in Language Planning: An Evaluation of its potential in Contemporary Wales. *Language Problems and Language Planning,* 5, (1), 57–73.

—1982, The Spatial Analysis of Welsh Culture, *Etudes Celtiques,* 19, 283–322.

WILLIAMS, D.T., 1937, A Linguistic Map of Wales, *Geographical Journal,* 89, (2), 146–57.

—1953, The Distribution of the Welsh Language, 1931–1951, *Geographical Journal,* 119, 331–35.

WILLIAMS, G. & ROBERTS, C., 1983, Language, Education and Reproduction in Wales. In B. BAIN (ed.), *The Sociogenesis of Language and Human Conduct.* London: Plenum.

WILLIAMS, R., 1981, *Culture.* Glasgow: Fontana.

WILLIAMS, V., 1971, The Construction of Standardized Tests for Welsh-Speaking Children. *Educational Research,* 14, (1), 29–34.

YOUNGMAN, M.B., 1979, *Analysing Social and Educational Research Data.* Maidenhead: McGraw-Hill.

Author Index

Subject Index